Summer Exhibition Illustrated 2020

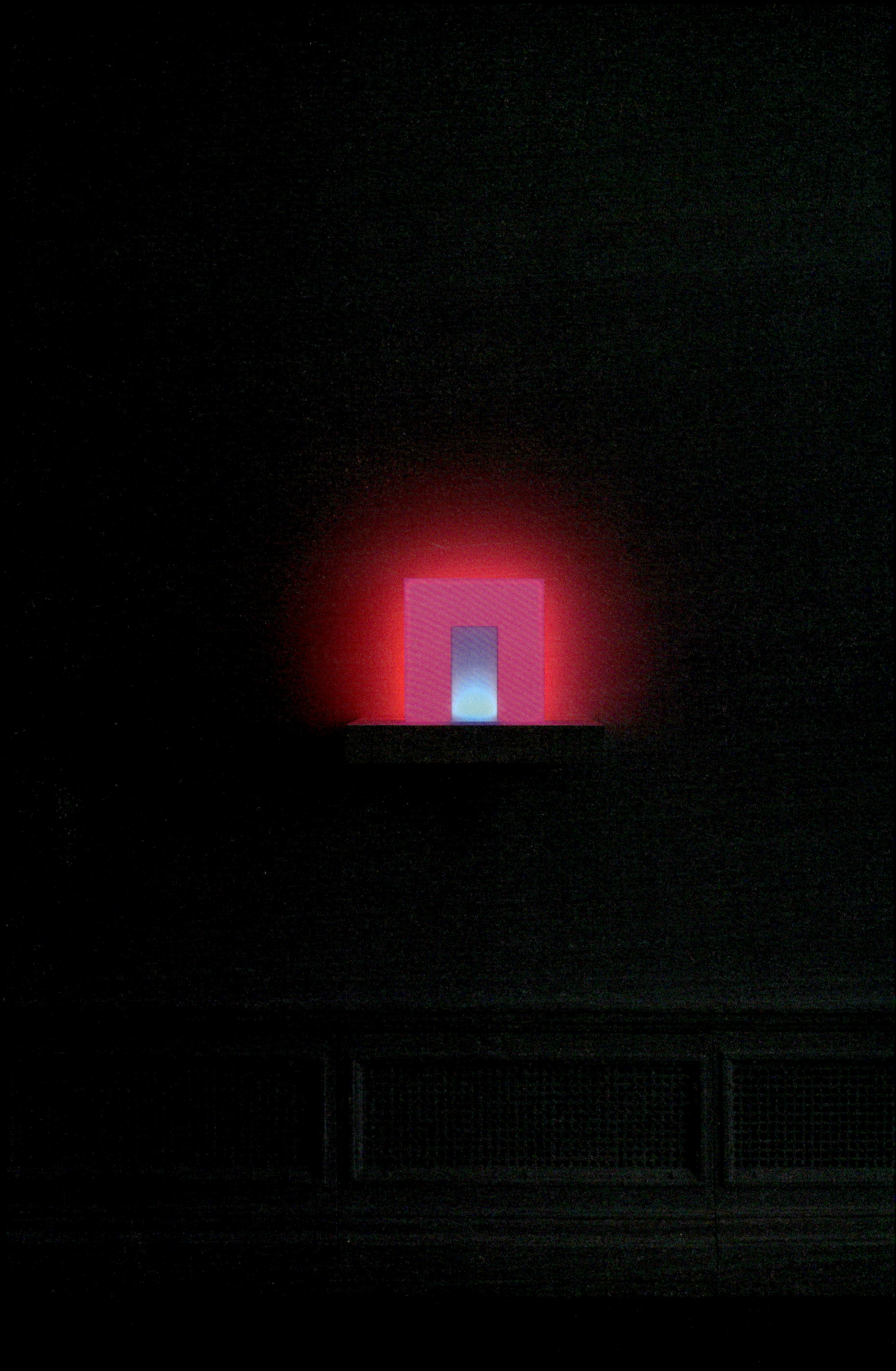

A selection from the 252nd Summer Exhibition
Edited by Jane and Louise Wilson RA

Winter

Summer Exhibition Illustrated 2020

Royal Academy of Arts

Sponsored by

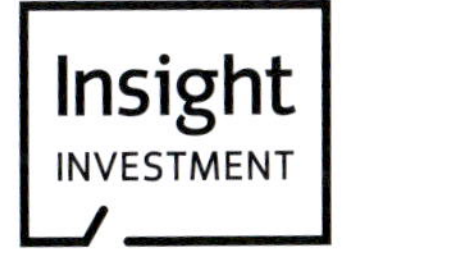

BNY MELLON | INVESTMENT MANAGEMENT

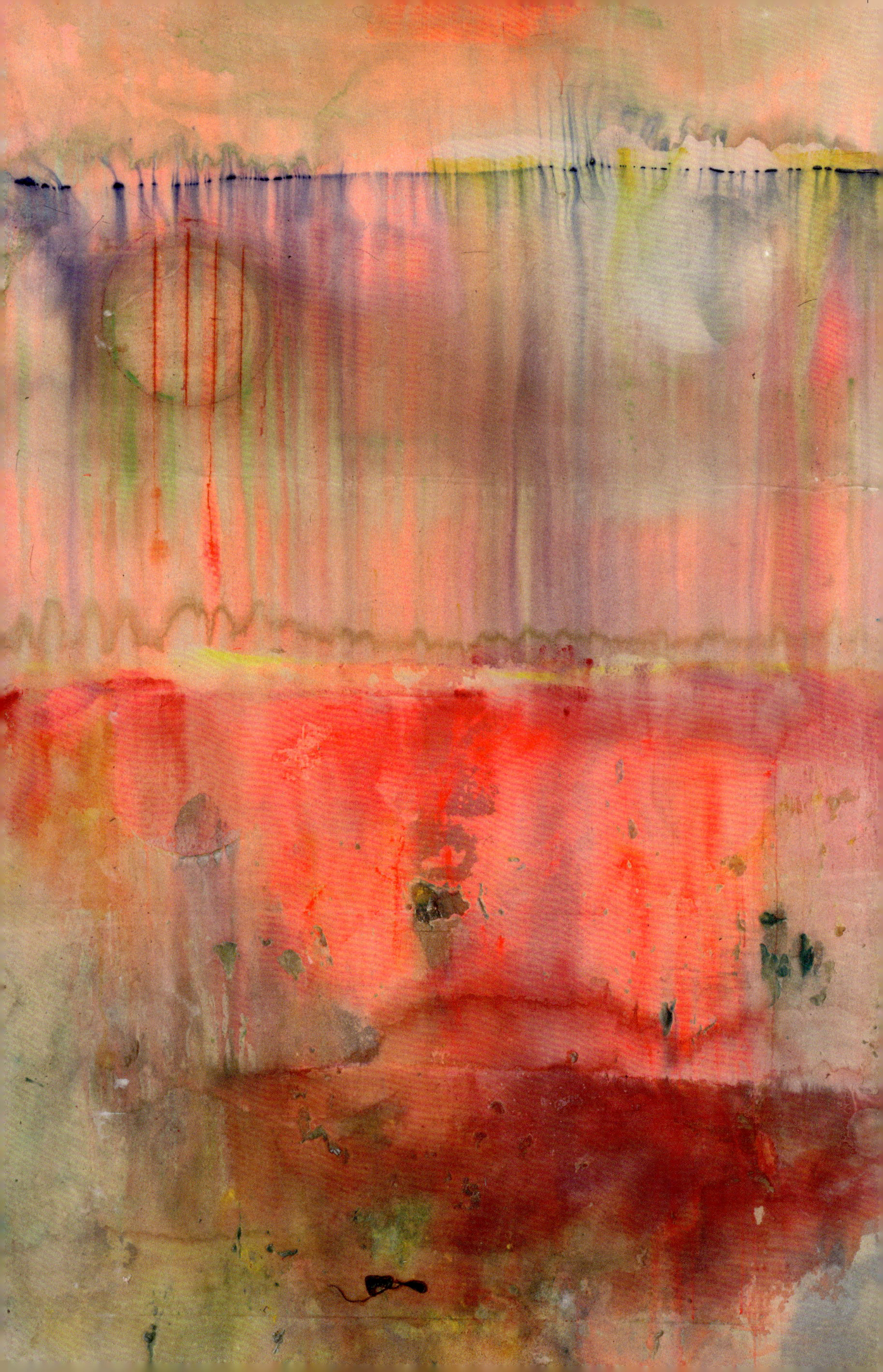

Contents

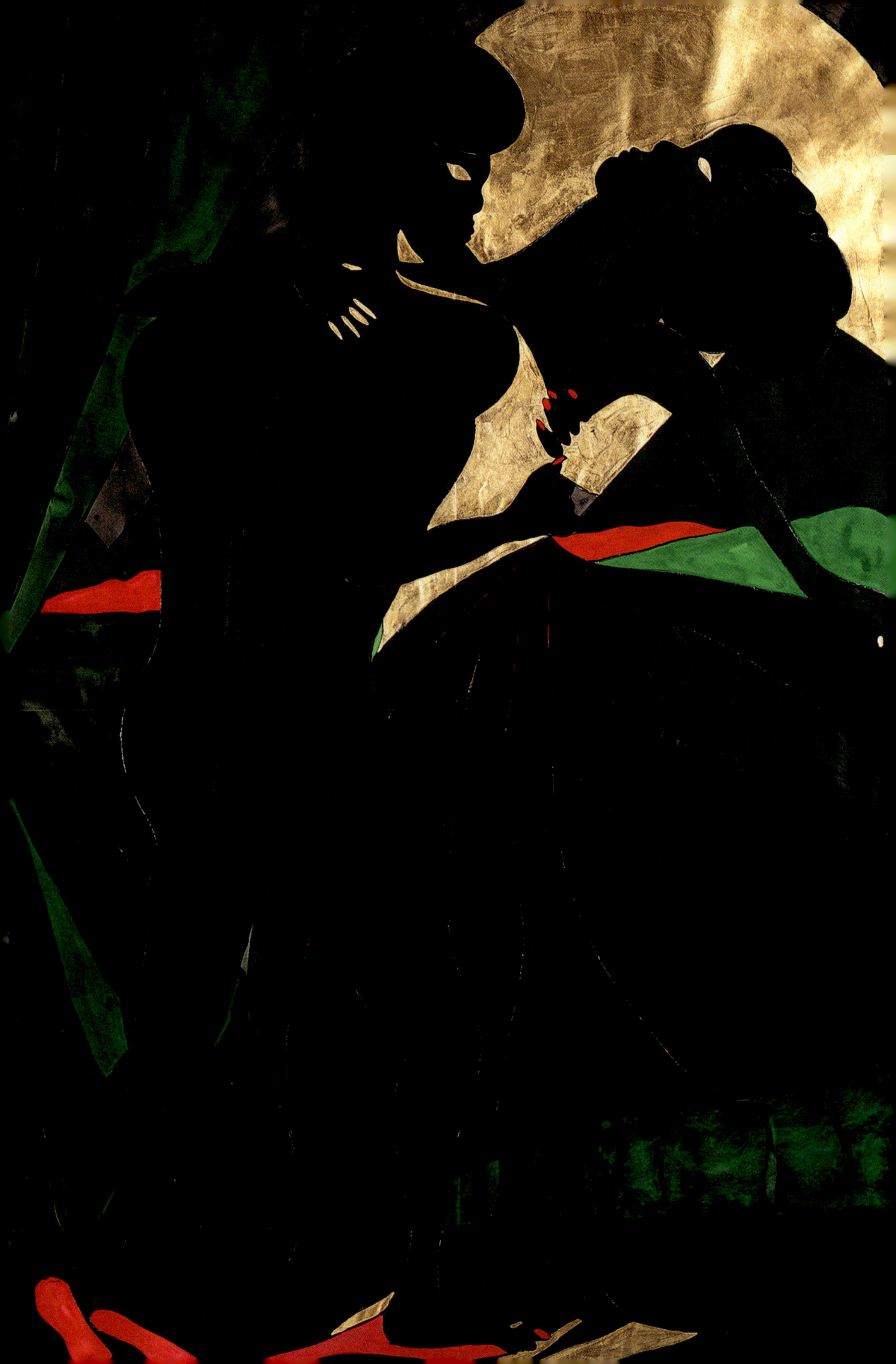

President's Foreword

2020 has been a uniquely difficult year of firsts for the Royal Academy. For four months over the spring and summer, we were forced to close to the public and, for the first time in our 252-year history, we have had to postpone our annual Summer Exhibition until the autumn. Perhaps more than ever before, this year's exhibition embodies the commitment and dedication to art and the nation's cultural life of not only the Royal Academy but also of individual artists and members of the public.

I would especially like to express my gratitude to our brilliant co-ordinators of this year's exhibition, Jane and Louise Wilson, and the members of the committee: Sonia Boyce, Eileen Cooper, Richard Deacon, Stephen Farthing, Eva Jiřičná, Isaac Julien and David Remfry. They have all been unfailingly positive in the face of uncertainty and have created a vibrant and welcoming Summer Exhibition.

We are proud that this year's exhibition includes works by a range of international artists who have never previously submitted their works to the Royal Academy, and who may not even have considered doing so without the encouragement of Jane and Louise Wilson and members of the committee. Galleries I and II, curated by Isaac Julien, stand as a tribute and memorial to one of the greatest curators of our time, Okwui Enwezor, who sadly died in 2019. Enwezor helped to expand the traditional borders of art history and the art world and was the first African curator of the Venice Biennale in 2015. At the Royal Academy we share his vision of a truly international world of art. We are also delighted to show works by Michael Armitage and Ajamu, recently acquired under the terms of the Chantrey Bequest, which supports acquisitions to the Tate Collection and is administered by the Royal Academy.

Sadly, within this exhibition we also mark the passing of four of our own Royal Academicians: the architects Ted Cullinan and Paul Koralek, the painter Jeffery Camp and the sculptor John Wragg. They are all sorely missed.

I would like to congratulate Diana Armfield and Trevor Dannatt, who both celebrated their 100th birthdays this year, but who have not yet had a chance to receive their ovations at the Academy. Both are still active and supportive Royal Academicians and we are so glad to have them in our midst.

On behalf of Council and my fellow Royal Academicians, I would like to thank the members of this year's Summer Exhibition Committee, the Royal Academy's staff and our loyal sponsors, Insight Investment, for their commitment and vision. They have all shown flexibility and ingenuity to overcome obstacles and ensure that we can brighten a troubled year with this glorious celebration of creativity. We never doubted that it could and would be held and I hope this year's exhibition will offer all our visitors both inspiration and optimism.

Rebecca Salter
President, Royal Academy of Arts

Sponsor's Preface

In a year in which many of the UK's most important cultural institutions are dealing with unprecedented challenges, it is hugely encouraging that the Summer Exhibition, the world's largest open submission contemporary art show, will not miss its 252nd year.

The exhibition is a significant cultural event which supports the exchange of ideas and experience of artists from all walks of life. The Royal Academy's determination to persevere to ensure its continuity demonstrates the important role that arts institutions play in shaping the cultural conversation.

Insight has sponsored the Royal Academy Summer Exhibition for fourteen years and we are proud to have supported the RA in 2020 as they strive to maintain the unbroken record of 252 consecutive Summer Exhibitions. We hope that everyone can continue to enjoy this wonderful event for many more years to come.

Abdallah Nauphal
Chief Executive Officer

Sponsored by

Insight
INVESTMENT

BNY MELLON | INVESTMENT MANAGEMENT

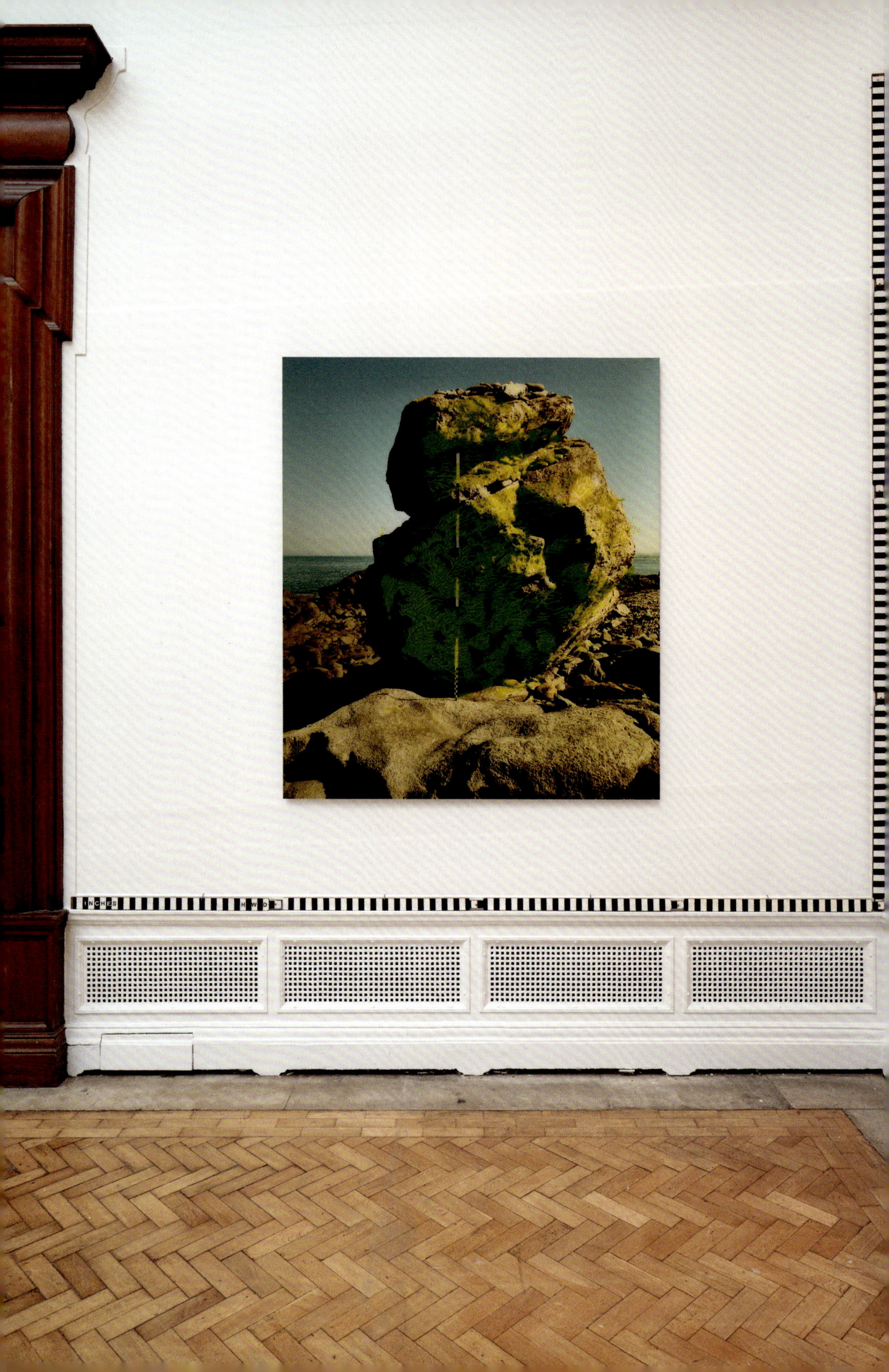
INCHES

Jane and Louise Wilson RA in conversation

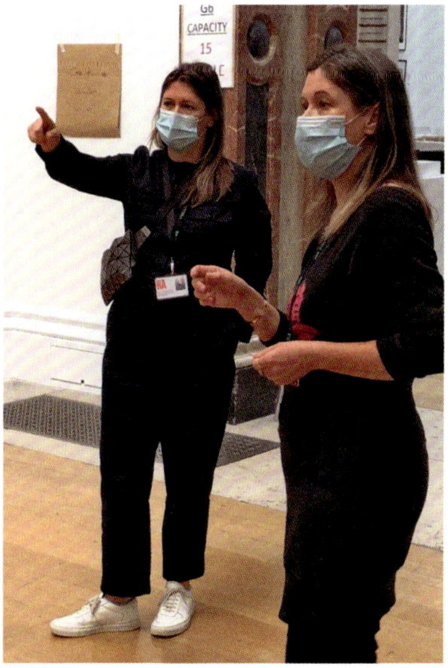

LW We first showed work at the Summer Exhibition in 2001, when Peter Blake was co-ordinating. Then, in 2016, we were invited by Richard Wilson to stage an installation on the staircase of Burlington House. We showed seven large photographs documenting the aftermath of the nuclear disaster in Chernobyl and the clean-up operation, thirty years after it happened. The exhibition took place during the refurbishment of the RA, as the building work was being completed, which meant we could remove the tarpaulin on either side of the staircase to expose the antique brickwork beneath. We wanted to reveal the texture and archaeology of the building. The installation was titled *Future Ruin* and the images were double hung and cantilevered from the bare walls to create a virtual space of fragility and a hubristic image of ruin. Richard's focus for that show was artist duos, and in 2018 we were elected as the second artist duo to be Royal Academicians.

JW It was interesting that the Academy chose to recognise the fact that we are a collaborative duo by electing us as a single Academician. Whether it's one position or two doesn't really matter, it's based on the work and the fact that the work is always a joint endeavour. The dialogue between us is instrumental. Neither of us feels the need to claim sole authorship – we're joint authors. Working together and collaborating during lockdown has been a pleasure, to be honest. It's been the one thing that's kept my brain ticking over – that and running! It's been so important to have things that keep you positive.

LW Obviously initially it was difficult getting into the studio, but actually I think a lot of artists have probably enjoyed some aspects of being in lockdown because it's provided time and space to reflect, which has led to a valuable and creative period for a lot of artists.

JW There have been fewer distractions, certainly, although we also have to be aware that there has been an extensive range of responses. The Summer Exhibition committee covers all ages and some of its members have been and still are shielding. For some people it's been an extremely stressful time and many have had to deal with their own health issues or those of loved ones – including us. We've been looking after our elderly parents who are both undergoing hospital treatment.

LW What's really unusual about the committee this year is that we've been so dispersed. Isaac Julien is currently living in the US and Stephen Farthing is living in Jordan. Eileen Cooper and Richard Deacon have been self-isolating. So it will be Sonia Boyce, Eva Jiřičná, David Remfry, Jane and me who are here in the galleries.

JW Stephen is in Amman and Isaac is in Santa Cruz and neither can get back! Life intervenes, doesn't it? The great thing is that everyone on the committee has stayed on board if they possibly can.

LW Which is really wonderful – amazing, actually.

JW Yes! You could totally imagine some people saying 'Oh, this is not the year, bye!'
LW Richard, Stephen, Isaac and Eileen will for the most part do their hang via Zoom. They'll be guided around their spaces on camera and will curate remotely in discussion with the art handlers on the ground.
JW They'll each have a dedicated install team to work with them. This year more than ever, we have to see the hang as a collective endeavour. Obviously we need to make sure everyone's safe in terms of social distancing, so in the spacing and placing of works we have to be aware that visitors must flow easily through the rooms and not dwell too long in the exhibition spaces. As a team we've come together to work on that and we're trying to avoid operating as in previous years when committee members were held solely responsible for 'their' room in a separated way. We're having a conversation and I think it's for the better that we are.
LW It feels relevant to have a more fluid approach this year, especially as we've all had to be flexible. We're extremely thankful to the committee for their incredible commitment, vision and support.
JW It feels like a different beast this year and we've had to keep very flexible. We don't have the same freedom to stage something in the Annenberg Courtyard that we would have done, nor in the stairways. Our proposed Courtyard installation will now happen next year. We've had to compromise and create public thoroughfares, as important areas to enter and negotiate the building. In previous years that's never been an issue. In the end, the committee are pretty philosophical about that. Everyone understands the reasoning behind it and it will be what it will be.
LW This year you won't be able to enter through the Wohl Central Hall. You'll start instead in Gallery I, and for the first time there will be a guided path through the exhibition, which will be an important change. It will feel different but hopefully not diminished. As you exit through the Central Hall we'll have works by Anne Hardy and Korakrit Arunanondchai, an artist raised in Bangkok who often works with film, performance and installation. He's created two beautiful paintings for the exhibition, a diptych that will create a sense of ritual cleansing as you exit.
JW It would have been great to have had a performance in the Central Hall. We can't do that now and people won't be able to go to St James's Church for the Artists' Service either, but something is planned in Gallery III to bless the building. Inevitably there's a very particular identity to this year's show, given what everyone has had to adapt to, but this could lead to new approaches in future Summer Exhibitions. And maybe good things can come out of this that won't just be seen as challenging.
LW Although I doubt there'll be a Summer Exhibition held in winter again!
JW No, probably not! Clearly the need for social distancing

Lawrence Lek
Unreal Estate
(The Royal Academy is Yours)
Video

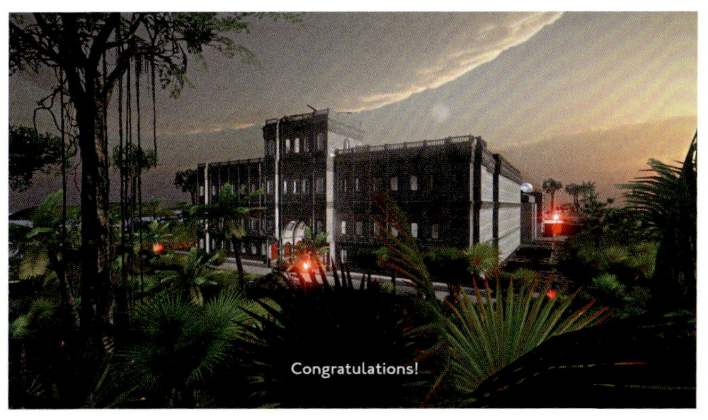

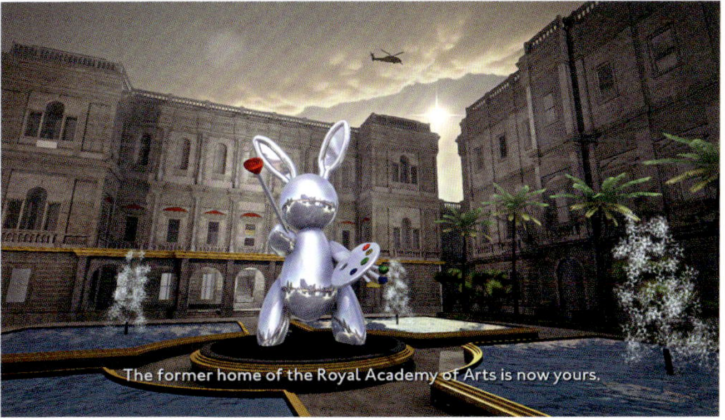

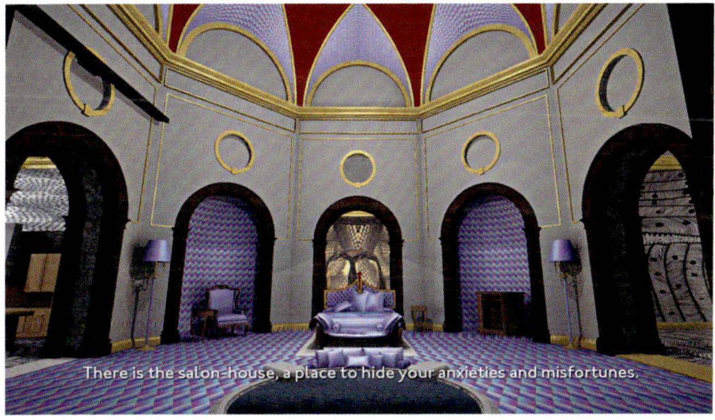

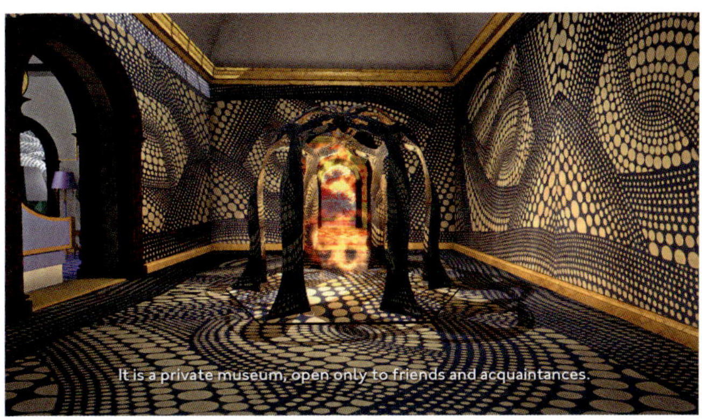

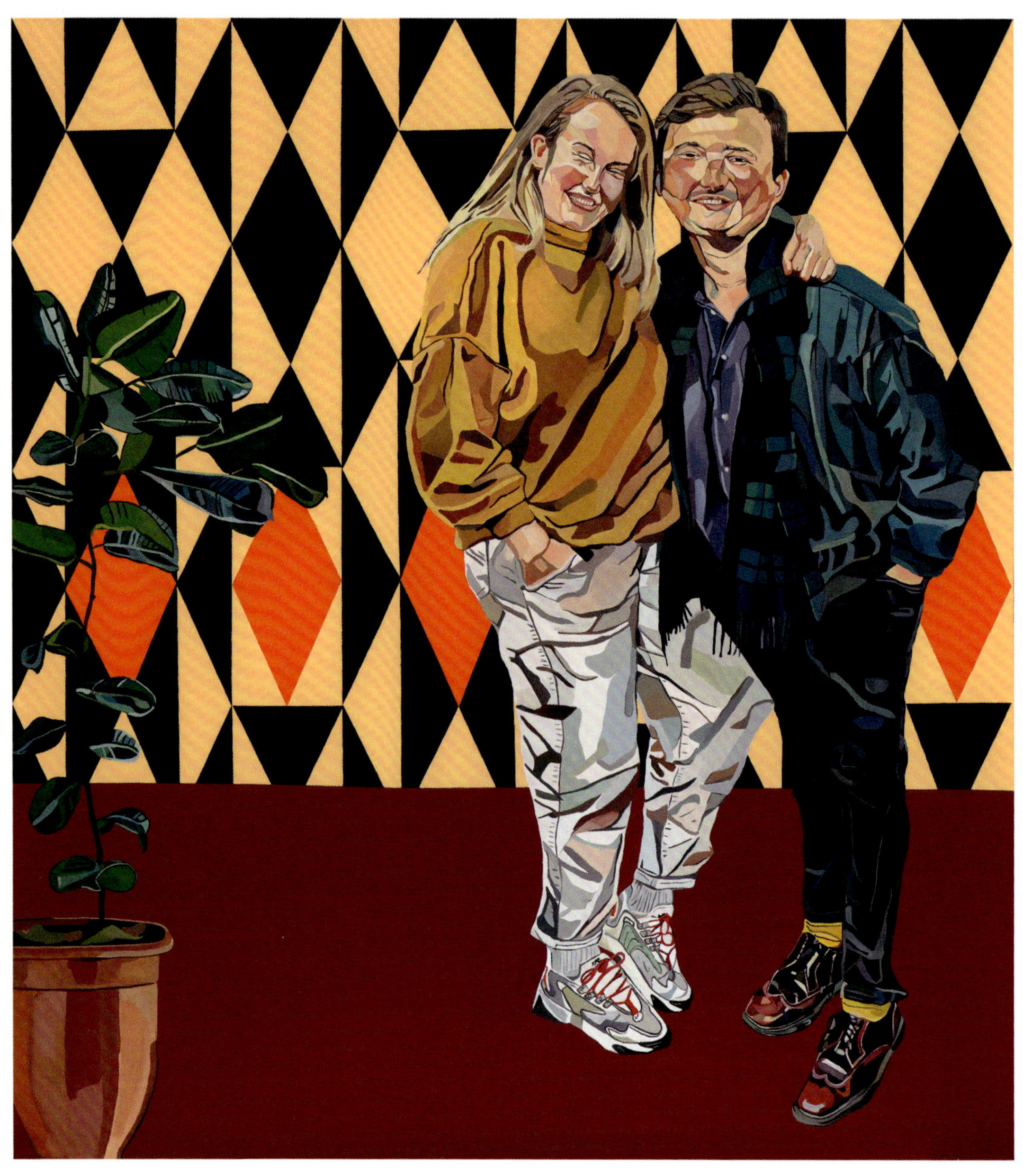

Joy Labinjo
Jenny and Louis
Oil
200 × 180 cm

has been a challenge and that's something no-one could have foreseen. We had planned to curate a screening programme to create a platform for longer-format film works, but that obviously can't happen this year because we can't have people gathering in one room for extended periods of time. We're still going to show digital works, but they'll have to be integrated in the exhibition overall, becoming more of a slow-form visual. They'll be interspersed with other work so you'll be able to dip in and out, hopefully creating a viewing experience that's more ephemeral and fluid. Young-Hae Chang Heavy Industries have submitted a piece, for example, which will be projected in the Small Weston Room. Our plans have had to change but it's great that video works can still feature in the exhibition.

LW Absolutely. We're also very excited to be able to include video works by John Smith, Soyoung Chung, Hilary Lloyd, Lawrence Lek, Yuri Pattison and Paul Walde.

JW The invited artists have all really come through amazingly. We have a new Rebecca Horn painting and powerful drawings from Michael Armitage and Mary Griffiths, as well as two new works by Joy Labinjo, an exciting young painter who recently graduated from Newcastle University.

LW There's an extraordinary large-scale drawing installation piece by Anne Hardy and beautiful paintings by Tomma Abts, Karen Kilimnik, Rosalind Nashashibi, Narbi Price, Laura Lancaster, Rachel Lancaster and David Lock as well as wonderful new sculptures from David Batchelor and Simon Periton.

JW We have fantastic collages from Hans-Peter Feldmann and Linder and two extraordinary pieces from Margaret Harrison and Conrad Atkinson. They're both in a more vulnerable age group, so it's a privilege to profile important works by them both. We appreciate that for some people this year has been really challenging. Some of the artists we invited were unable to submit for health reasons or other issues and that's entirely understandable.

LW We're tremendously grateful to the invited artists who are showing such significant works, including a new sound installation by Brian Eno and photographic works by Reza Aramesh, Sarah Jones, Ori Gersht and Ajamu.

JW It's exciting to see what can grow out of this. There will be a lot of young and emerging artists showing alongside established and mid-career artists. When we were selecting from the open submission in March, before lockdown, we were looking at themes surrounding identity and climate emergency, but we were also very conscious of identities, minorities and disabilities and the importance of representing the diversity of the art world. It was crucial to have Isaac and Sonia on the committee, to make clear that there is a very important voice within the Academy that needs to be articulated in the context of the Summer Exhibition. BAME rights are hugely significant given

Black Lives Matter, the global campaign against violence and systematic racism towards Black and ethnic minority people, as well as the understanding of how Covid-19 has impacted some communities a lot harder than others.

LW In his selection in Galleries I and II, Isaac will be paying tribute to Okwui Enwezor, the deeply influential Nigerian curator, poet and educator whose passing in 2019 was a devastating blow to the art community. It's a timely reminder for us all of Okwui's powerful and uncompromising vision, one that exposed how the history of violence against Black people in Africa and the African diaspora often goes unacknowledged. He really confronted colonial histories in both the US and the UK and questioned how our traumatic histories are represented. Among the artists Isaac has invited to show this year are Theaster Gates, Wangechi Mutu, Oscar Murillo, Peter Doig, Njideka Akunyili Crosby, Glenn Ligon, Chris Ofili and Zanele Muholi.

JW It's important that the art world can give a platform to a lot of different voices and accept that practice comes in all forms. It was so interesting to see the range of submissions. Although it's an exhausting process to go through all 18,000 applications, you don't want to miss anything! It's an epic endeavour, but fortunately we had the rest of the committee with us so, fingers crossed, we didn't miss anything. In the end, it's a collective endeavour and we managed to pull out some really important works. I think it's key that, where possible, every single submission to the Summer Exhibition is looked at by the committee as a whole.

LW We're seeing more and more how creative practice is not about hierarchies. When you consider Outsider Art, what children are producing, or the elderly, or perhaps those struggling with dementia, it's fascinating to see what's being produced. And it's such an affirmation of creativity that people are choosing to express themselves in so many creative ways, probably as a direct result of lockdown.

JW They're doing it together and that's the main thing: it's much more about the collective now. I think we've become much more conscious about our relationships to other people. We've really had to understand how we have to work together to protect ourselves and to protect others. Usually when you're going to work and keeping your head down on the commute you don't really have a perception of where you sit in your community. But now you're looking out for other people on your street, maybe you've done their shopping. You suddenly start to see your neighbours, see your streets, see your community.

LW That's perhaps something that will come through in next summer's exhibition, by which point people will have processed and reflected on this period. This year obviously the majority of the works we've selected were created before lockdown. But actually, it's just important that we have artworks on show, so

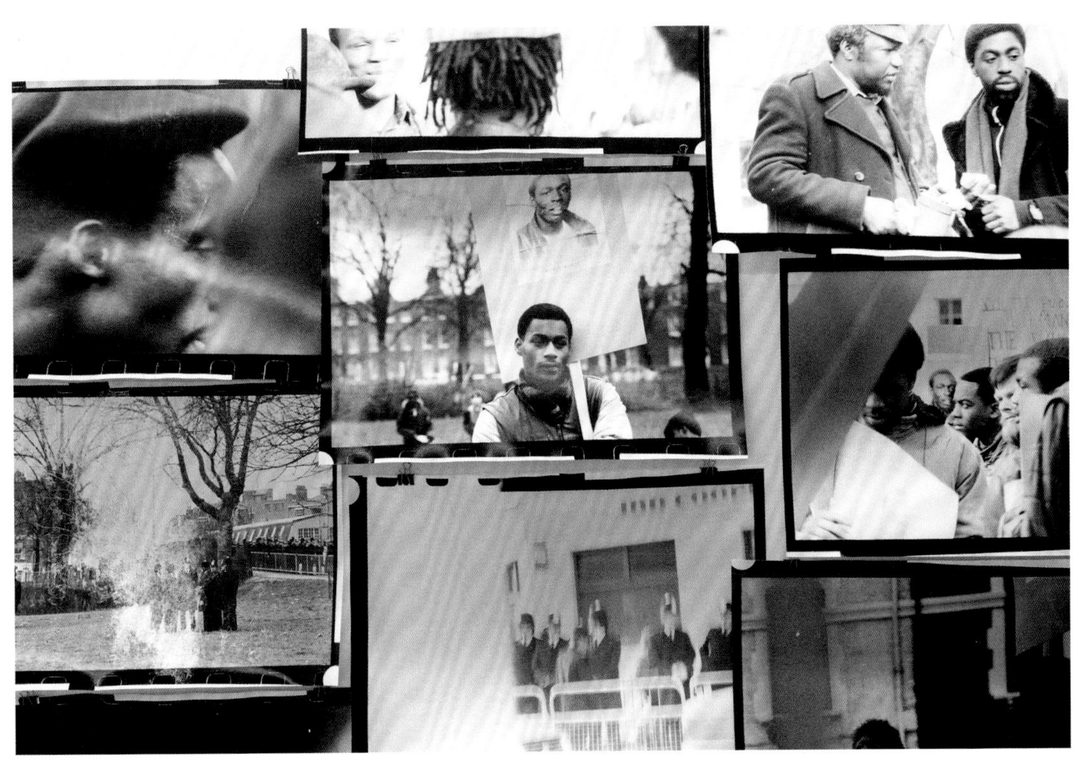

Isaac Julien CBE RA
Lessons of the Hour, London 1983 – Who Killed Colin Roach? (detail)
Silver gelatin prints
180 × 760 cm

MY PAPERS?
WHAT PAPERS?
WHY PICK ON ME?

Young-Hae Chang Heavy Industries
C.D.C. Warns of 'Aggressive' People Searching for Food During Shutdowns
Video

Jane and Louise Wilson RA
Turban Shell, Seaweed and Measure II
Photographic print
42 × 59 cm

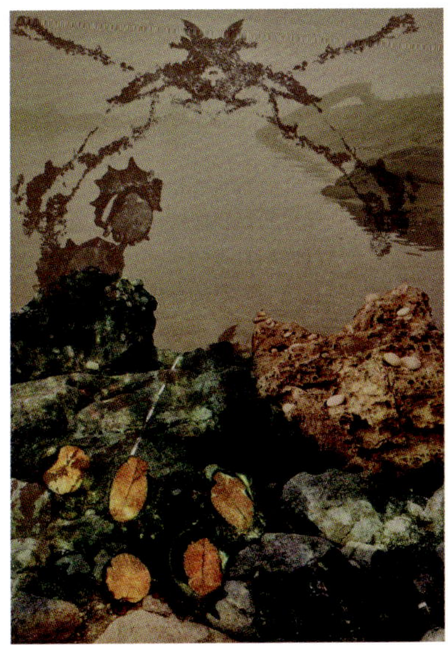

that people can come and see art again, and to recognise that there have been collective acts of outpouring – like people standing up and clapping for the NHS on a Thursday. We want people to experience that feeling of celebration from visiting an exhibition in person, and to be able to take joy and pleasure from engaging with the collective act of encountering art again.
JW Exactly. As important as anything is to state that we want the exhibition to be a celebration. The artistic community is suffering and has been hit very hard. Most artists are self-employed, struggling to make their way, to cover studio rents, to access materials, to be able to continue their practice at all. The fact that 1,200 artworks have been selected and that so many artists are going to show their work is really something to celebrate.
LW A lot of artists, including us, have had exhibitions cancelled or postponed, but the Summer Show – now Winter Show – is an important acknowledgement that artists still continue to practise.
JW Art endures! And what's so unique about the Summer Exhibition is that visitors will be seeing professional and non-professional artists rubbing up against each other, artists working in different mediums, from different margins, different minorities, different groups. We're trying to understand how the collision of all these different voices and approaches can come about in one exhibition. What's not to celebrate about that? What's not to celebrate about that enduring and being sustained? It's a very fragile existence for a lot of artists, and that must be acknowledged. Given the economic devastation that's already happened and the economic uncertainty to come, there is going to be a lot of hardship, so we must embrace and celebrate these voices now. It's an ecology that struggles to be there most of the time and it's great it's coming out on show in the Summer Exhibition.
LW Our original exhibition theme of 'Rapture in Fracture' is reflected in one of the images that we're showing this year, of a free-standing lava rock taken on the South Korean island of Gapado. It's a carbon neutral island and is home to the Haenyeo, the female free-divers who live there. Each small stone represents an act of faith placed there before each dive, a shamanic offering that's kind of an elemental prayer.
JW The free-divers are all of a certain age – on average between sixty and eighty. These women are remarkable but their communities and traditions are dying out. It's something we're very conscious of. Economies and ecologies are fragile and they exist by sheer tenacity and resilience – a lot like the artist economy.
LW Not quite molluscs on a rock, but…!
JW It hangs on in there, doesn't it? It's important that we acknowledge that in the Summer Exhibition. Our artists' ecology continues to exist and our artistic community endures.

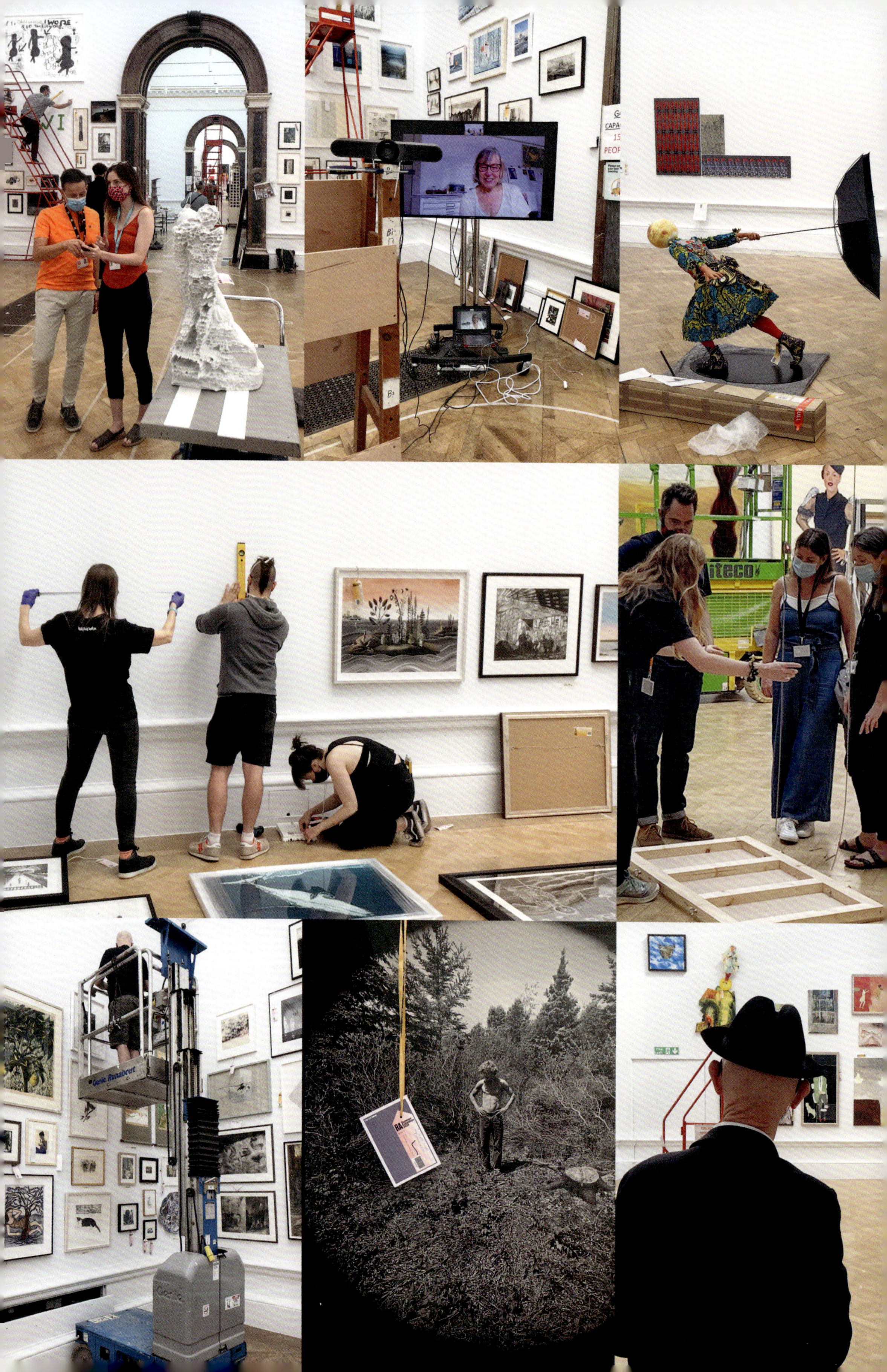

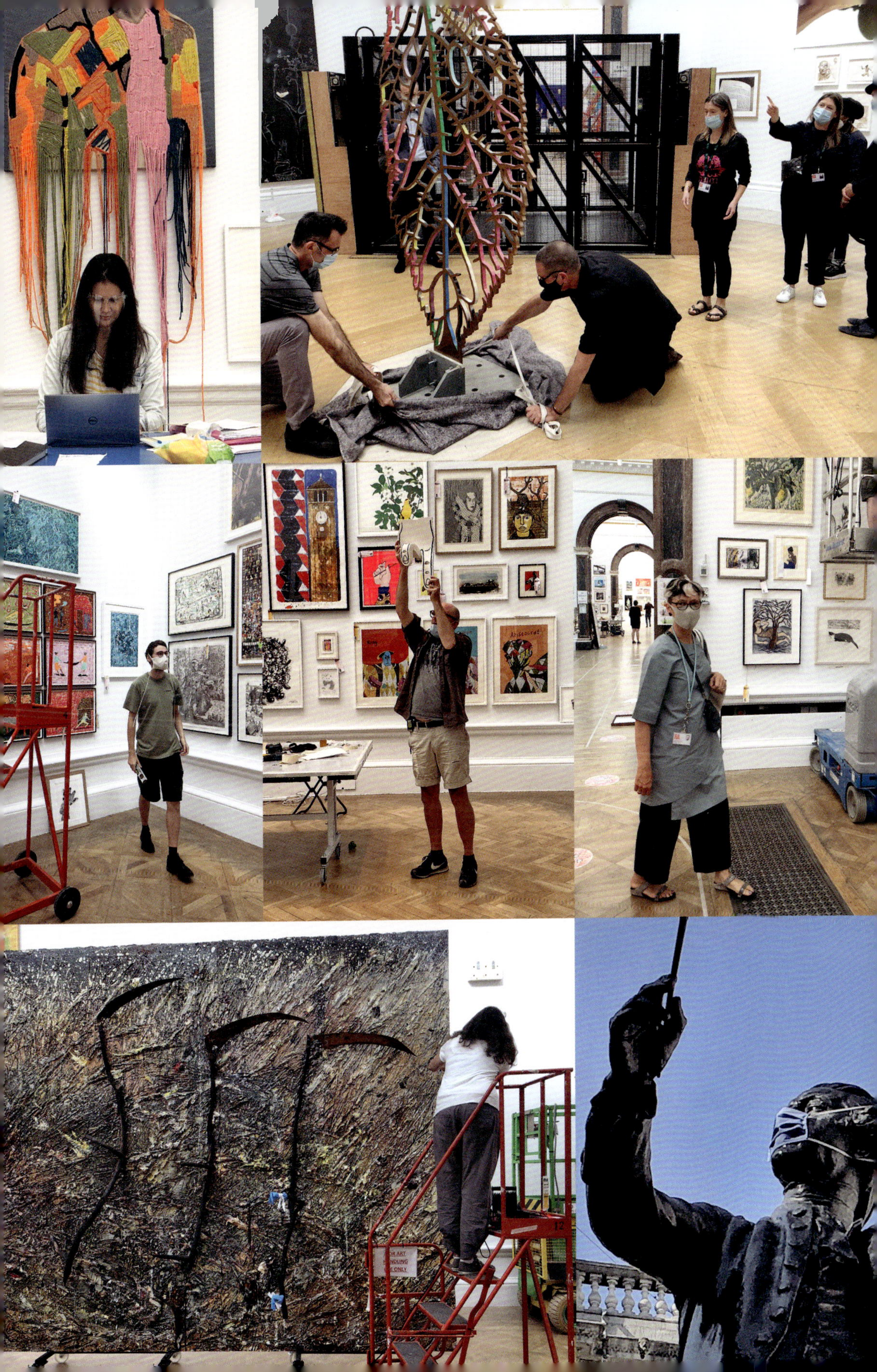

Oscar Murillo
Manifestation
Mixed media
220 × 350 cm

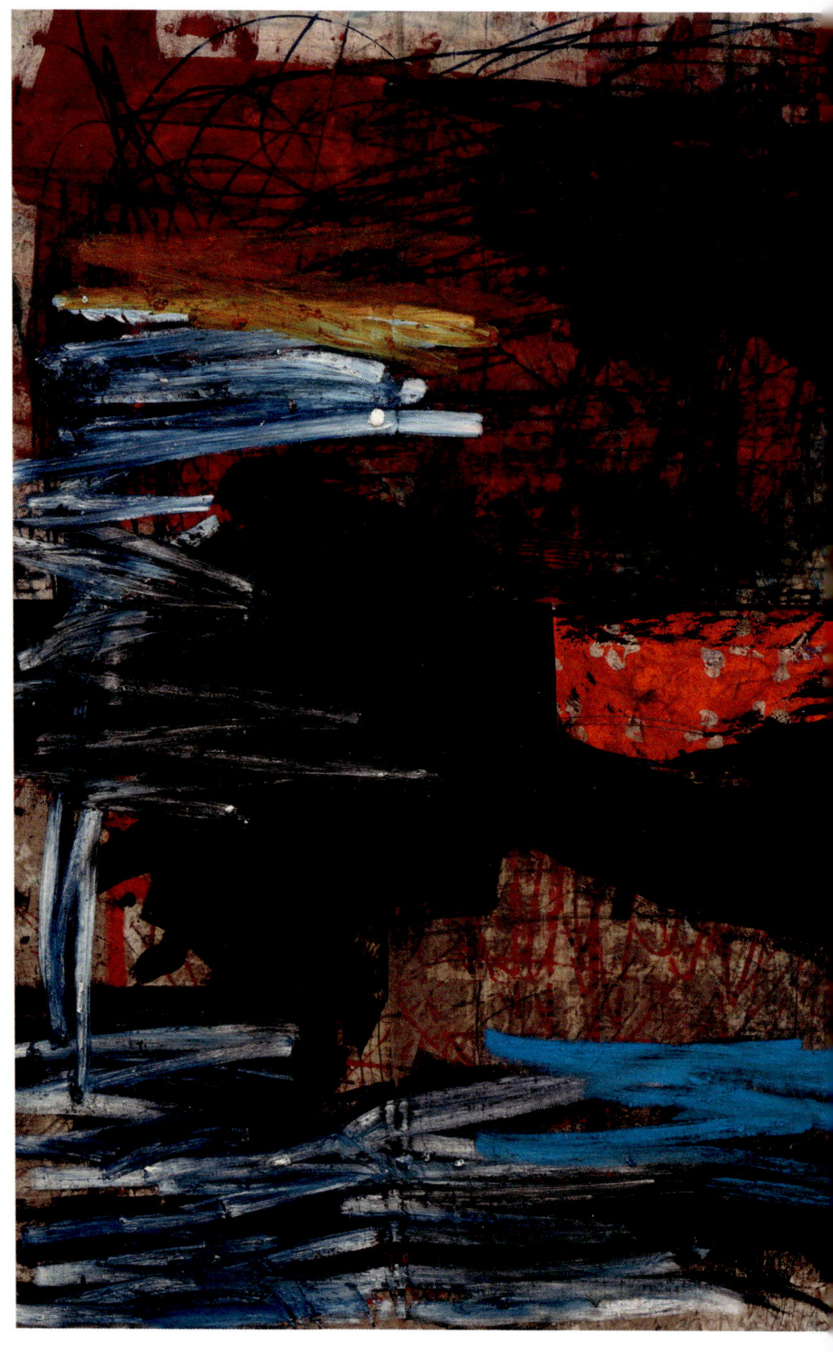

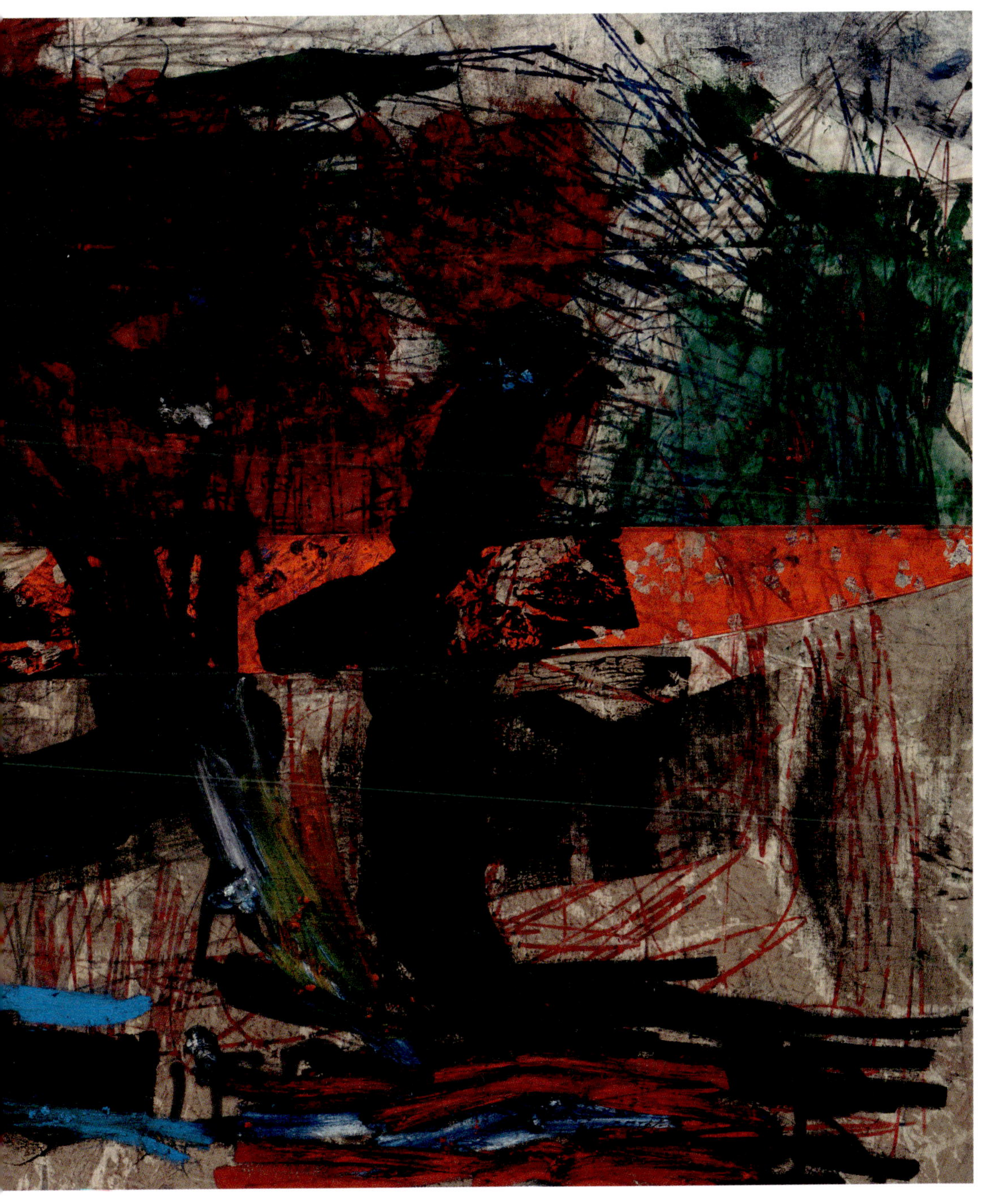

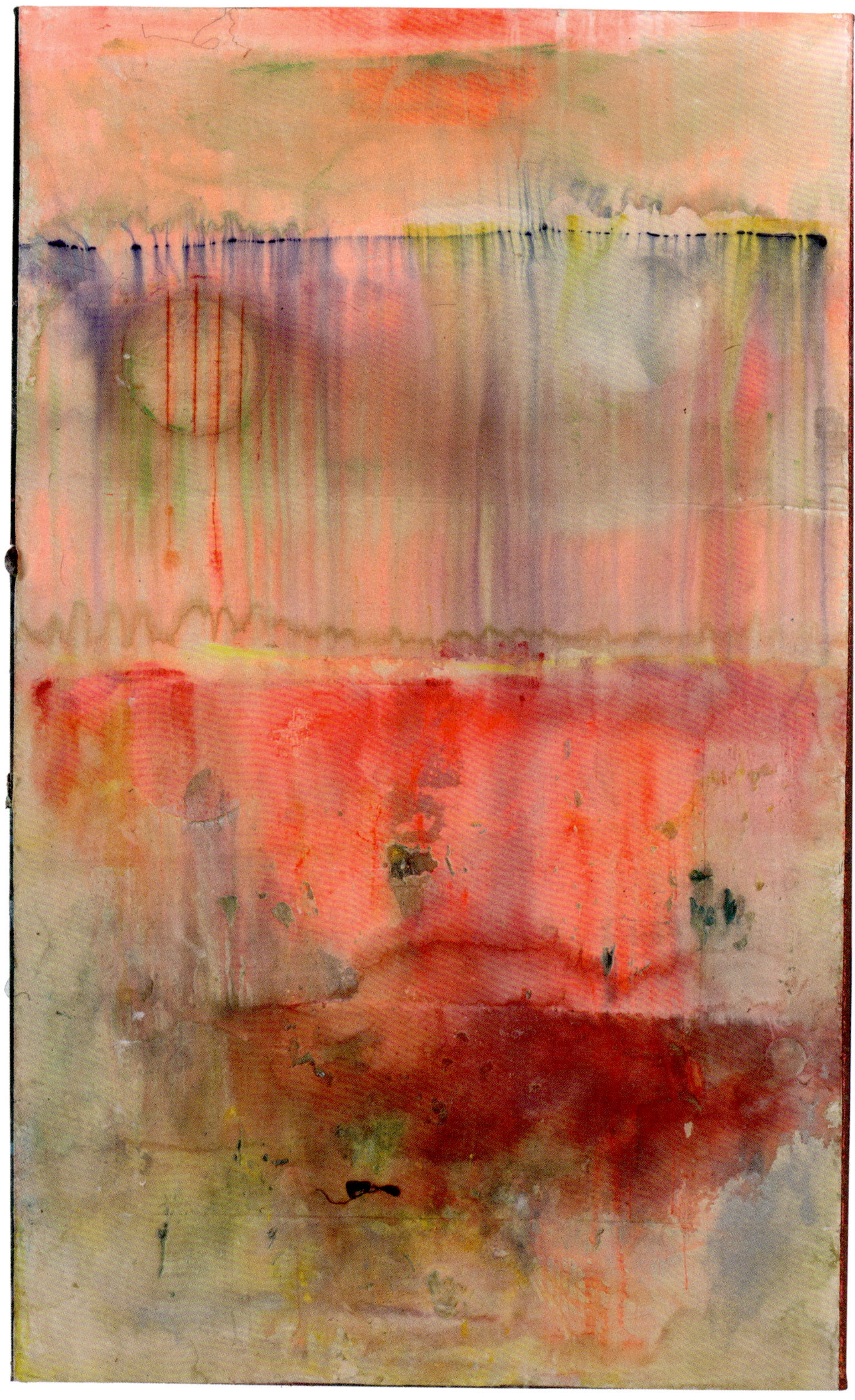

Frank Bowling OBE RA
Watermelon Bight
Acrylic
297 × 185 cm

Yinka Shonibare CBE RA
Air Kid (Girl)
Mixed media
H 148 cm

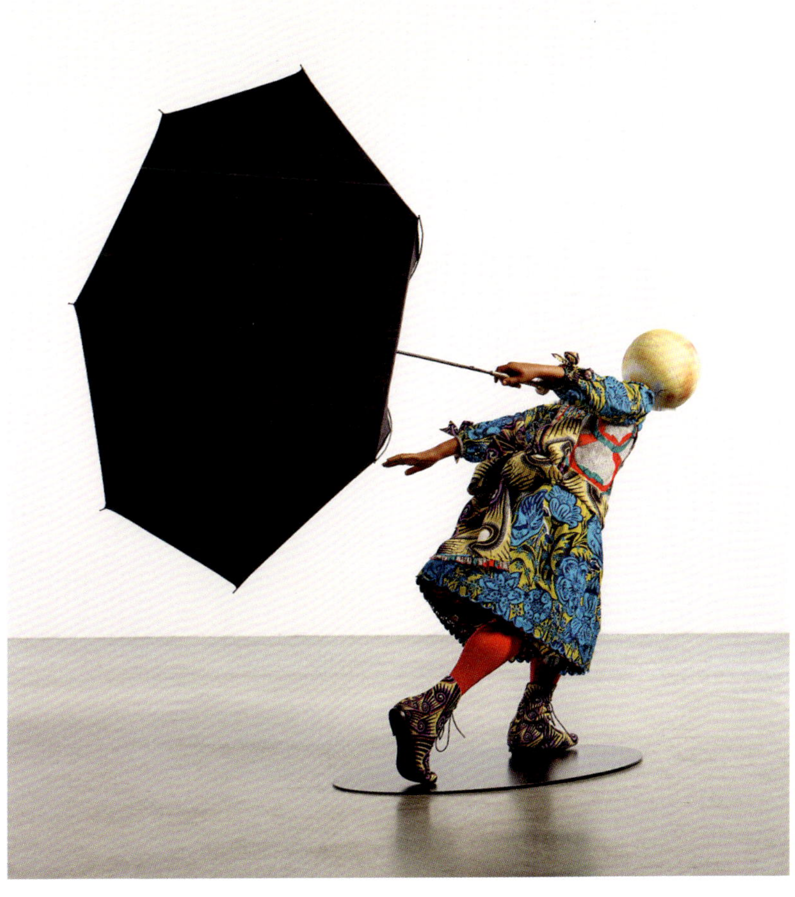

Njideka Akunyili Crosby
Blend In – Stand Out
Mixed media
243 × 314 cm

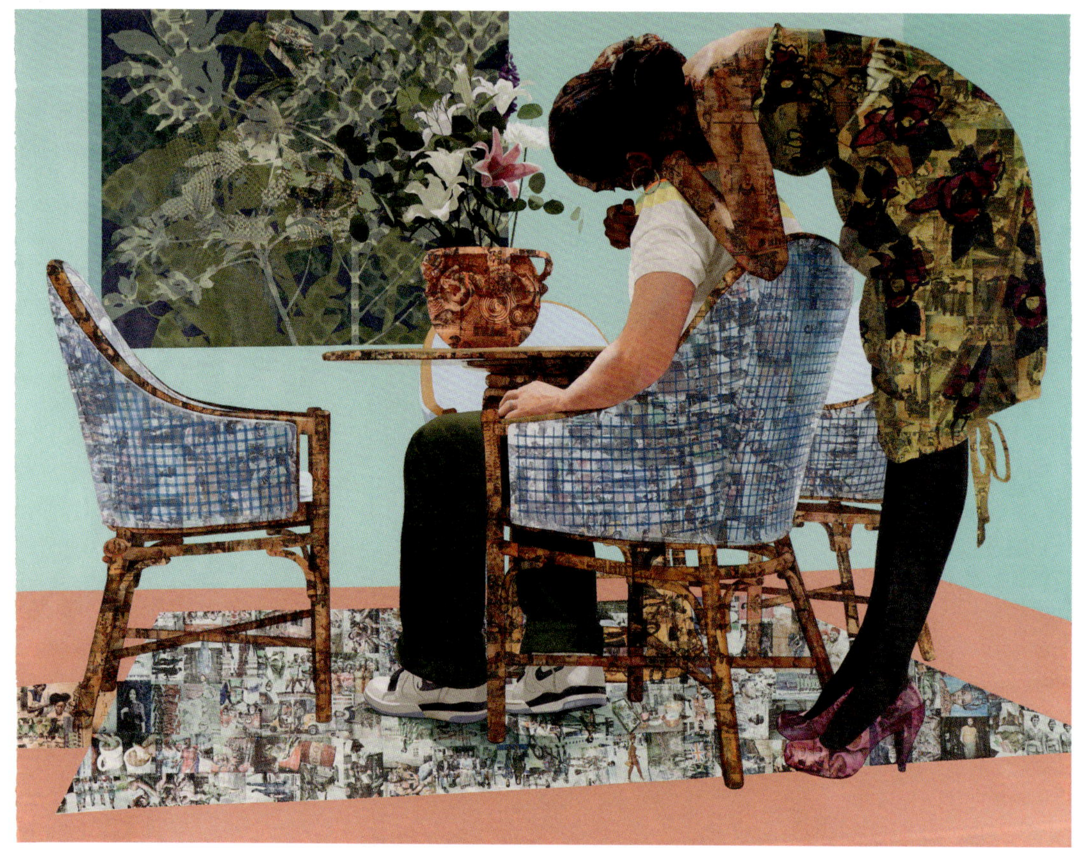

Isaac Julien CBE RA
The Lady of the Lake (Lessons of the Hour)
Photographic print
154 × 207 cm

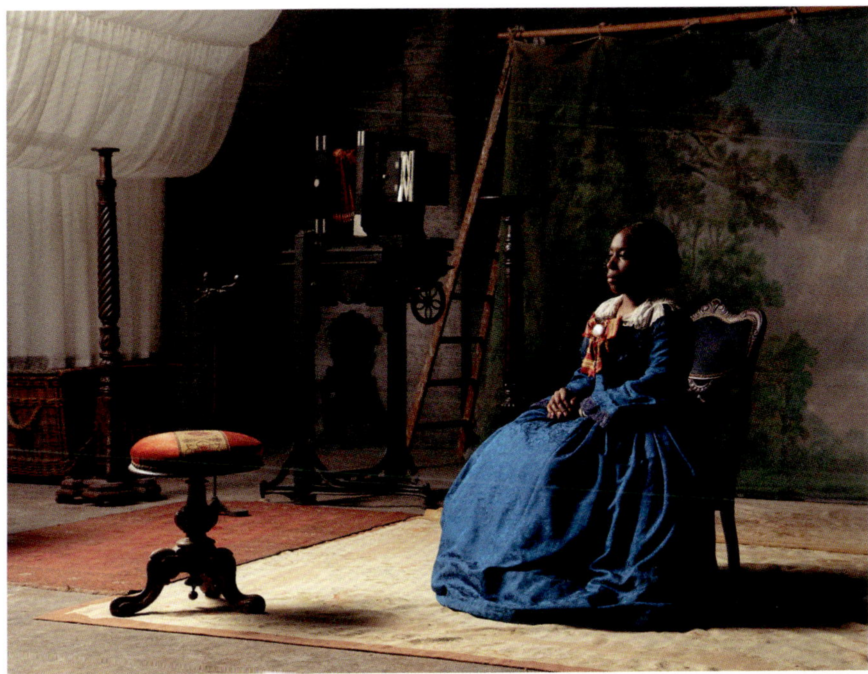

Prof El Anatsui Hon RA
Castle in the Cloud
Mixed media
270 × 410 cm

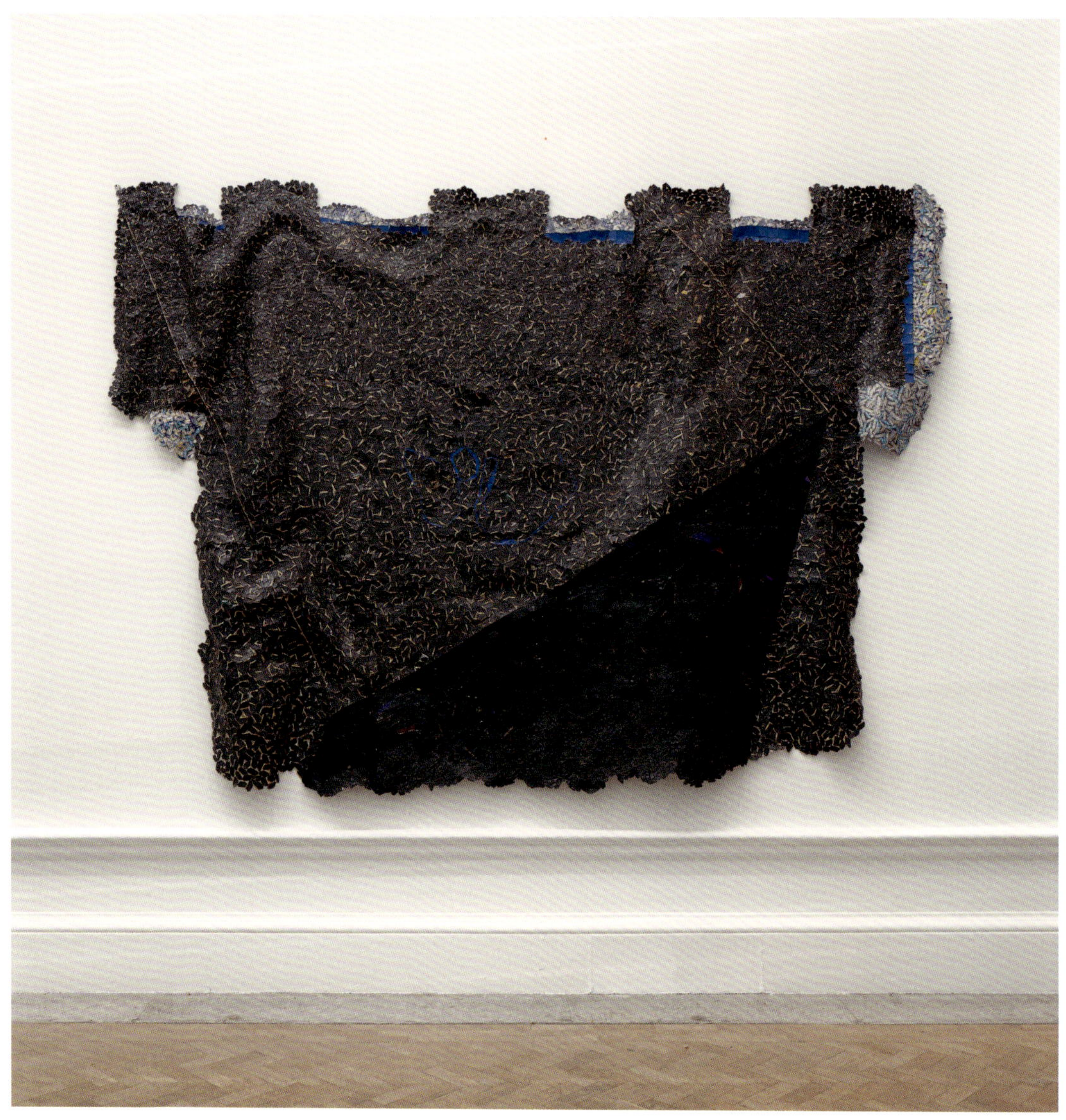

Prof Sonia Boyce OBE RA
Underworld-Overworld: Shaggy Bear Repeat
Photographic print
120 × 80 cm

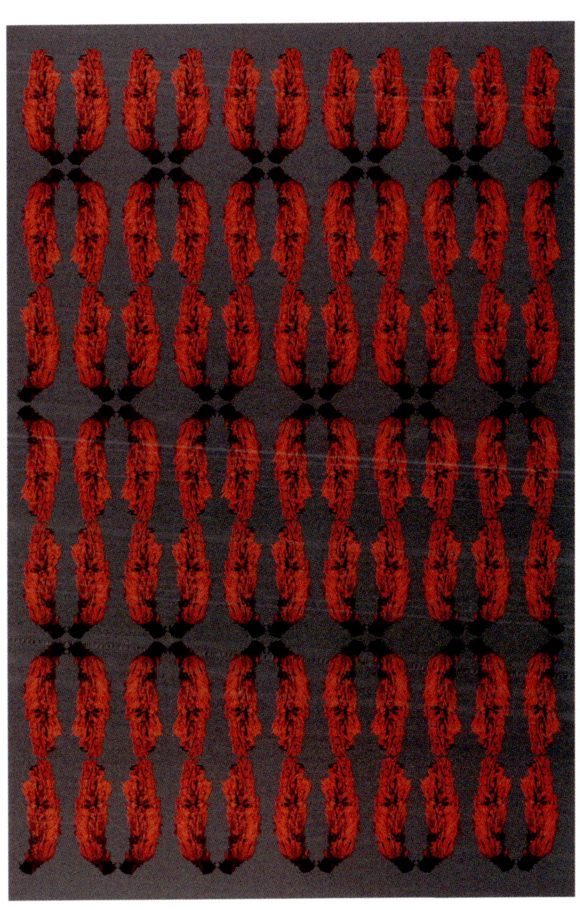

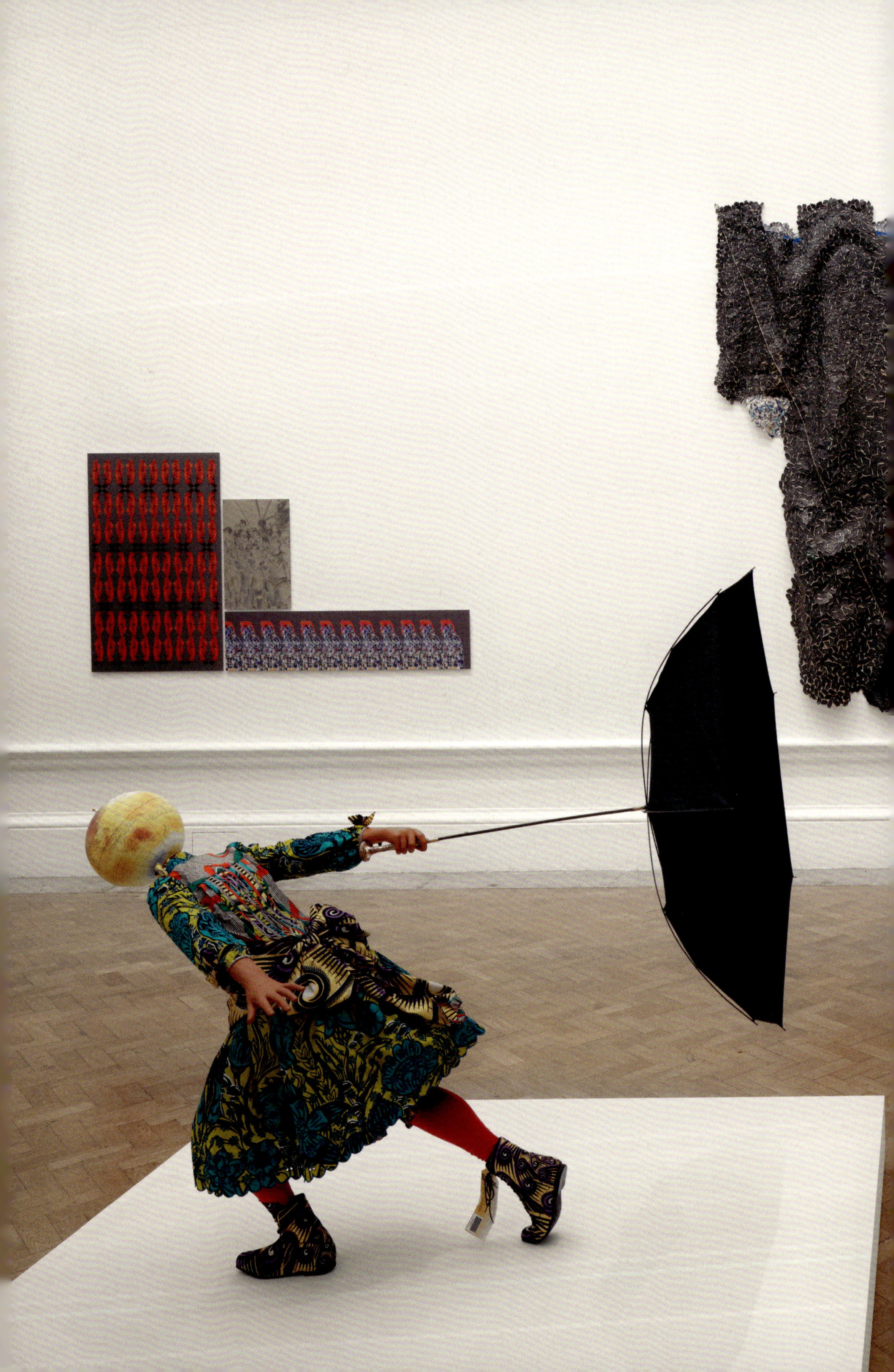

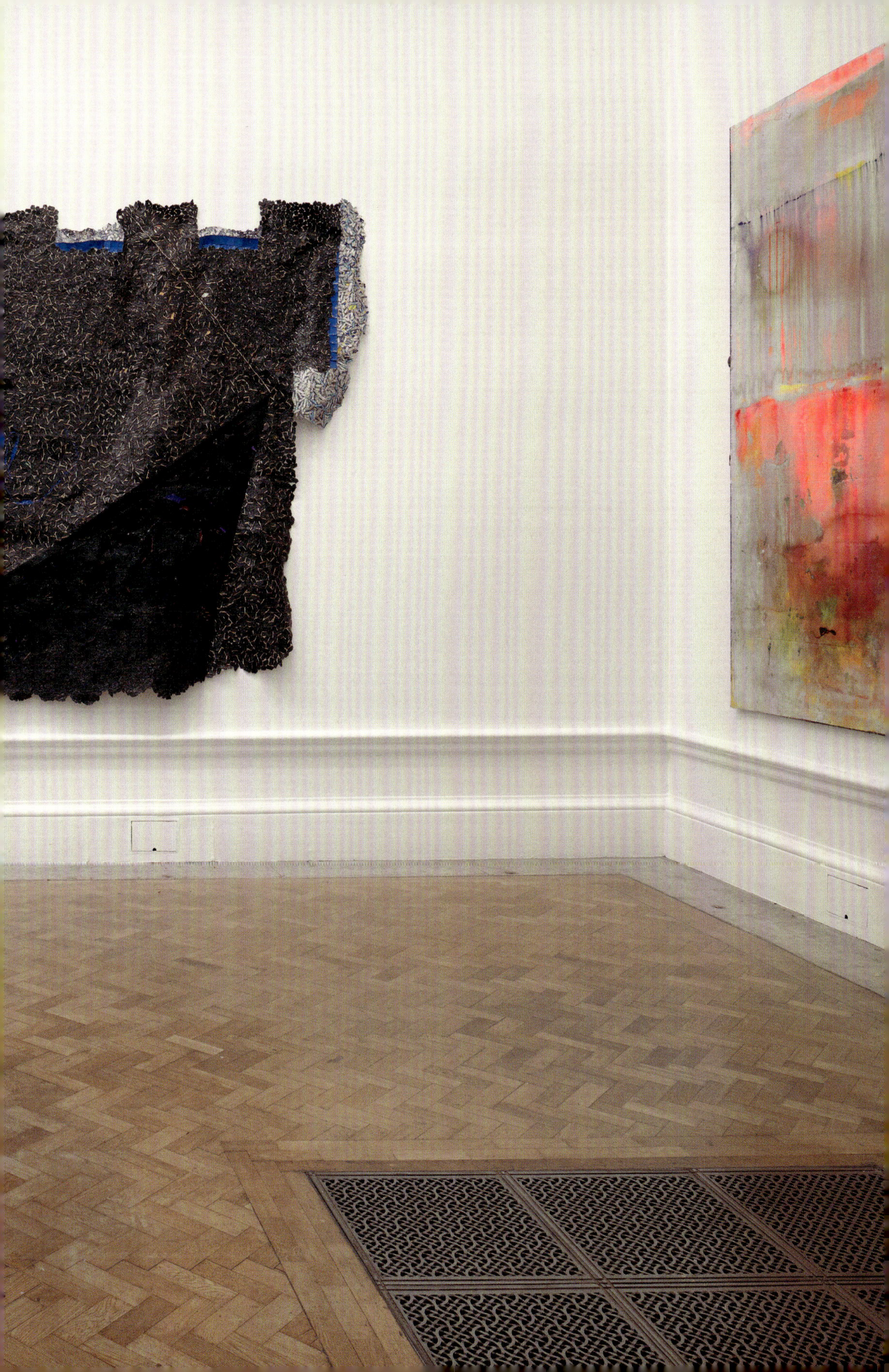

Chris Ofili
Cha Cha Cha (Triptych)
Mixed media
199 × 130 cm (each)

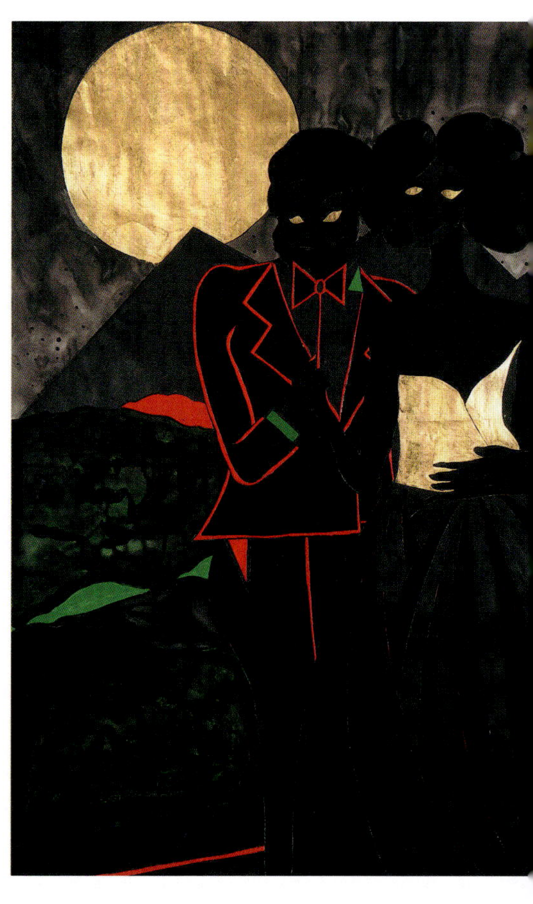

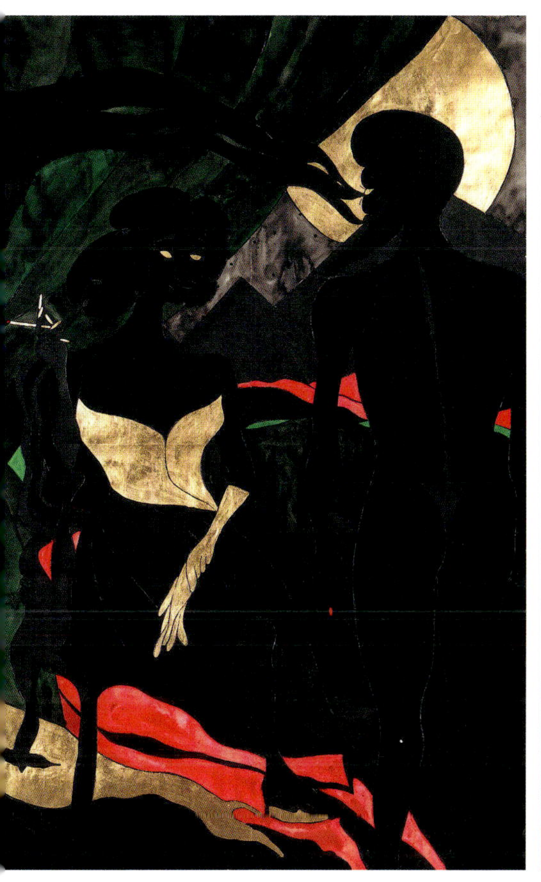

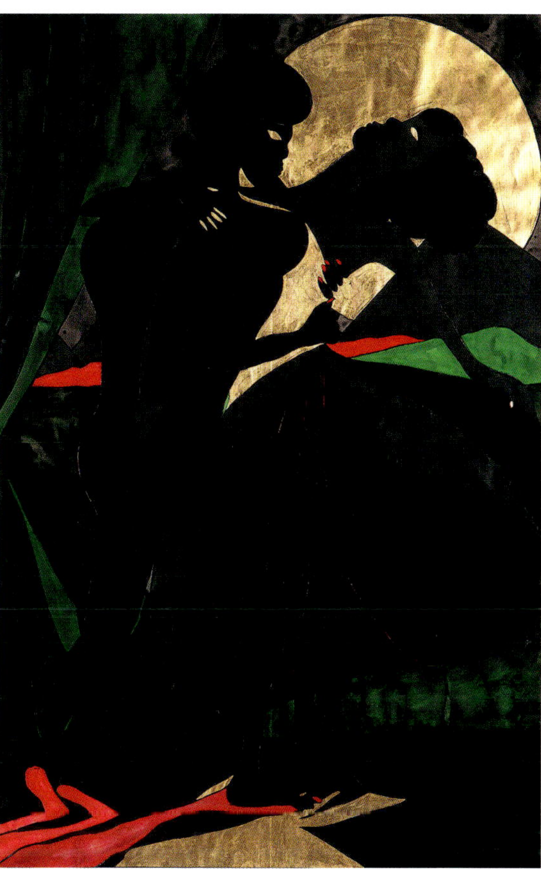

Glenn Ligon
Correspondence
Aquatint and drypoint
122 × 99 cm (each)

Wangechi Mutu
Sentinel IV
Mixed media
H 216 cm

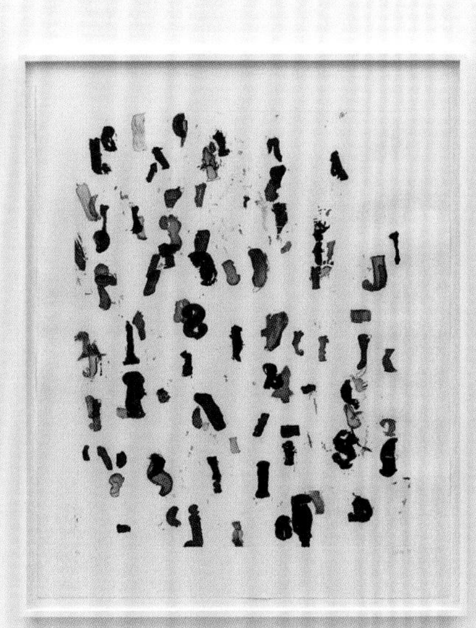

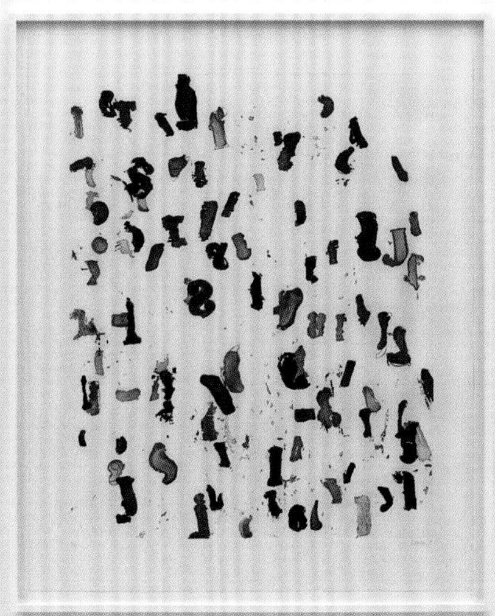

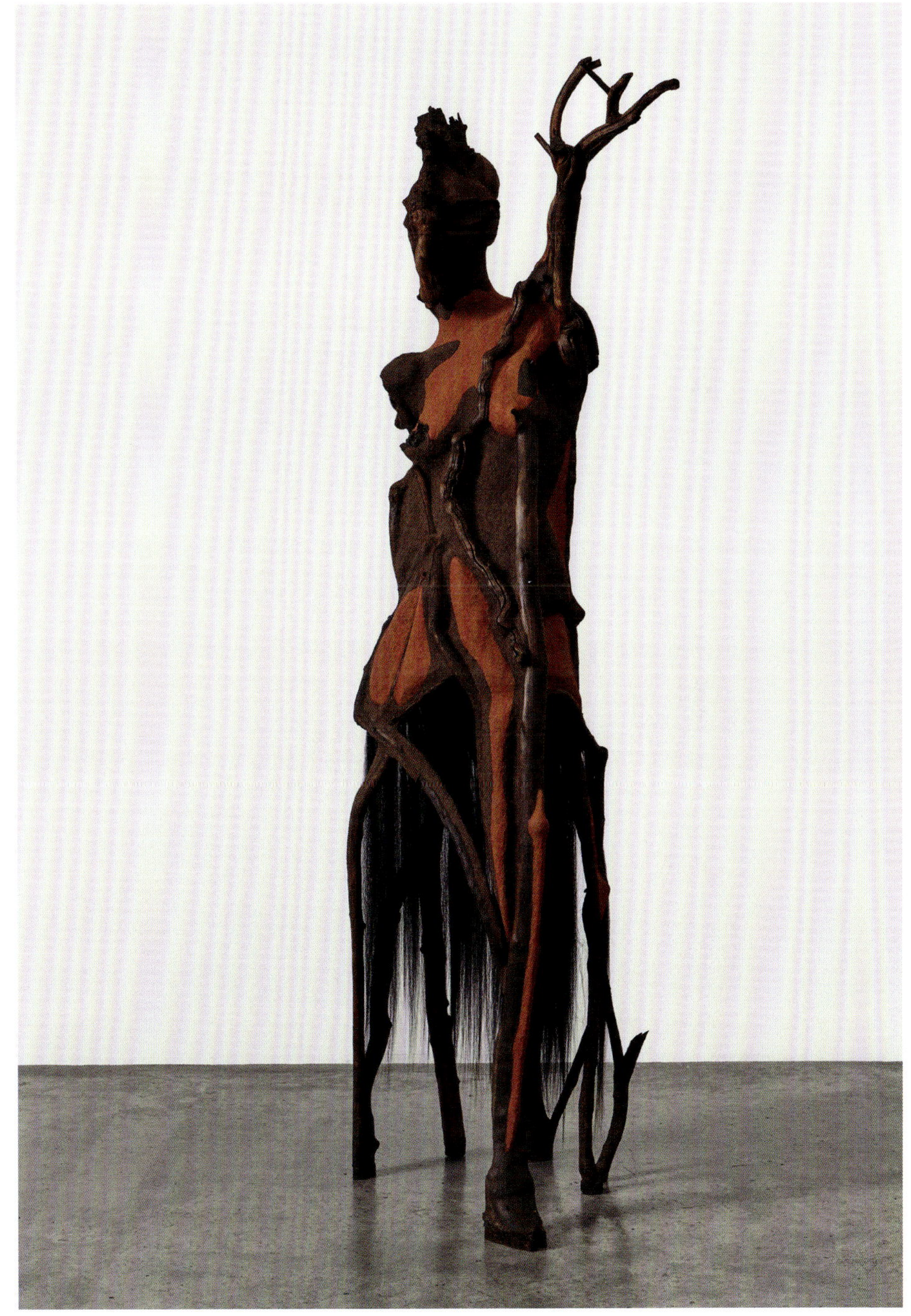

Theaster Gates
American Tapestry
Fire hose and wood
152 × 297 cm

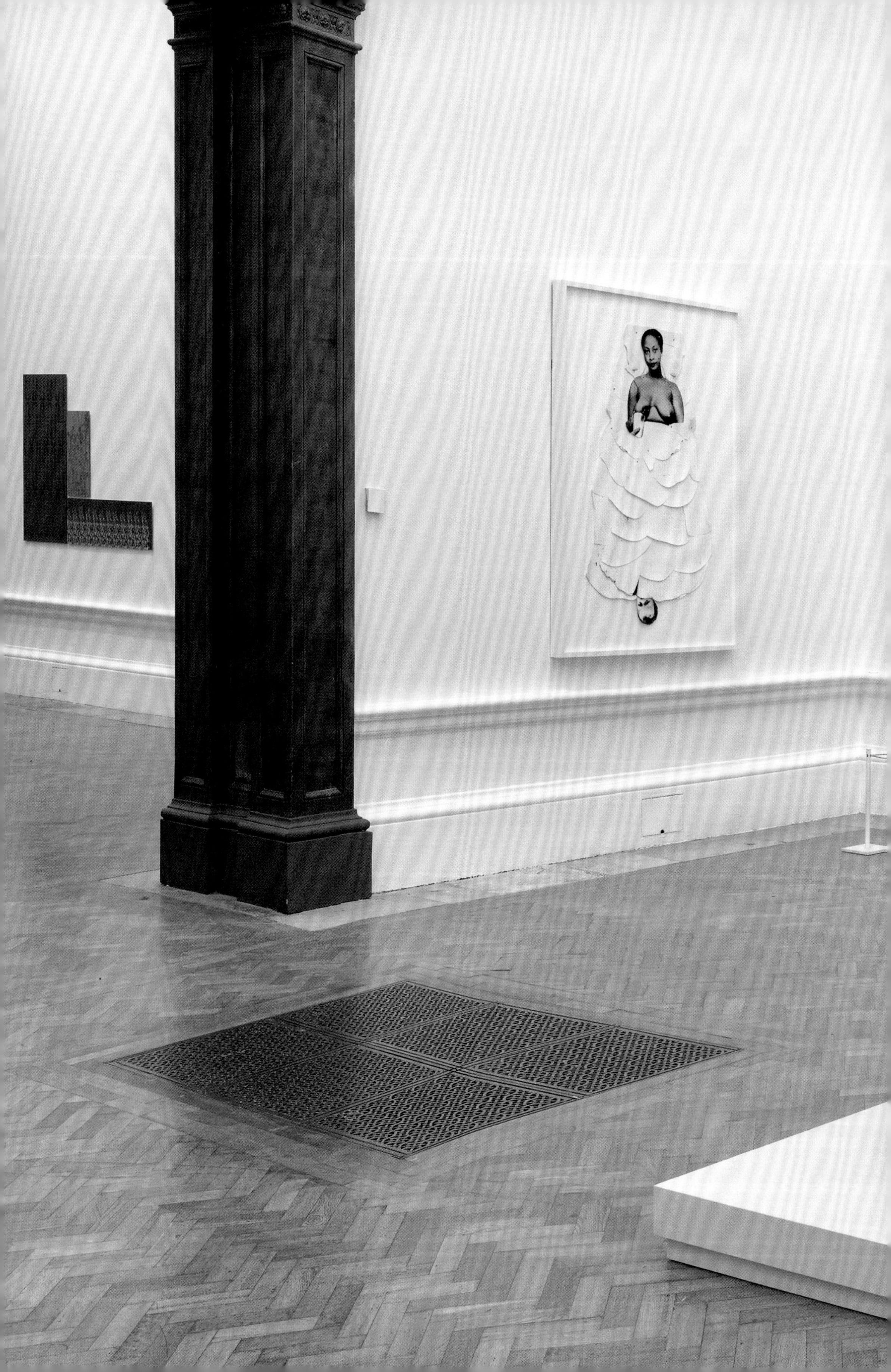

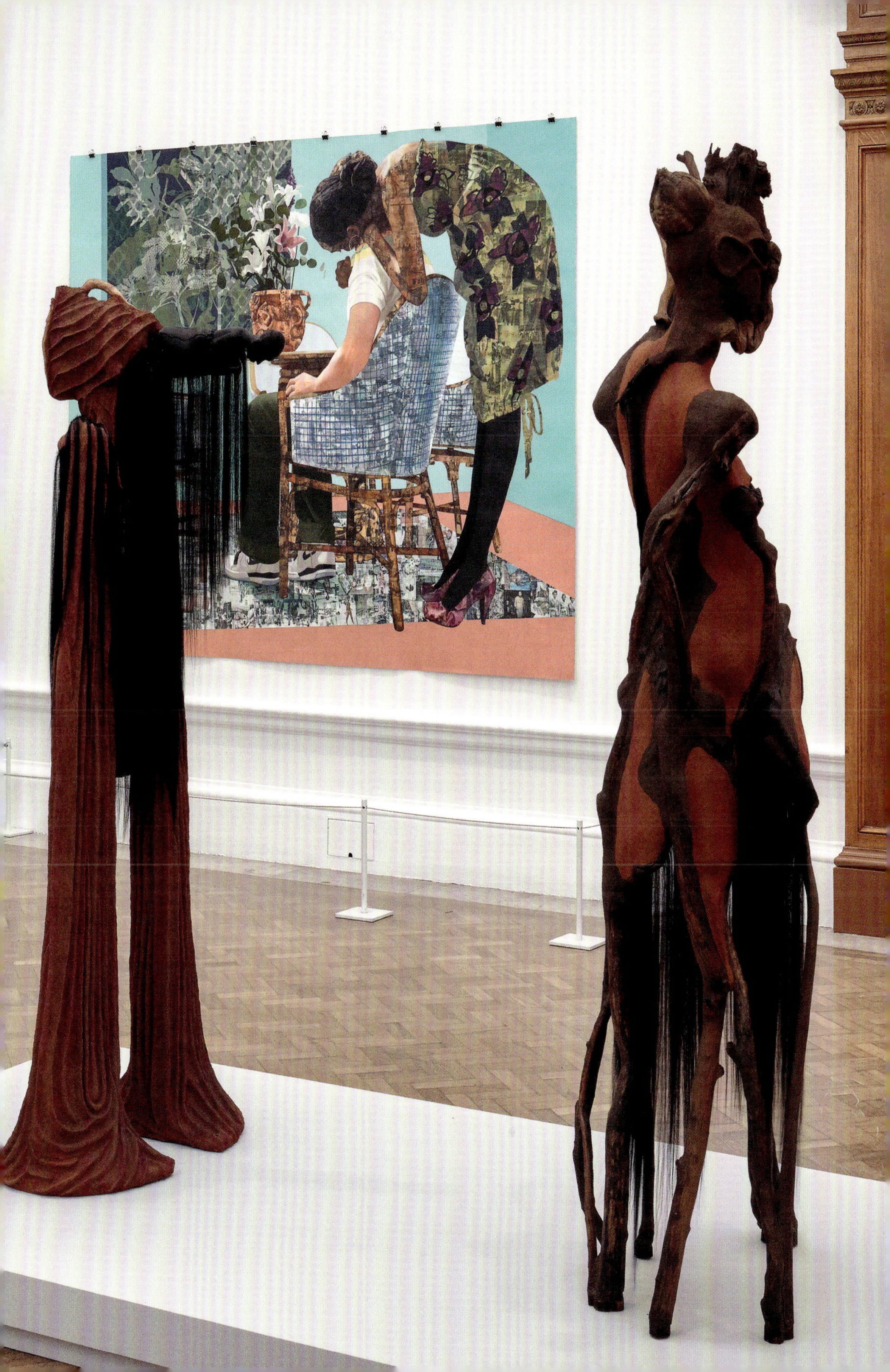

Conrad Atkinson
Vincentsear Uncovered and Euphonious Wound
Machine embroidery
64 × 168 cm

Karen Kilimnik
The Chinese Pavilion in Green Park
Oil
46 × 36 cm

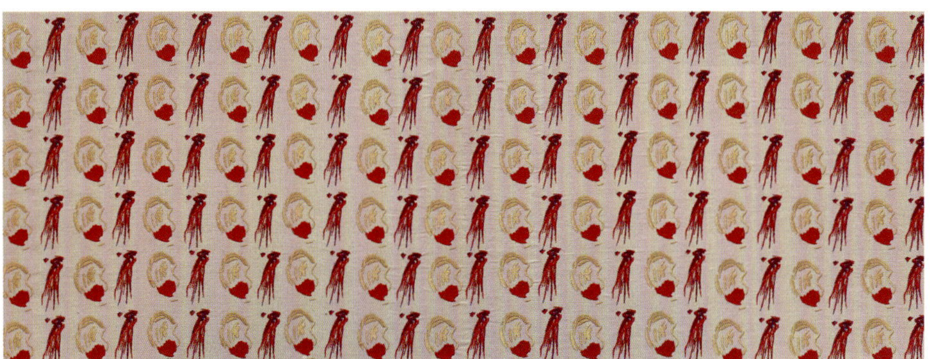

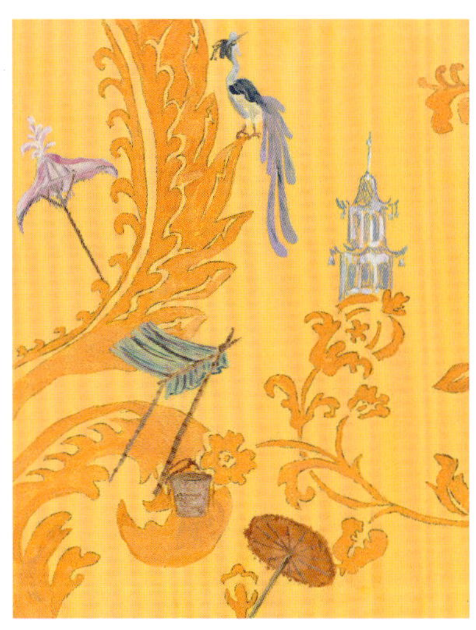

Jane and Louise Wilson RA
I'd Walk With You But Not With Her
Photographic print
34 × 34 cm

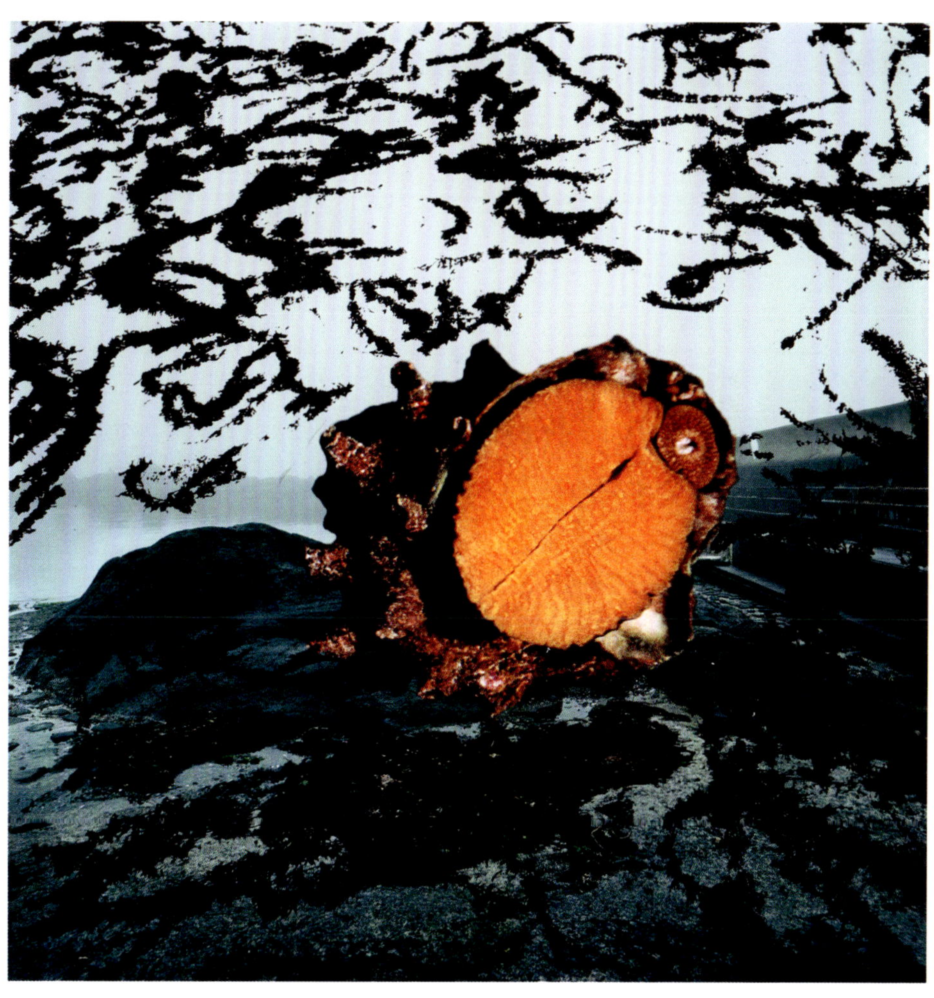

Gary Hume RA
The Sun Loved the Moon
Gloss paint
142 × 112 cm

Charles March
Shifting Sands 6
Giclée print
60 × 84 cm

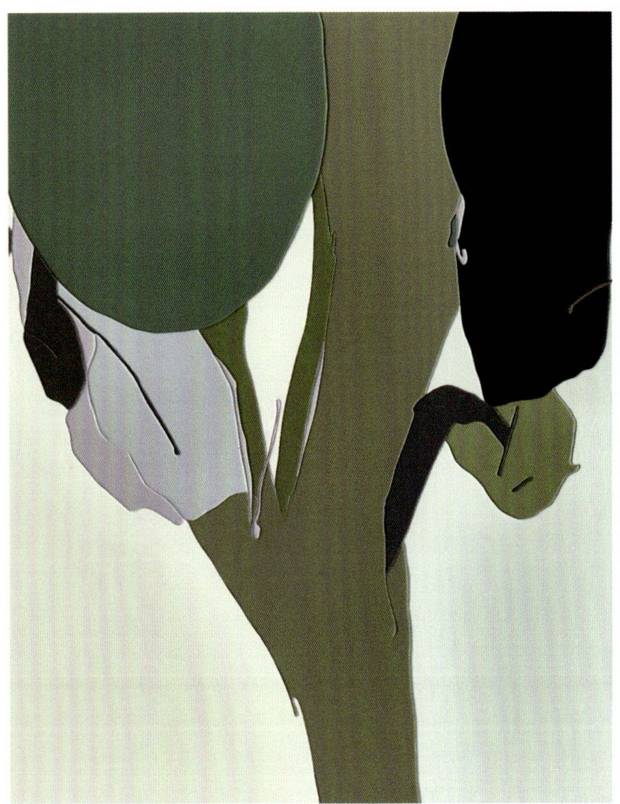

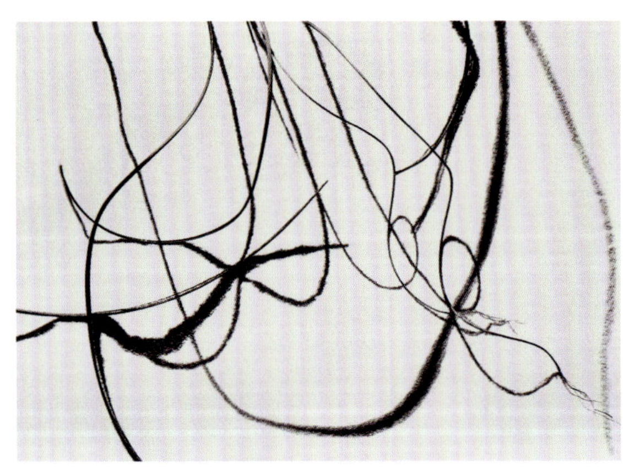

Joy Labinjo
Breakfast with Violet and Adam
Oil
150 × 200 cm

Yuri Pattison
transparent form (for user,space)
Video

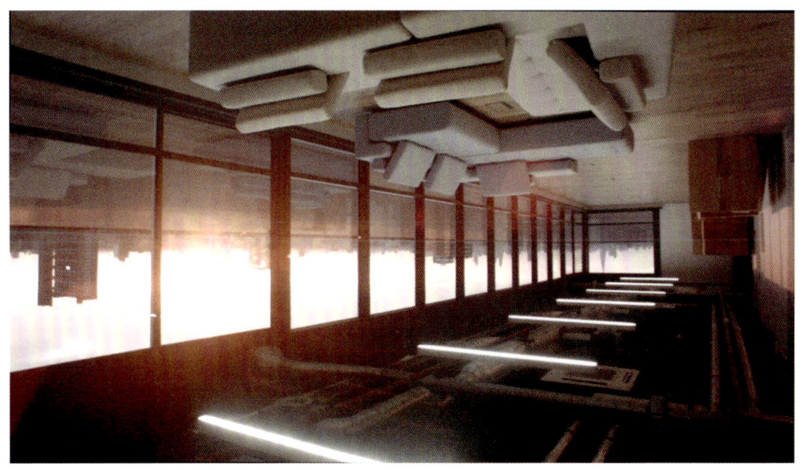

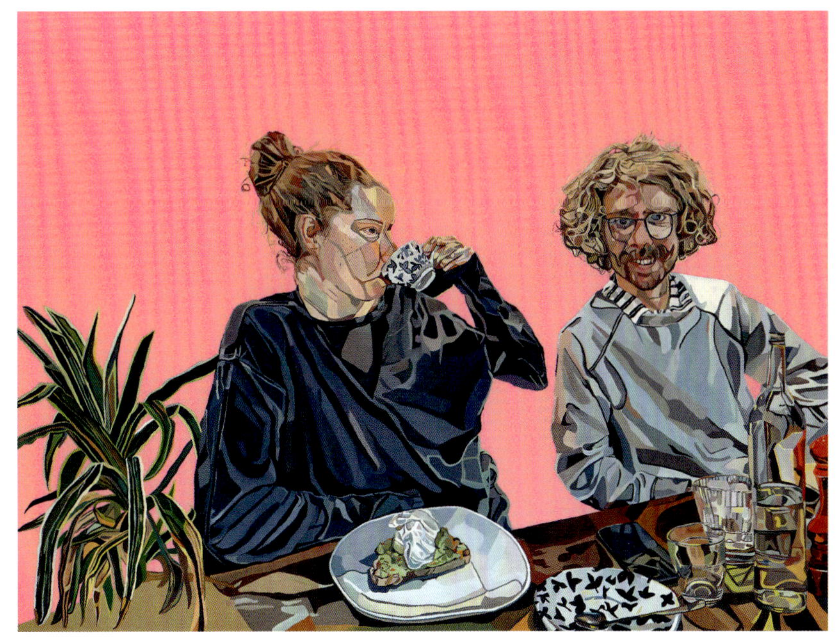

David Batchelor
Inter-Concreto 25
Acrylic and concrete
H 181 cm

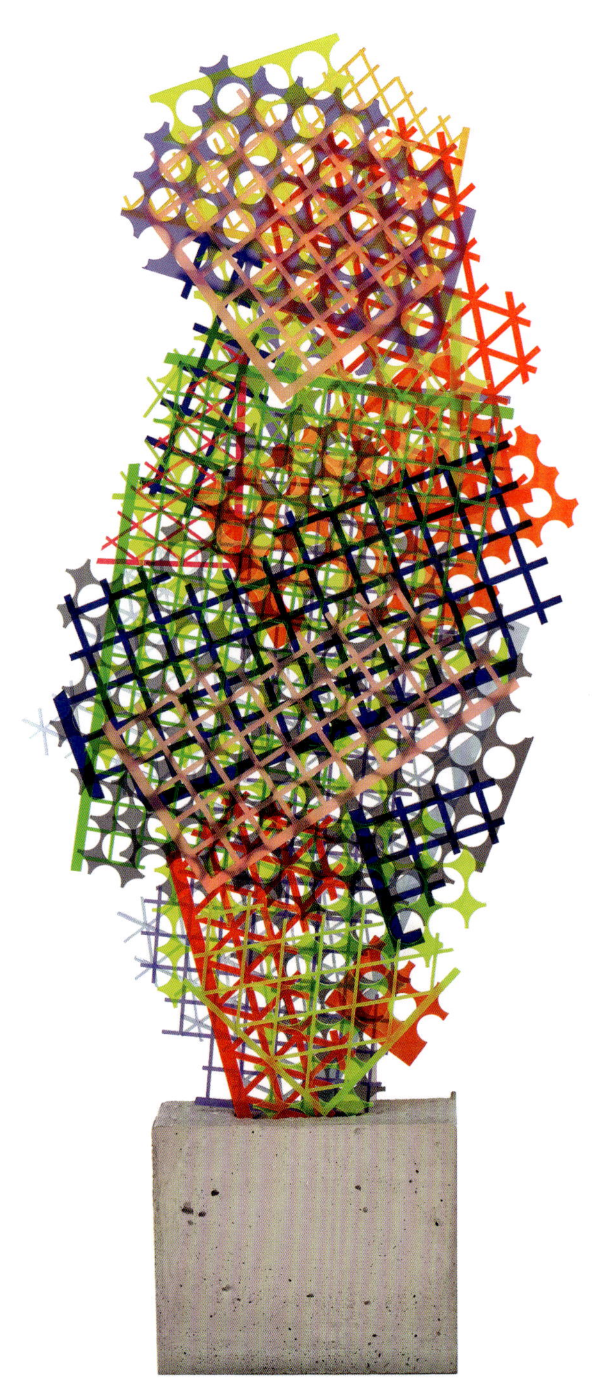

William Tucker RA
Wall Relief
Aluminium
H 255 cm

Prof Fiona Banner RA aka The Vanity Press
Intermission
Sunburnt paper
30 × 42 cm

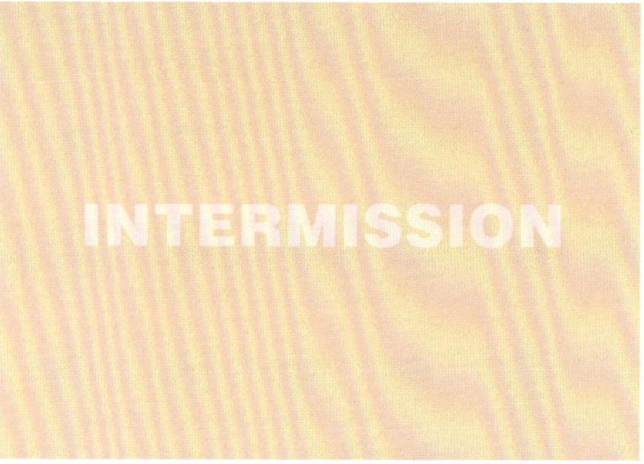

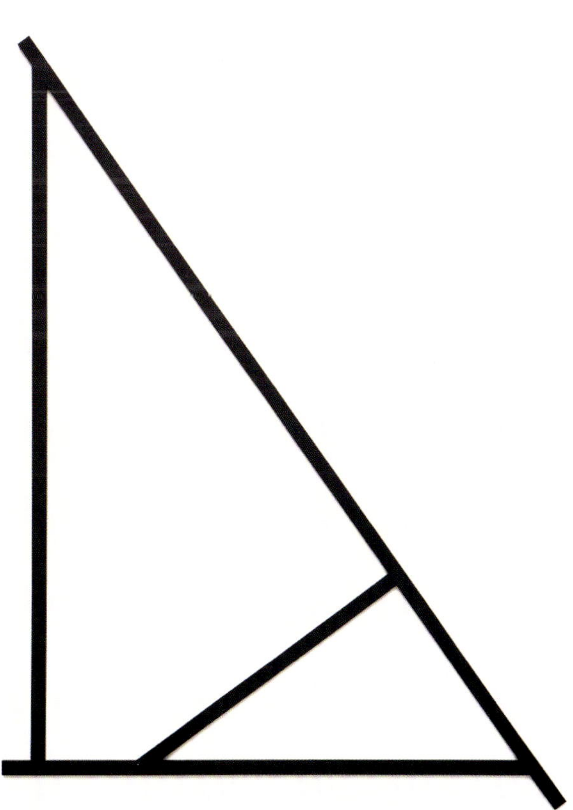

Margaret Harrison
Pain, Pleasure and Power
Mixed media
213 × 162 cm

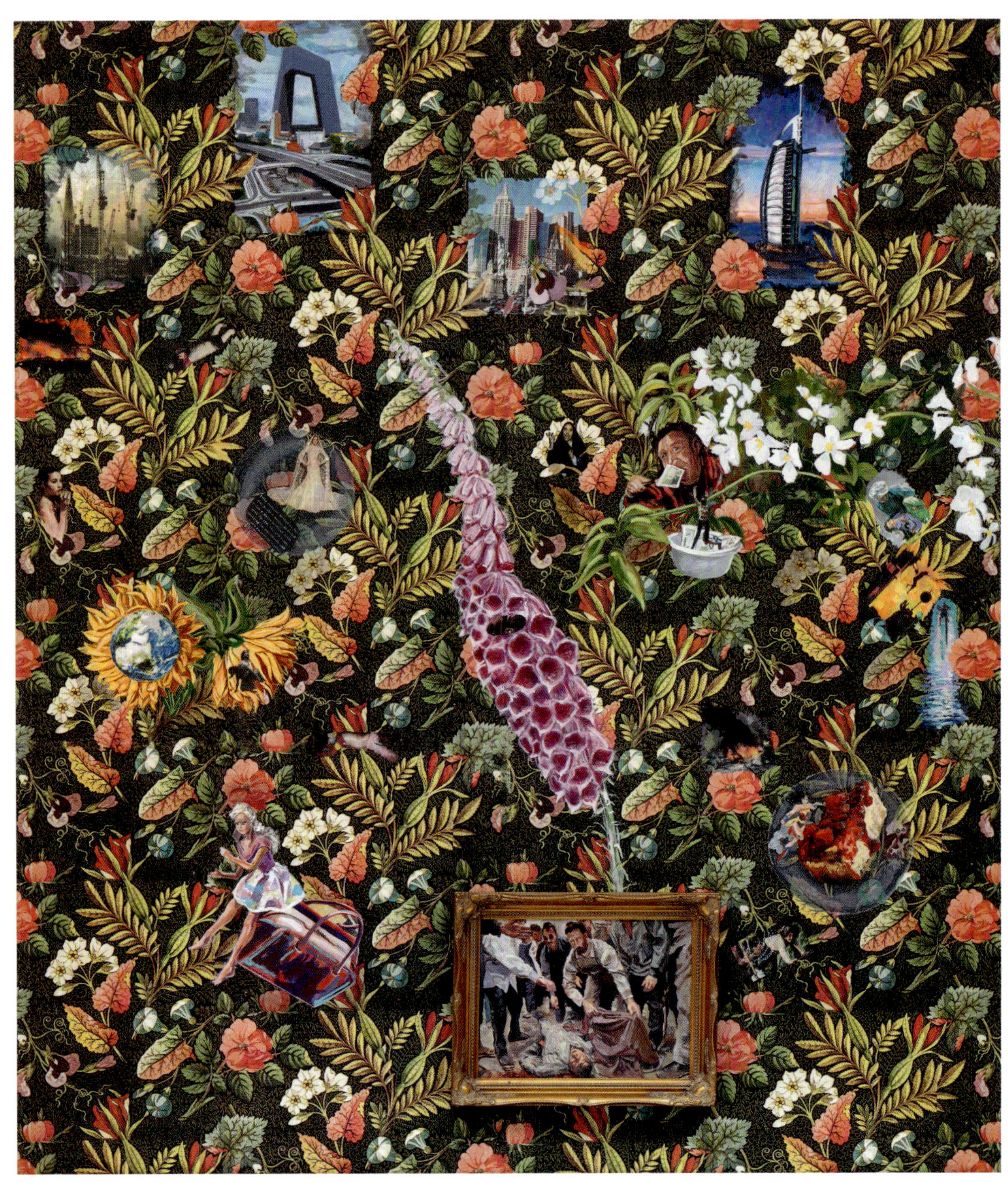

Simon Periton
The Lookout
Copper-plated steel
H 101 cm

Tomma Abts
Leko
Acrylic and oil
48 × 38 cm

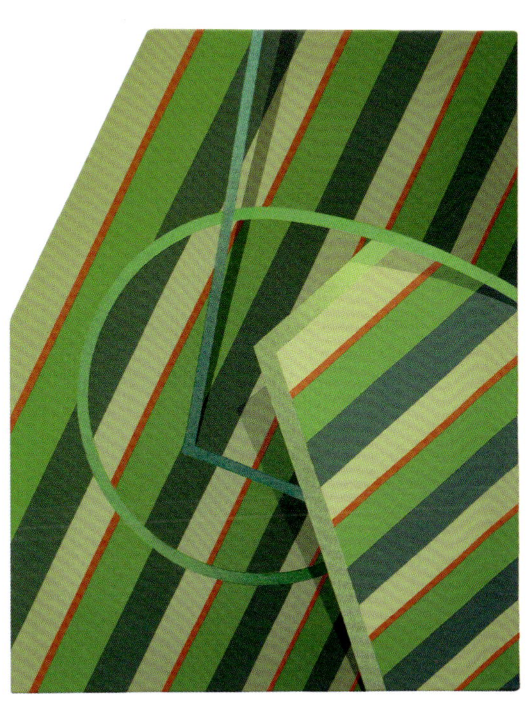

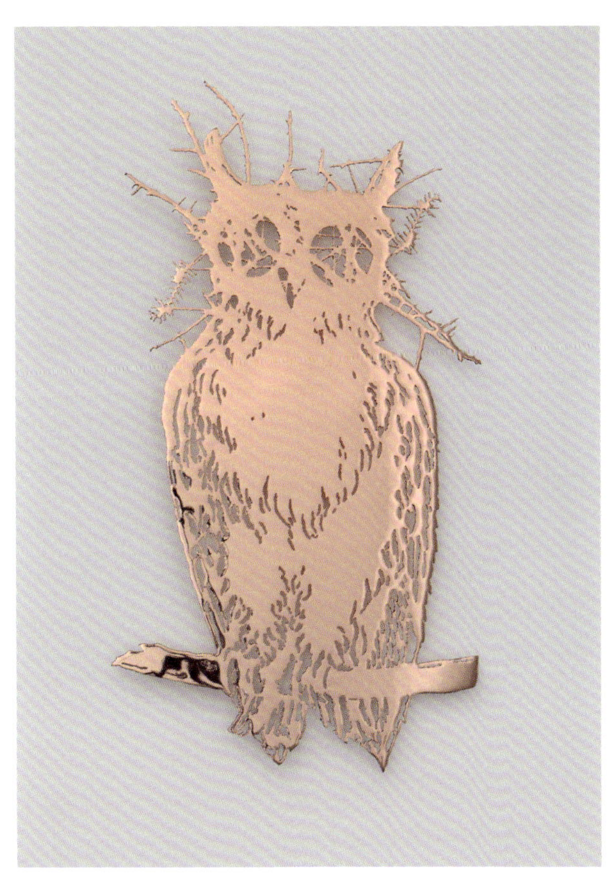

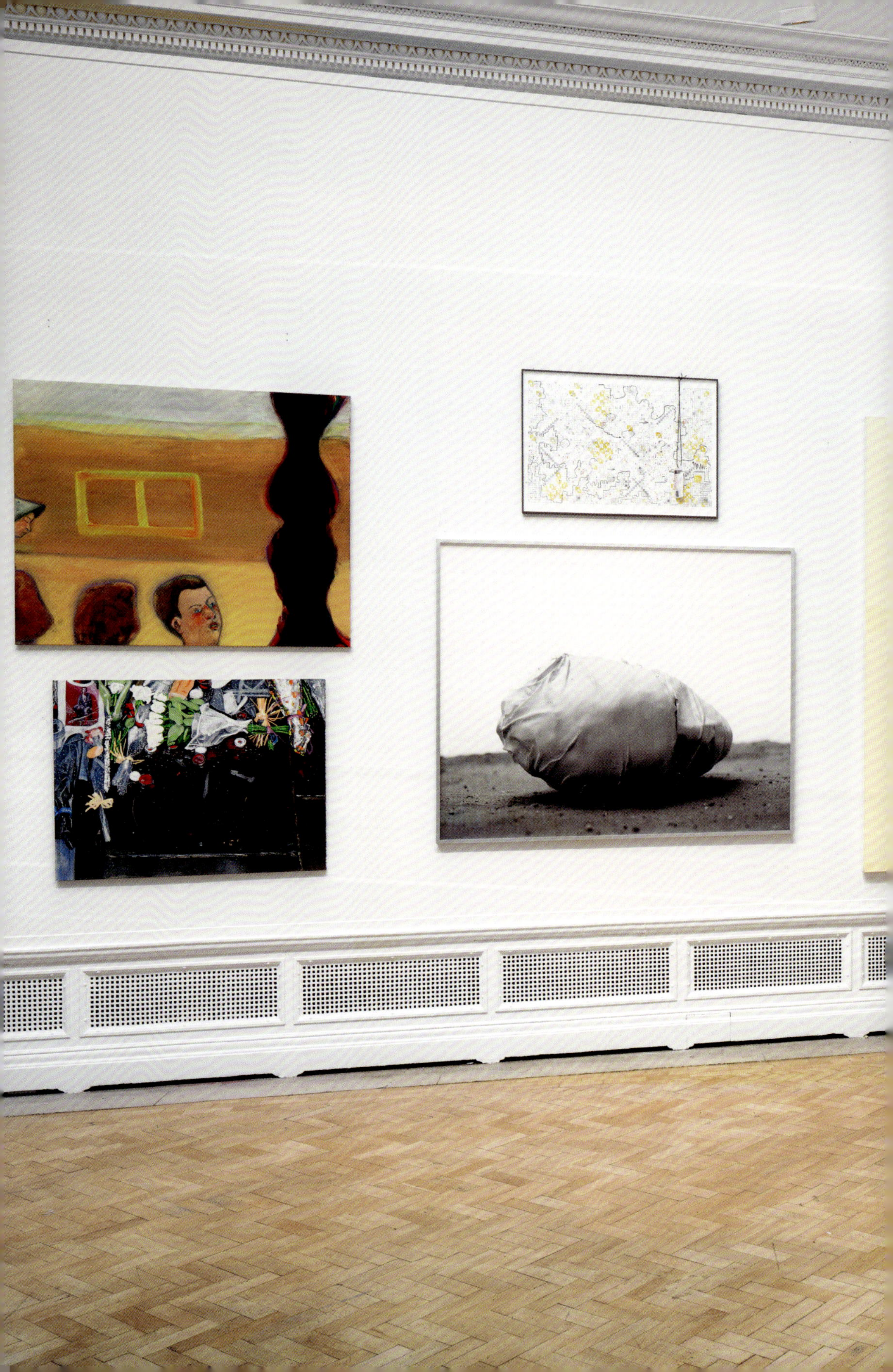

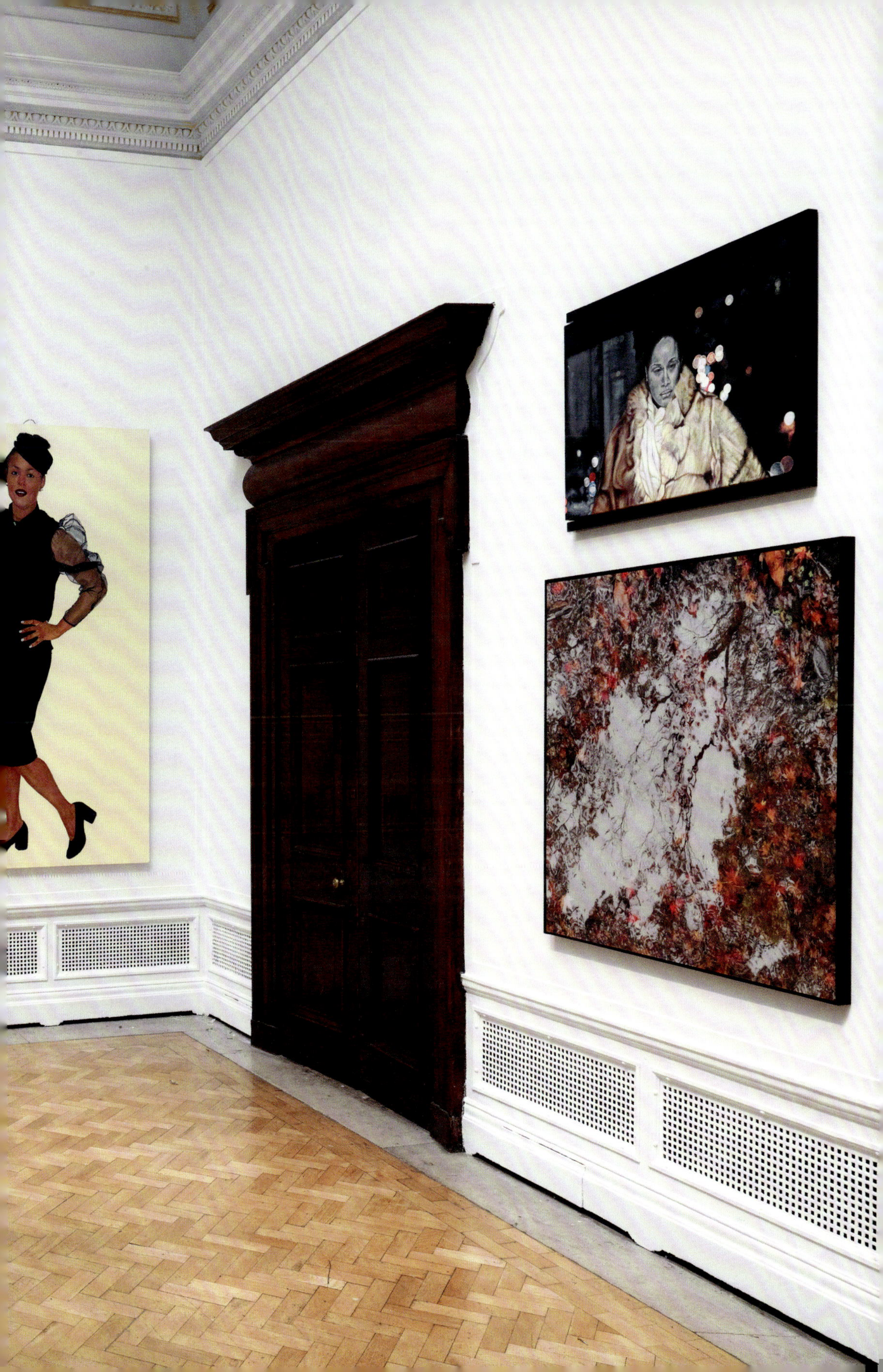

Ori Gersht
Floating World Melting World 02
Photographic print
120 × 120 cm

Eddie Peake
Sweat
Screenprint
76 × 60 cm

Prof Rebecca Horn Hon RA
Oracle
Acrylic and pencil
181 × 150 cm

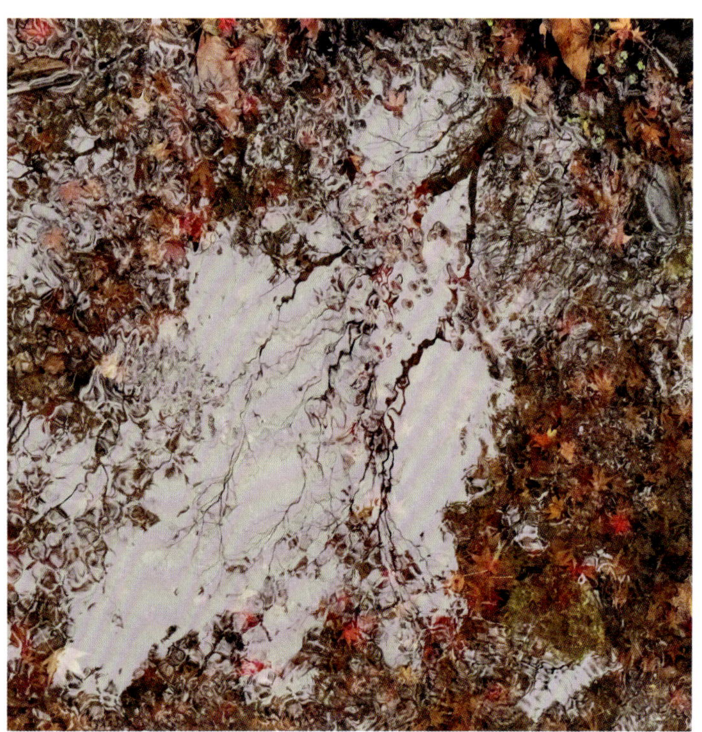

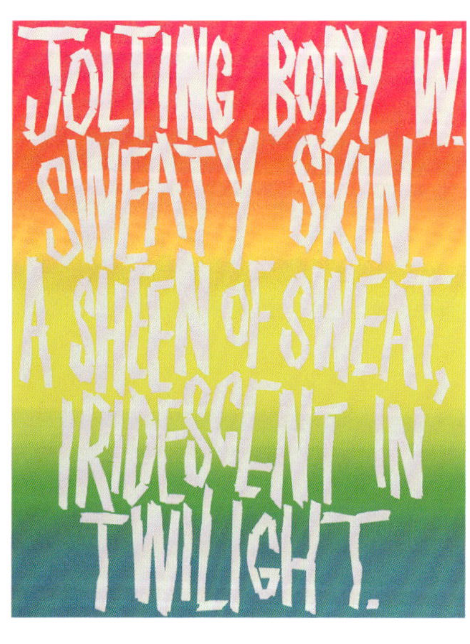

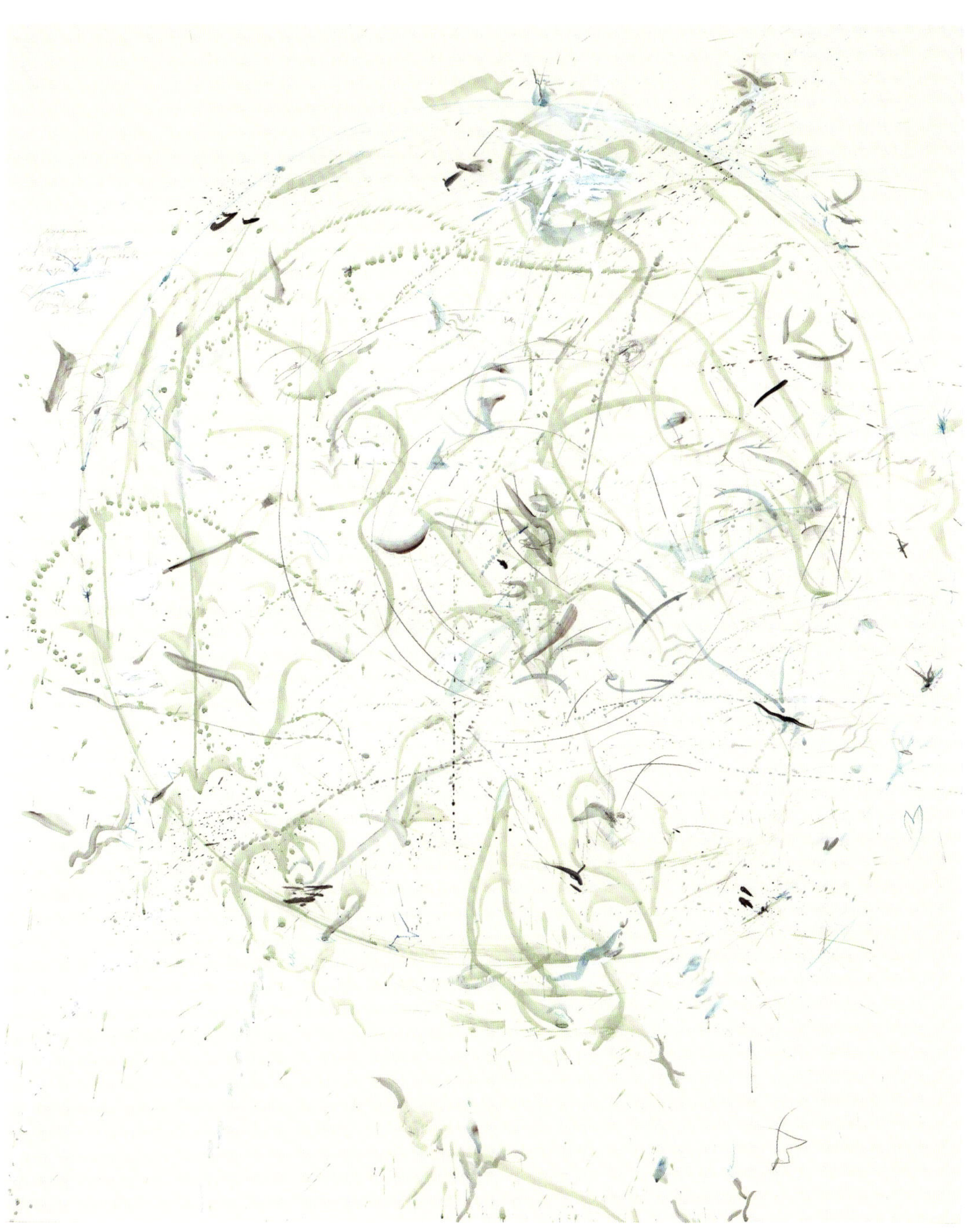

Gillian Wearing CBE RA
Lockdown Portrait
Watercolour
48 × 36 cm

Linder
Superautomatism IV
Enamel on magazine
26 × 19 cm

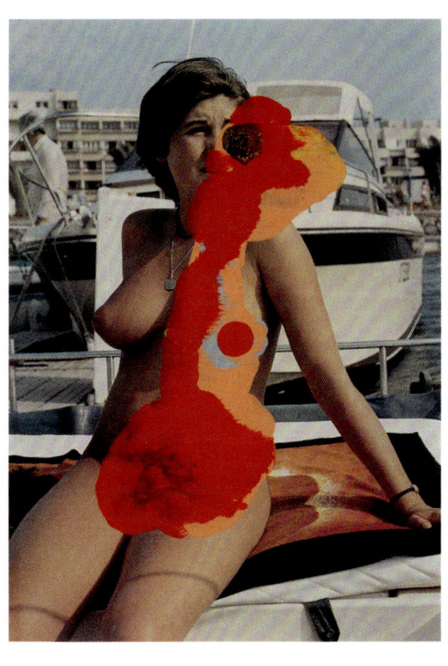

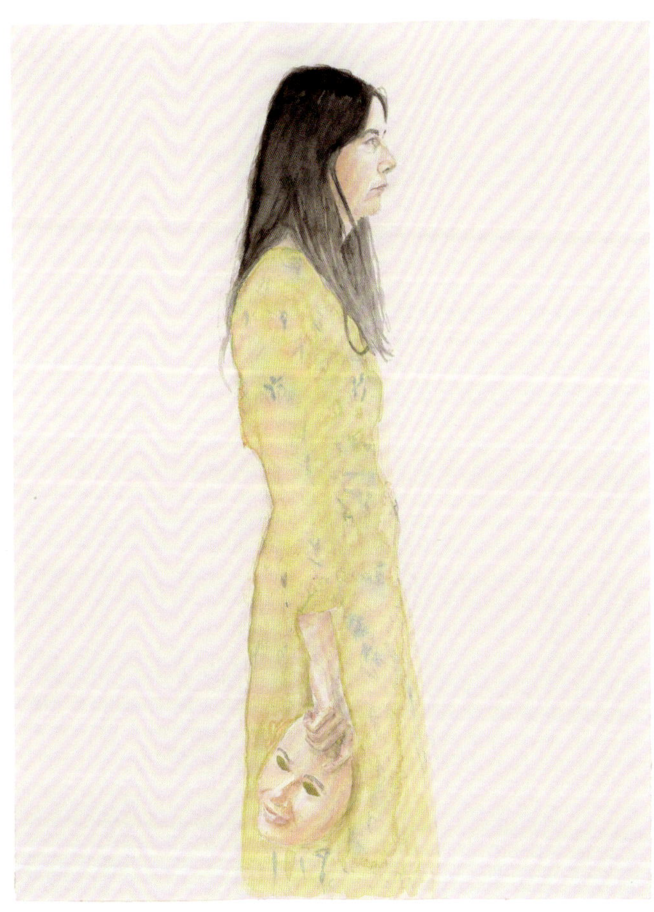

Hans-Peter Feldmann
Legs
Photographs
80 × 100 cm

Reza Aramesh
Action 116: Study of the Head as Cultural Artefact
Photographic print
148 × 184 cm

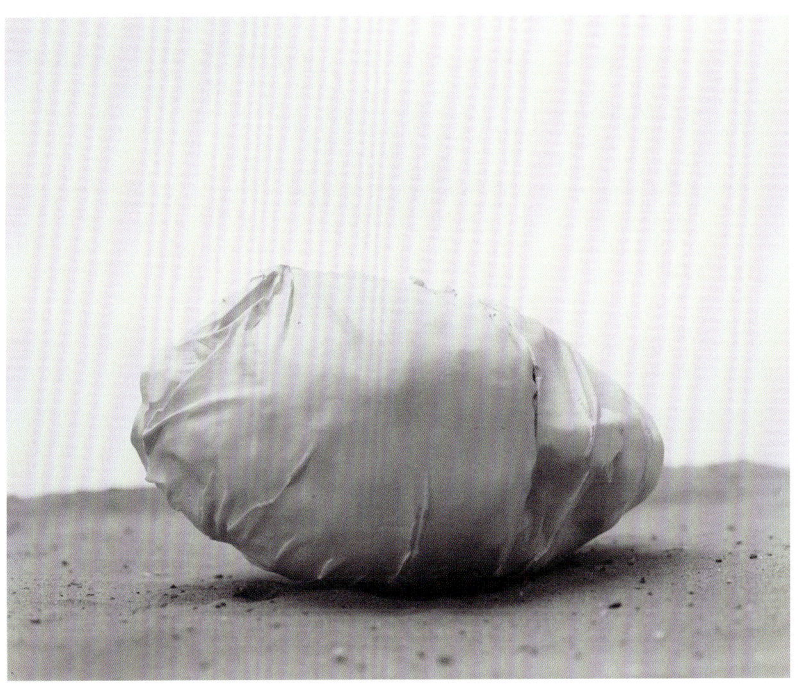

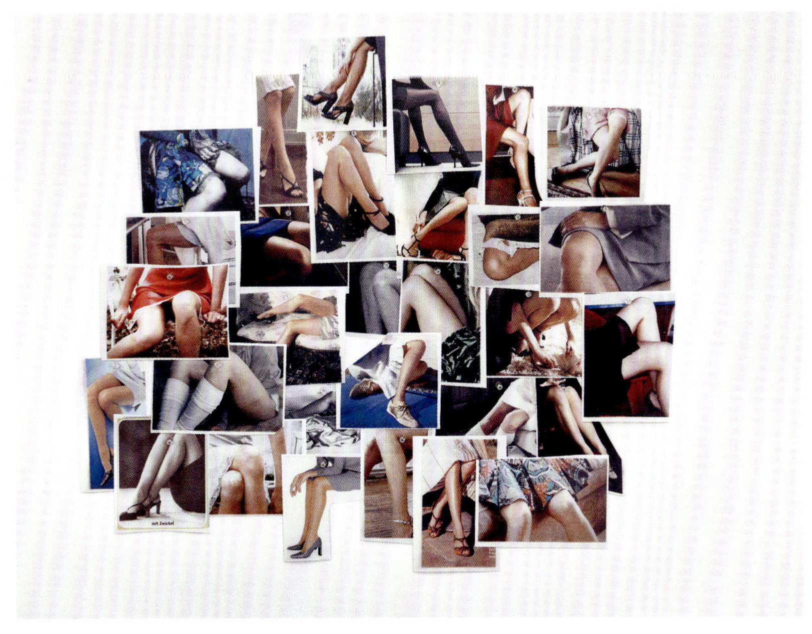

Prof Stephen Farthing RA
Study for a Portrait of a Fat Cat in the Age of the Oligarchy
Acrylic
60 × 100 cm

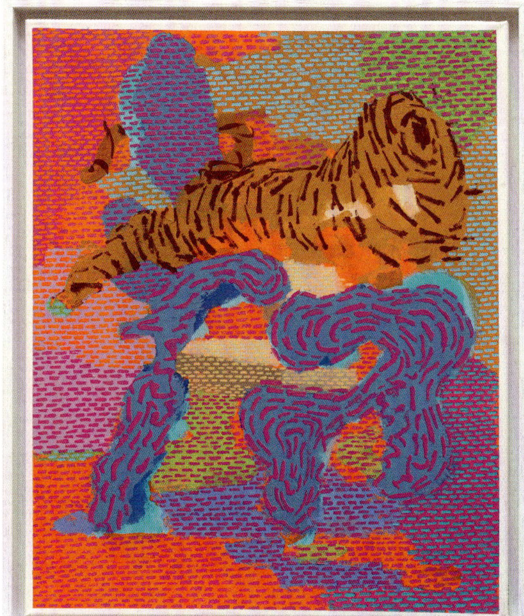

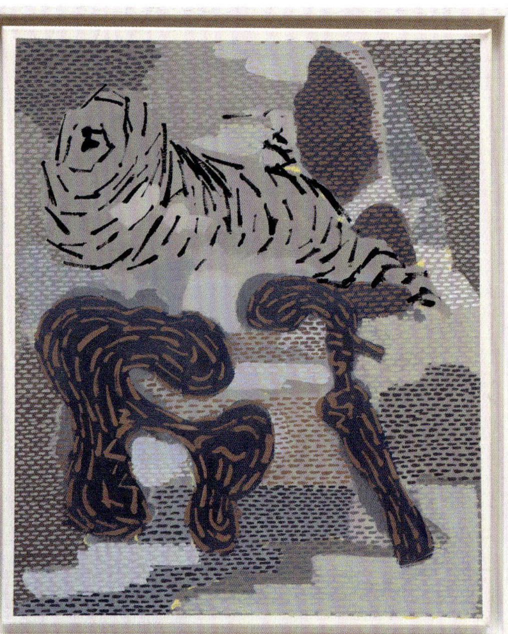

Vanessa Jackson RA
Spin Off
Oil
183 × 183 cm

Anthony Whishaw RA
Openings II
Acrylic
31 × 31 cm

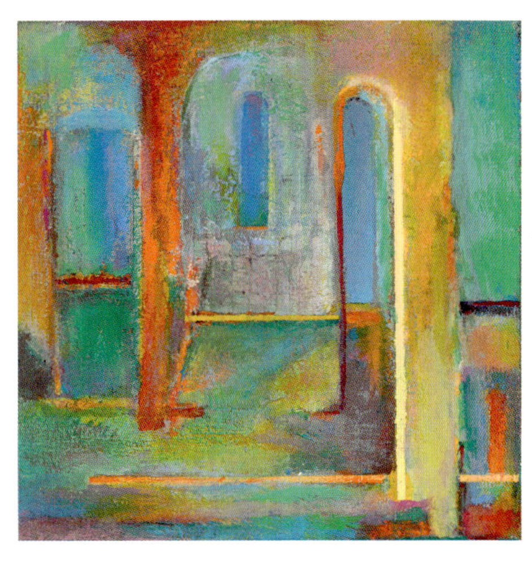

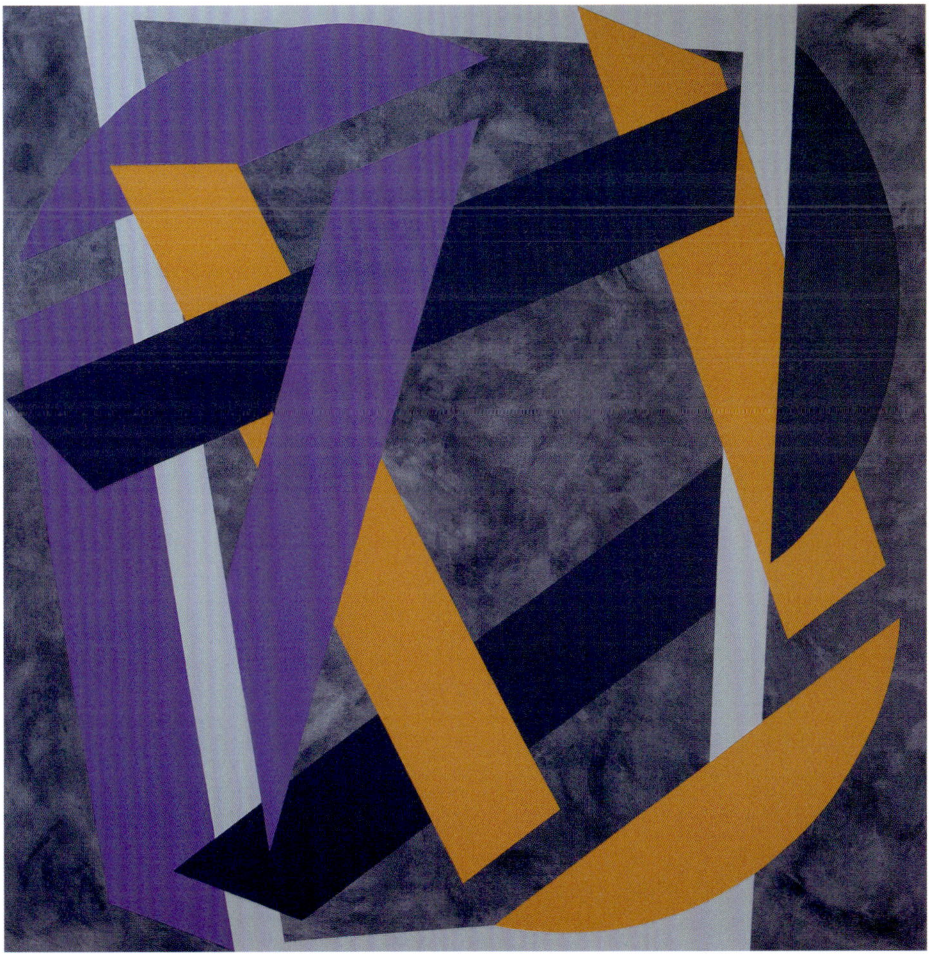

Sir Michael Craig-Martin CBE RA
Untitled (with glasses)
Acrylic
122 × 122 cm

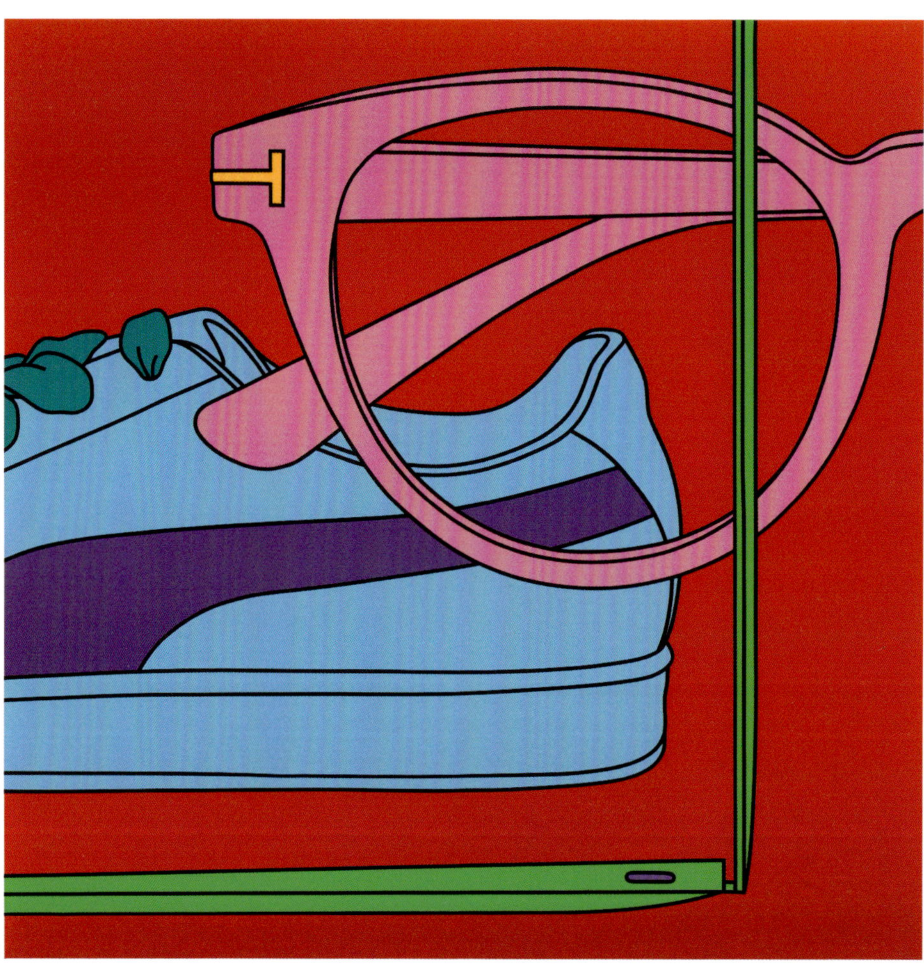

Prof Paul Huxley RA
Fermata 1
Acrylic
117 × 117 cm

Tess Jaray RA
Full Stop
Acrylic
80 × 309 cm

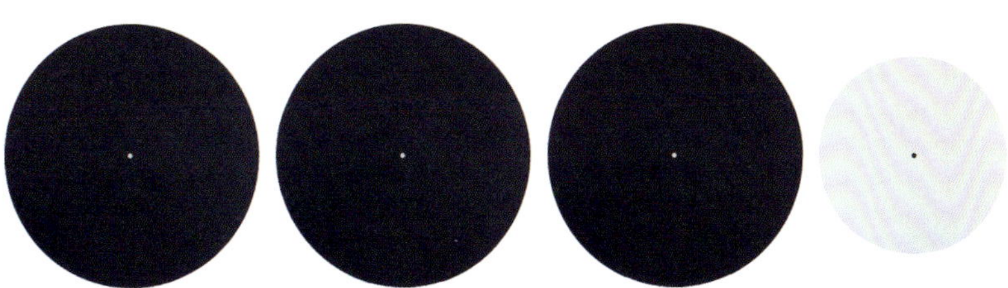

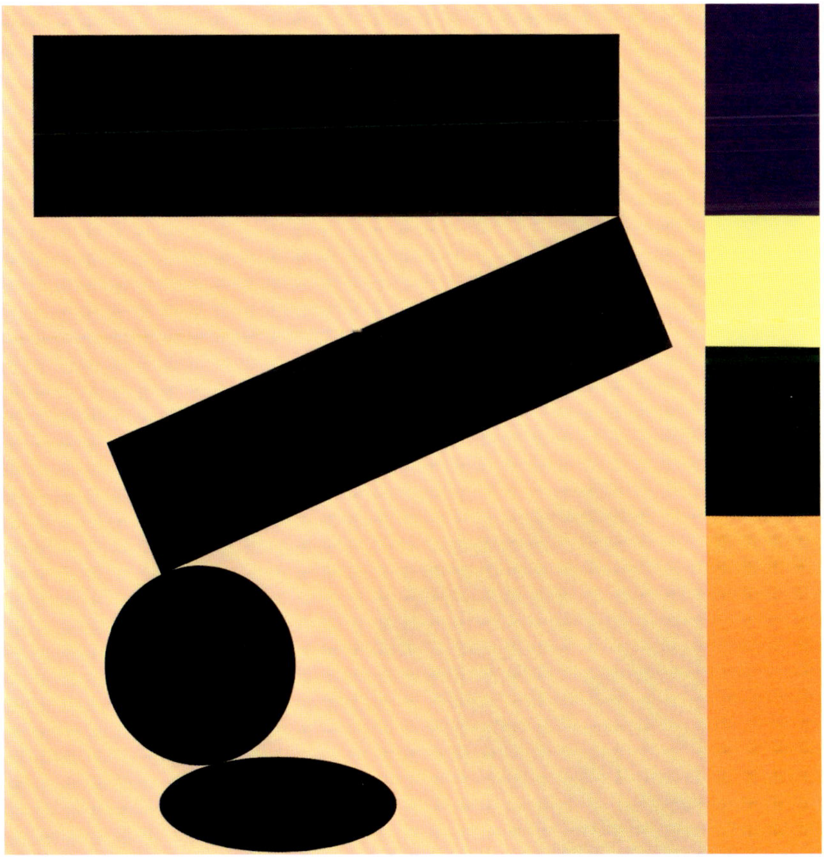

Jock McFadyen RA
Lost Boat Party
Oil
153 × 339 cm

Joe Tilson RA
The Stones of Venice, Contarini Fasan
Polyptych and acrylic
182 × 457 cm

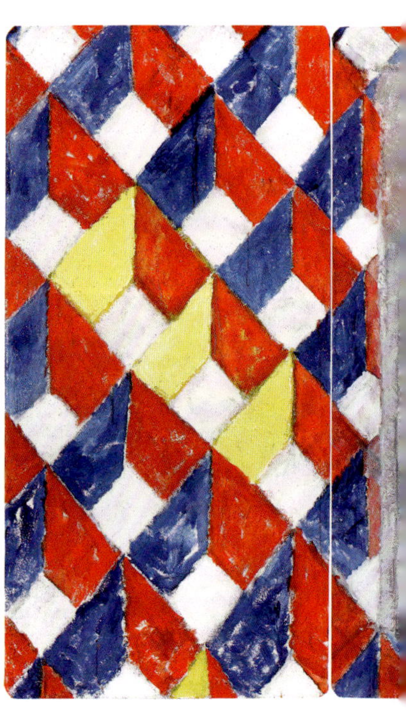

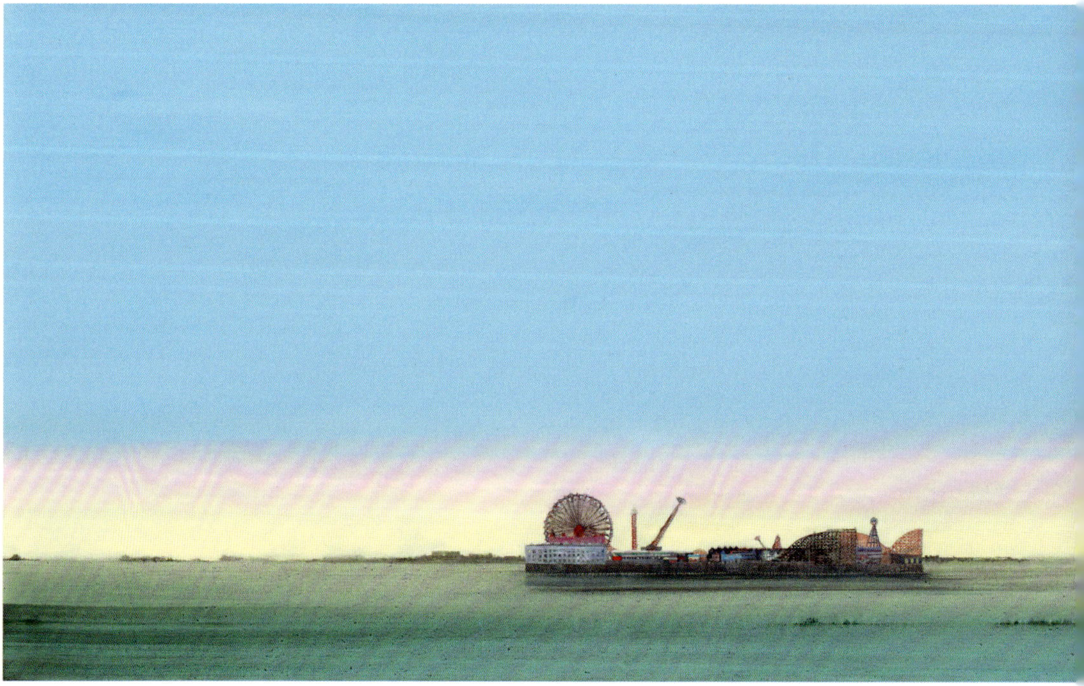

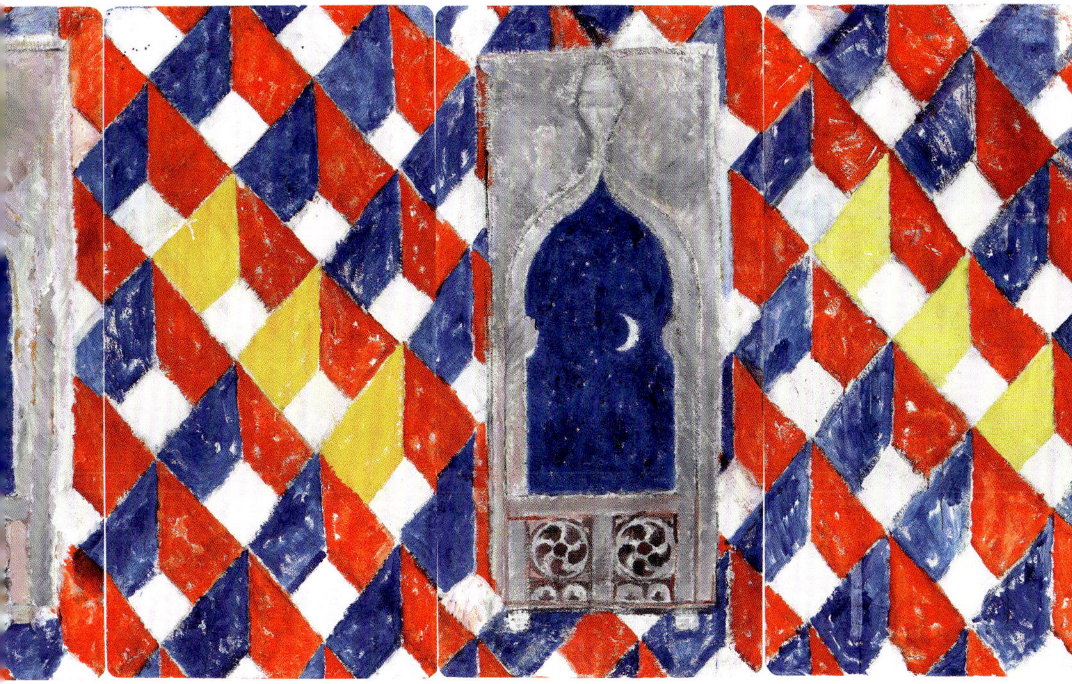

Ken Howard OBE RA
Drying Saris, Manmandir Ghat
Oil
51 × 61 cm

Frederick Cuming Hon DLitt RA
February Landscape, Peasmarsh
Oil
71 × 92 cm

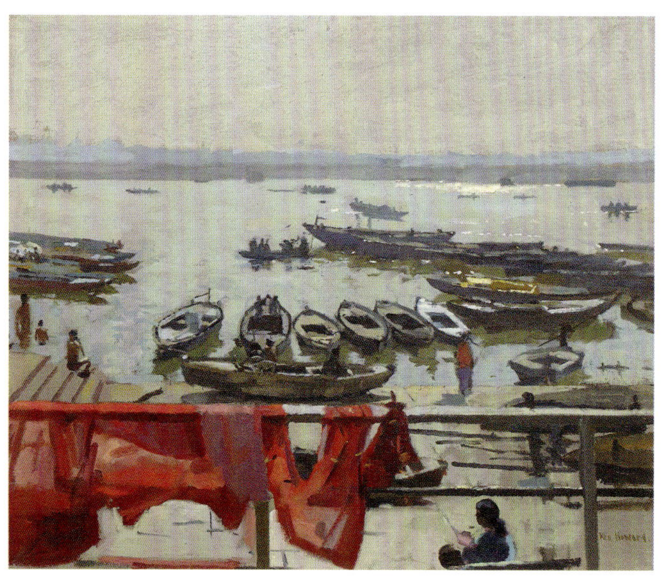

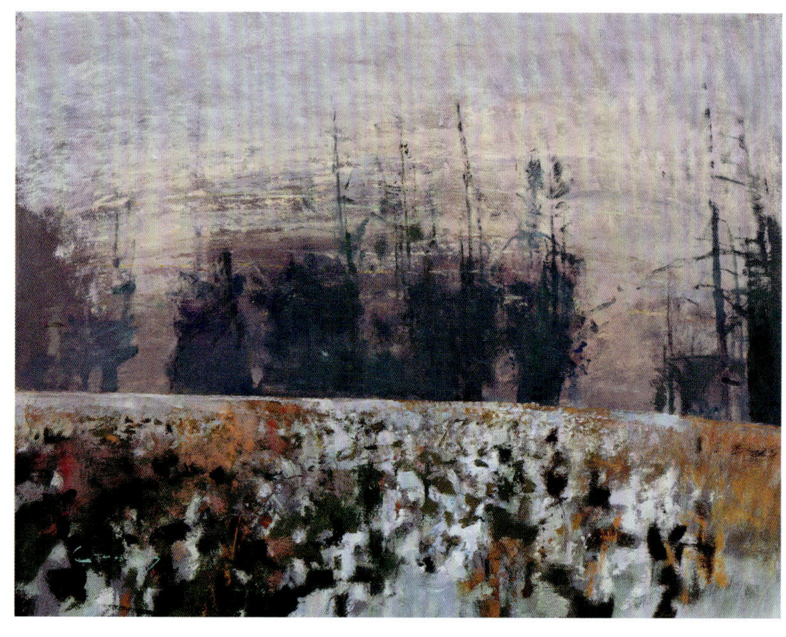

The late Jeffery Camp RA
Fling
Oil
125 × 325 cm

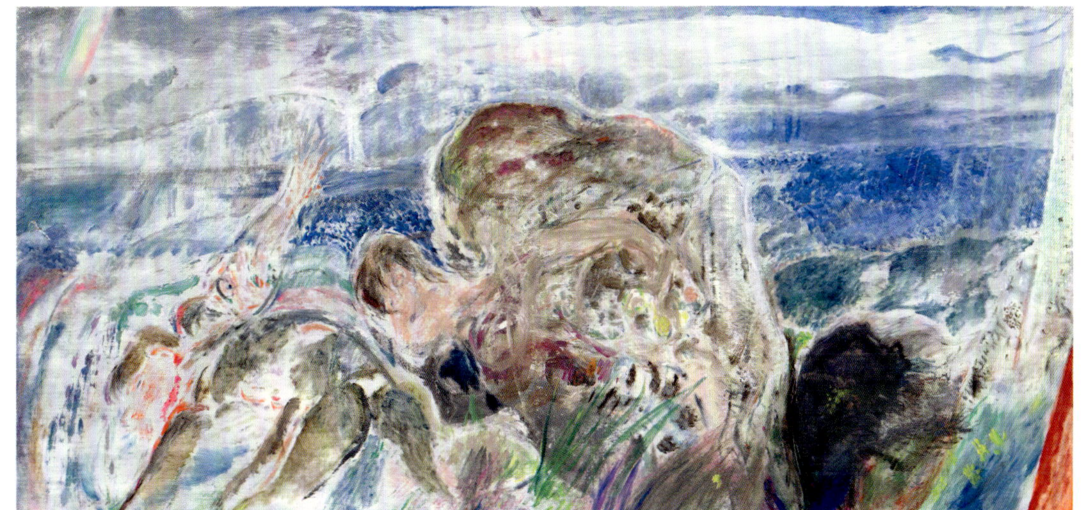

Hughie O'Donoghue RA
Wake
Mixed media
183 × 243 cm

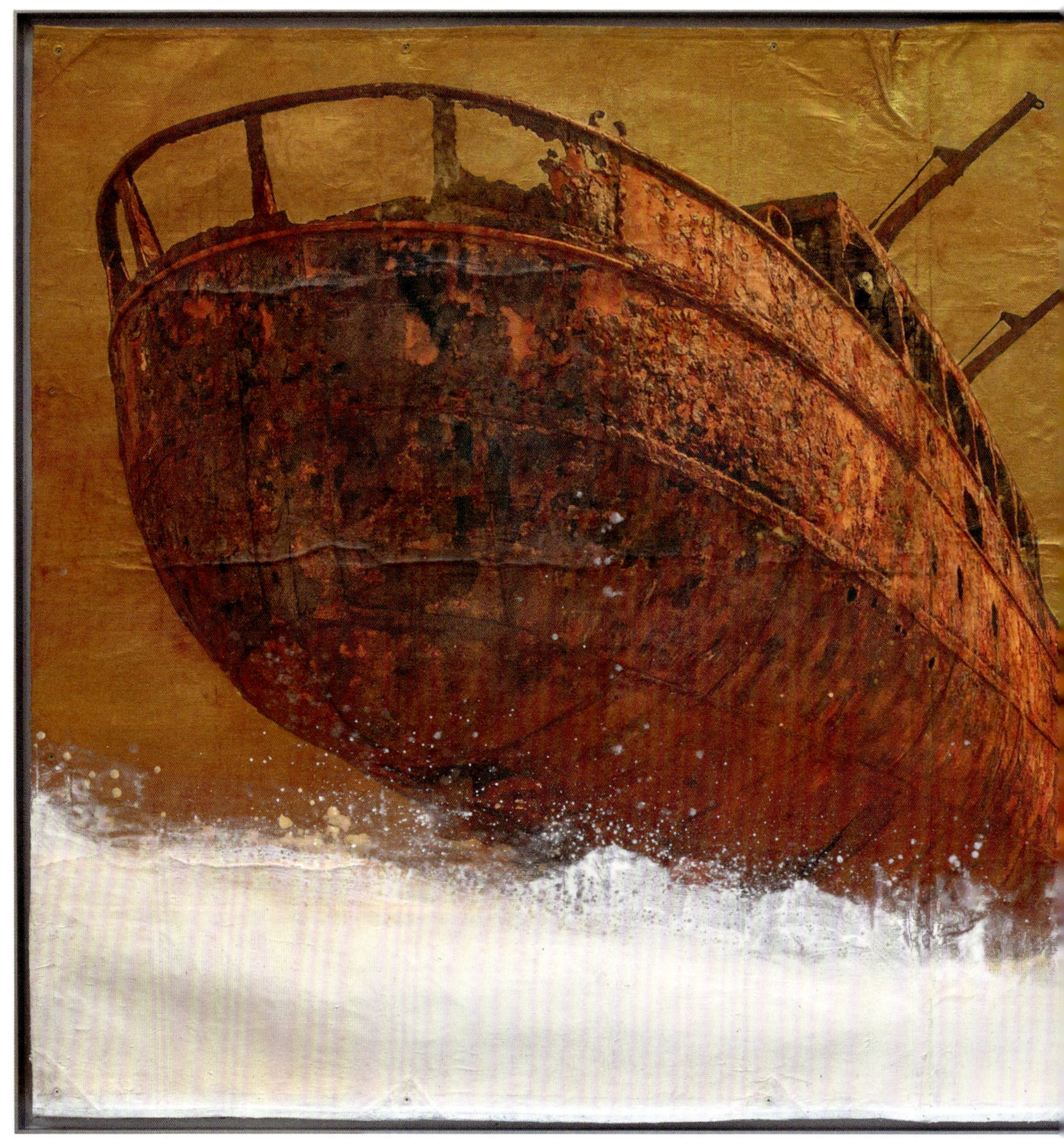

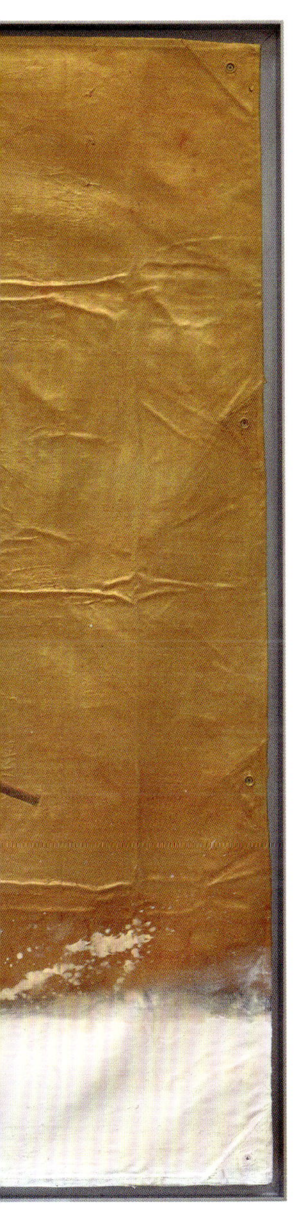

Terry Setch RA
Squall
Wax and pigment
27 × 36 cm

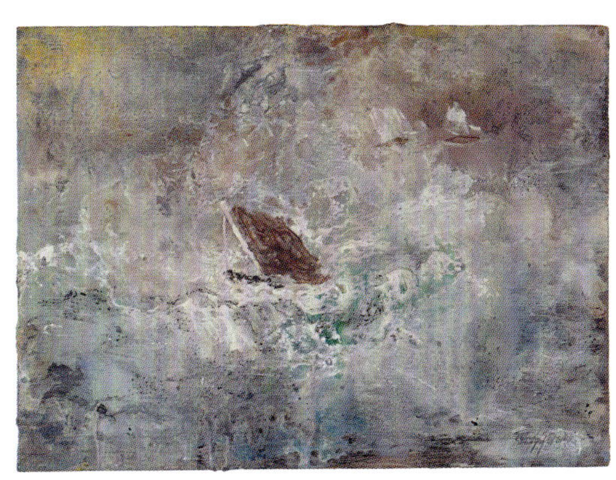

Humphrey Ocean RA
Now You See Me
Oil
122 × 153 cm

Philip Sutton RA
I Heard a Buzz
Oil
128 × 127 cm

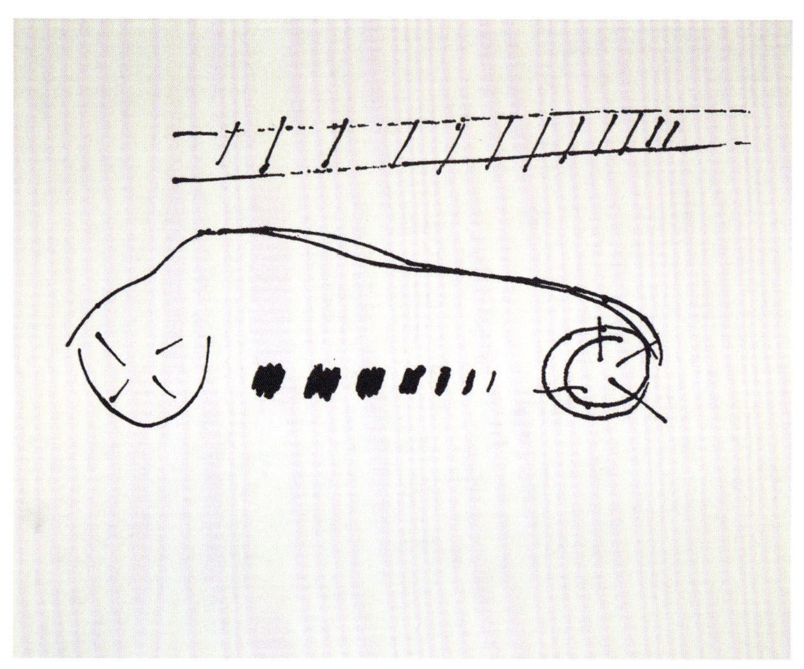

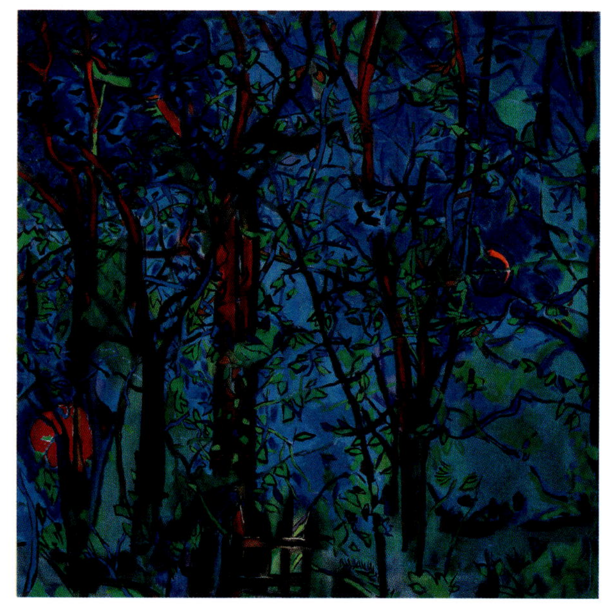

Mimmo Paladino Hon RA
Notturno (Nocturnal)
Mixed media
200 × 300 cm

Anselm Kiefer Hon RA
Vier Plus Eins
Mixed media
330 × 570 cm

Julian Schnabel Hon RA
Untitled (Bez)
Oil
335 × 234 cm

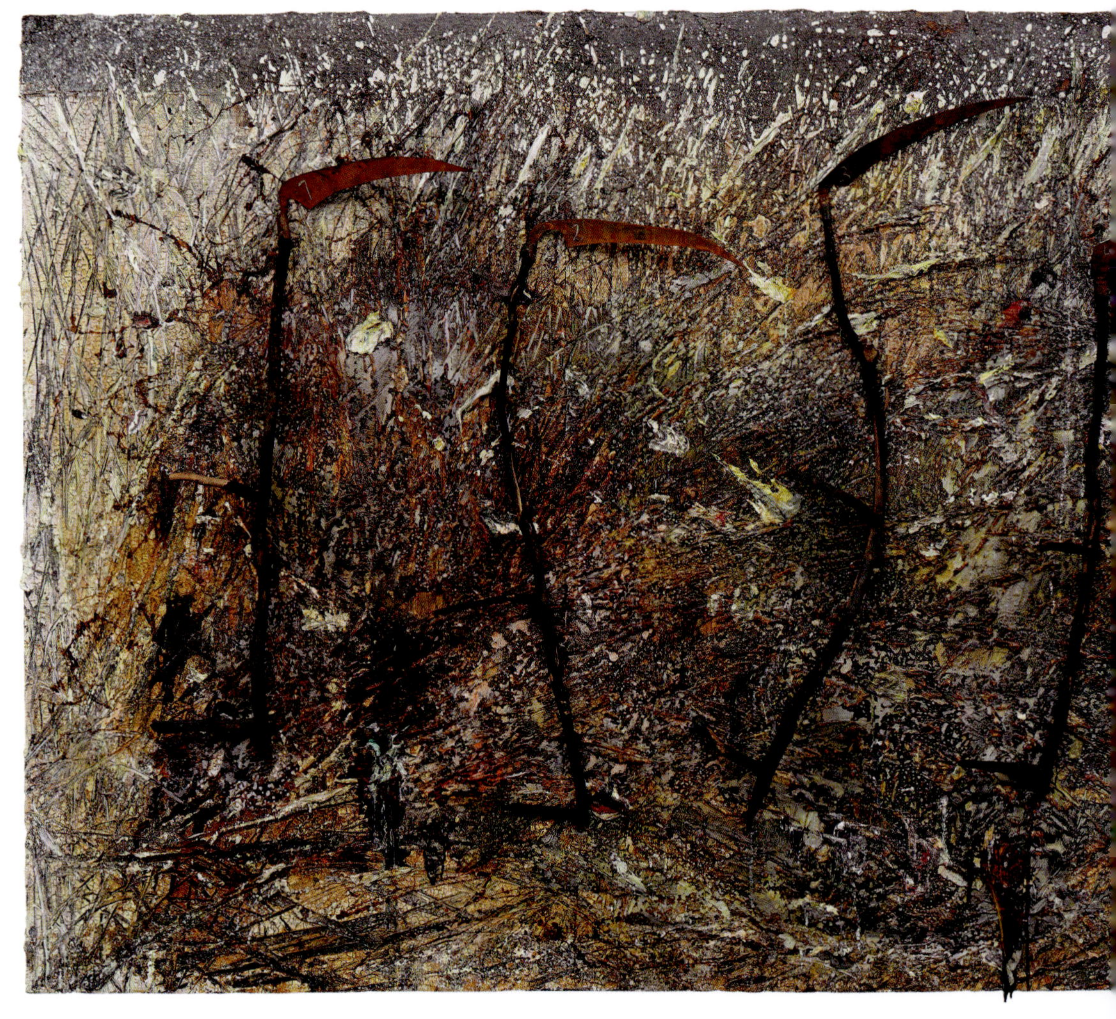

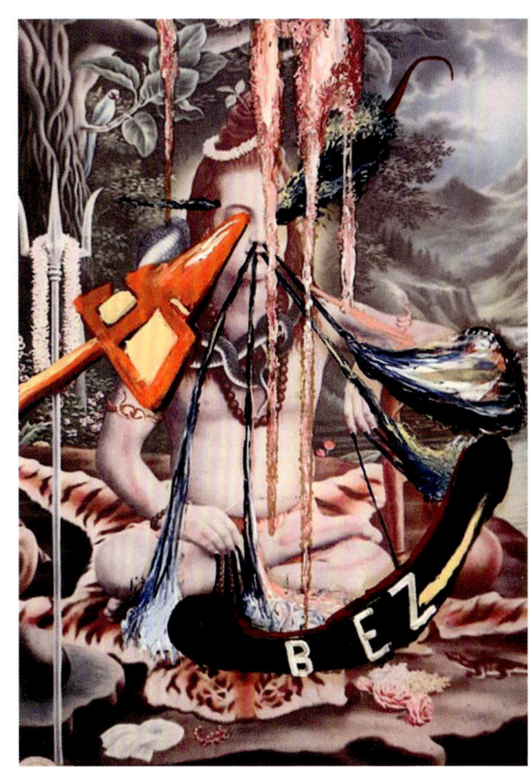
BEZ

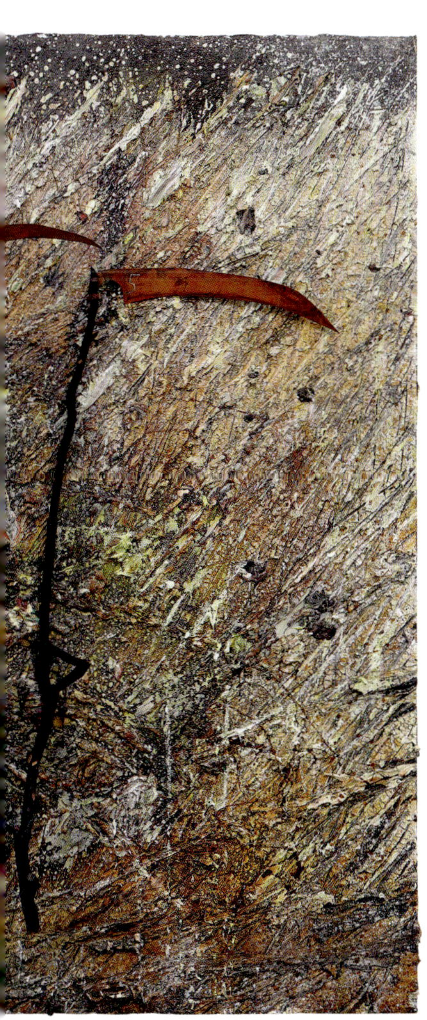

Christopher Le Brun PPRA
Colour Notes 2
Paper relief print
56 × 76 cm

Mali Morris RA
Vermont I
Acrylic
23 × 28 cm

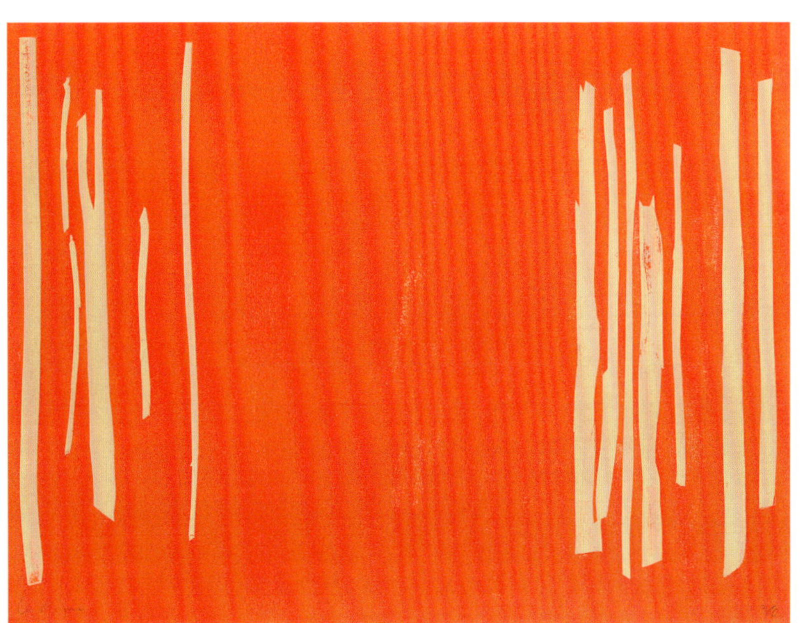

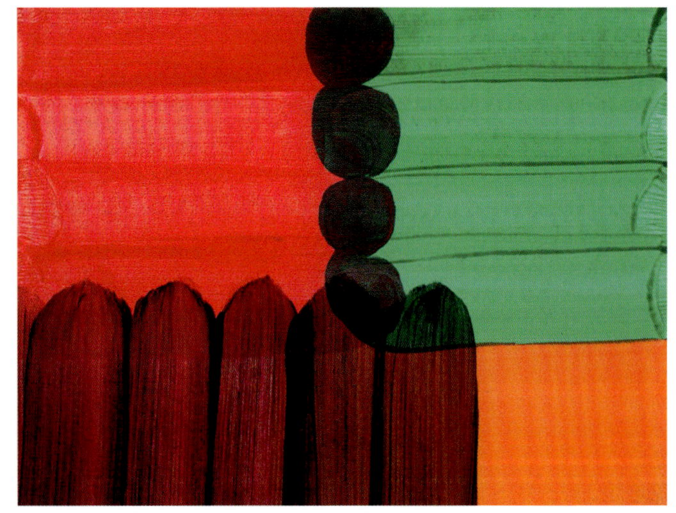

Basil Beattie RA
Divided Loyalties
Oil and wax
156 × 126 cm

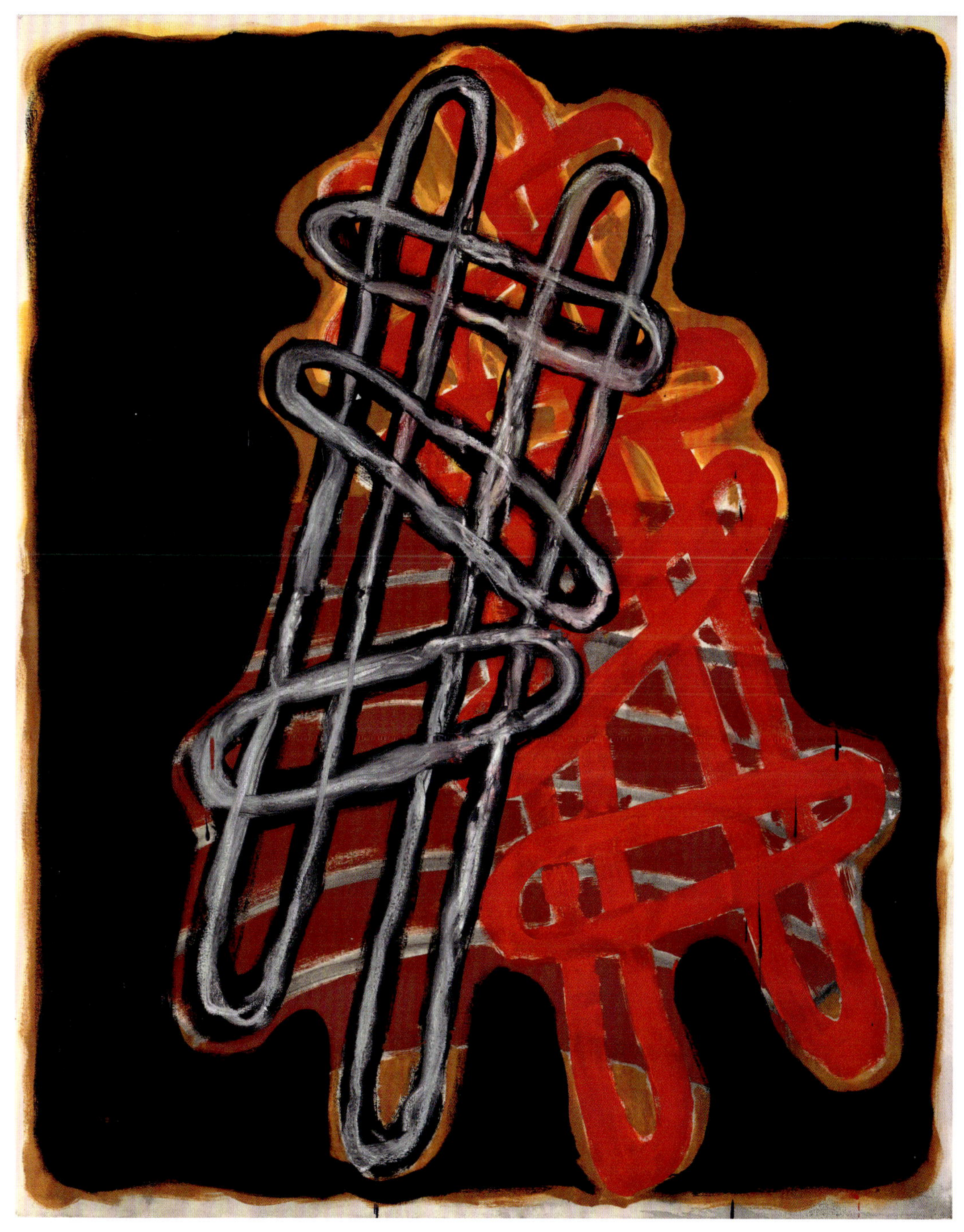

Timothy Hyman RA
They Enter the Market Café
Oil
61 × 91 cm

James Butler MBE RA
Joseph Banks and James Cook
Bronze
H 34 cm

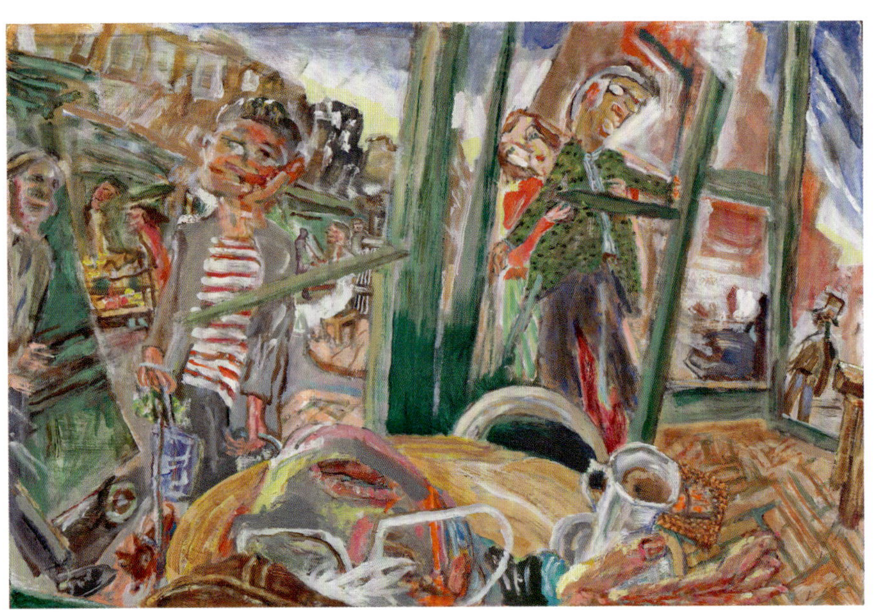

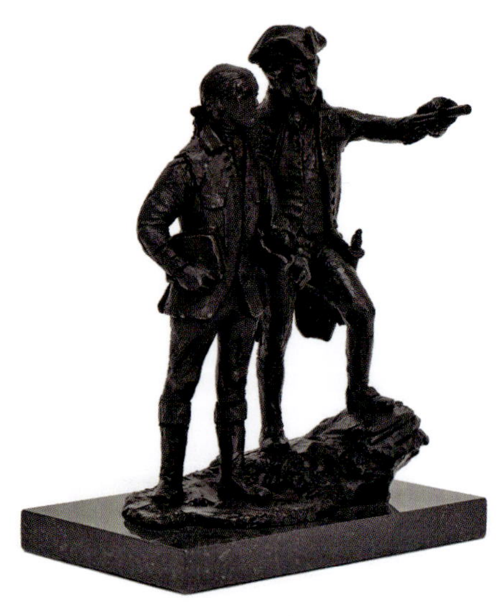

Michael Rooney RA
The Pilgrim Road
Gouache and tempera
76 × 102 cm

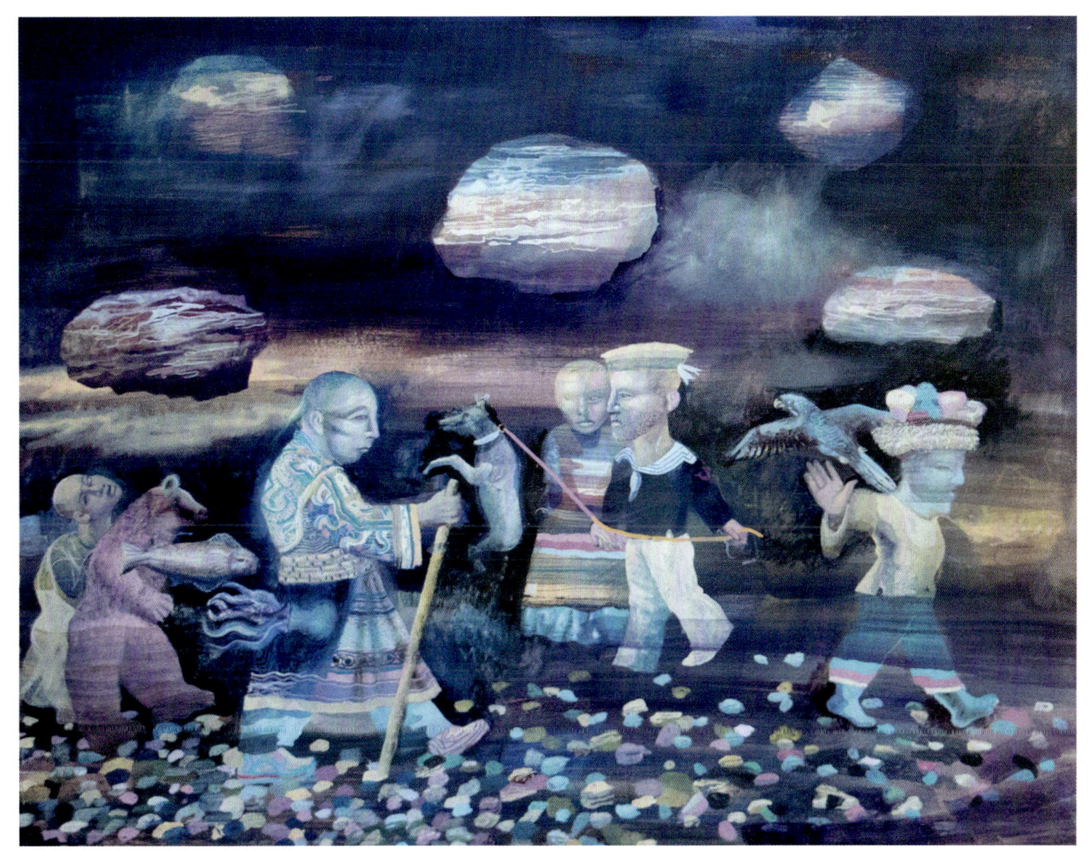

The late John Wragg RA
The Connoisseur
Acrylic
84 × 69 cm

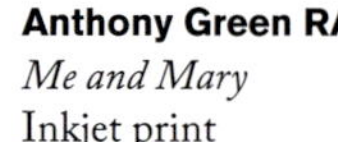

Anthony Green RA
Me and Mary
Inkjet print
41 × 29 cm

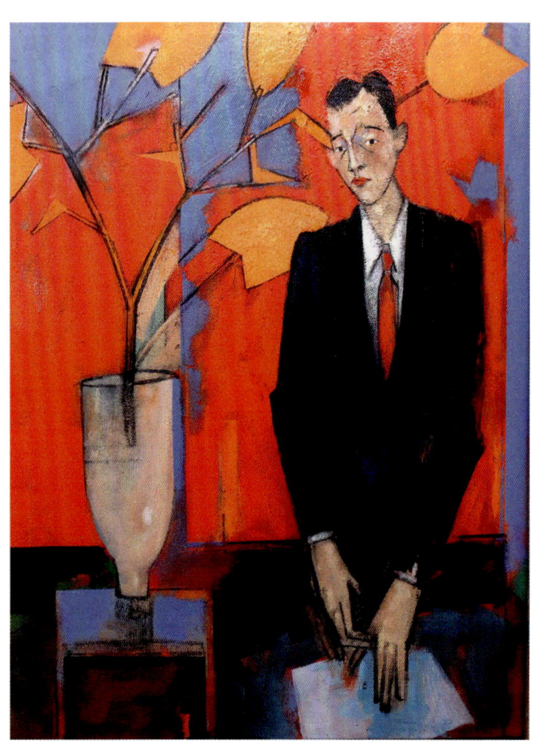

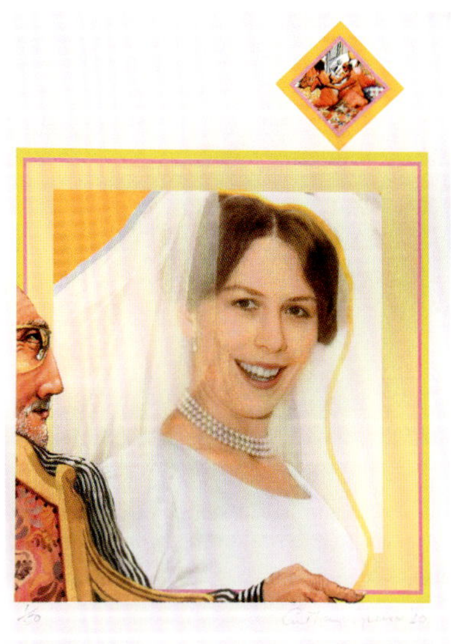

Allen Jones RA
Cacophony
Oil
180 × 180 cm

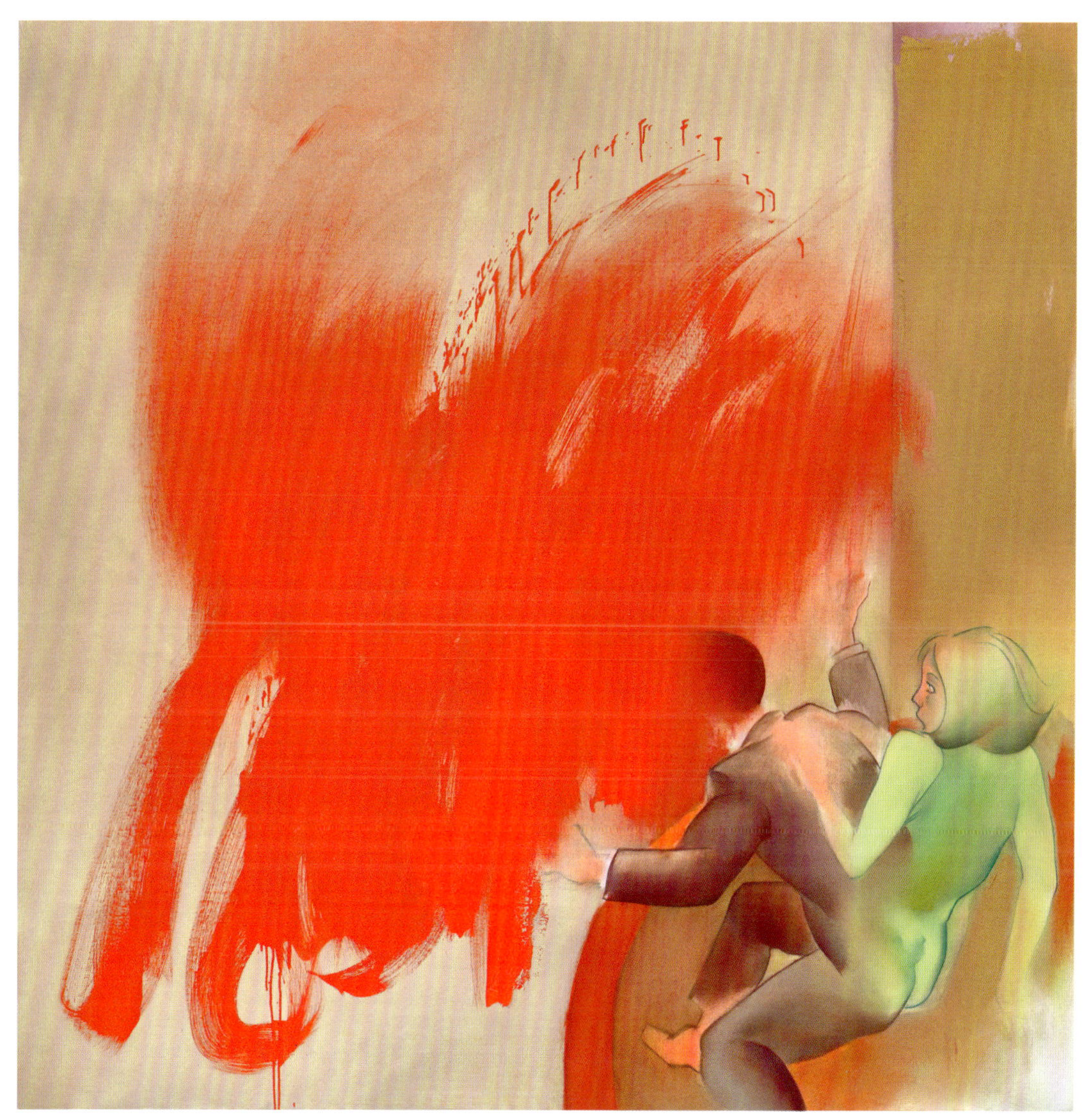

Bill Jacklin RA
Road Through the Field at Night
Oil
122 × 135 cm

Mick Moon RA
Northern Lights
Mixed media
122 × 140 cm

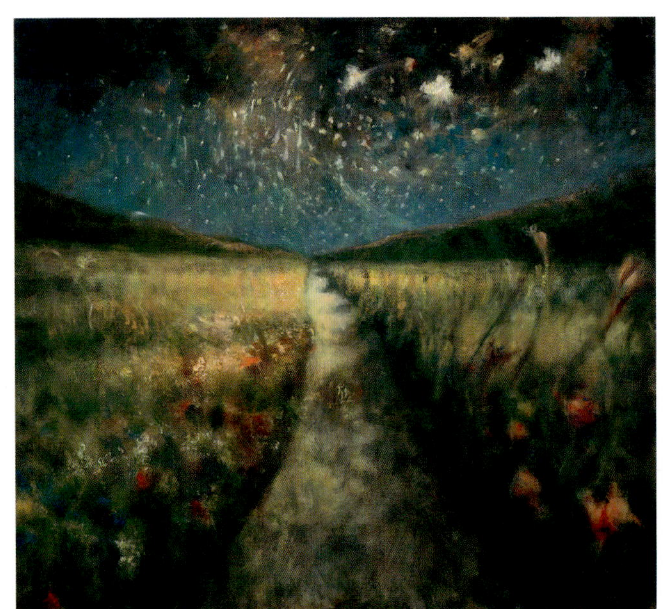

Prof Ian McKeever RA
Henge XI
Oil and acrylic
240 × 285 cm

Tony Bevan RA
Tree (PP1845)
Acrylic and charcoal
85 × 121 cm

Chantal Joffe RA
Nat and Vita in Their Doorway (11.4.2020)
Oil
30 × 24 cm

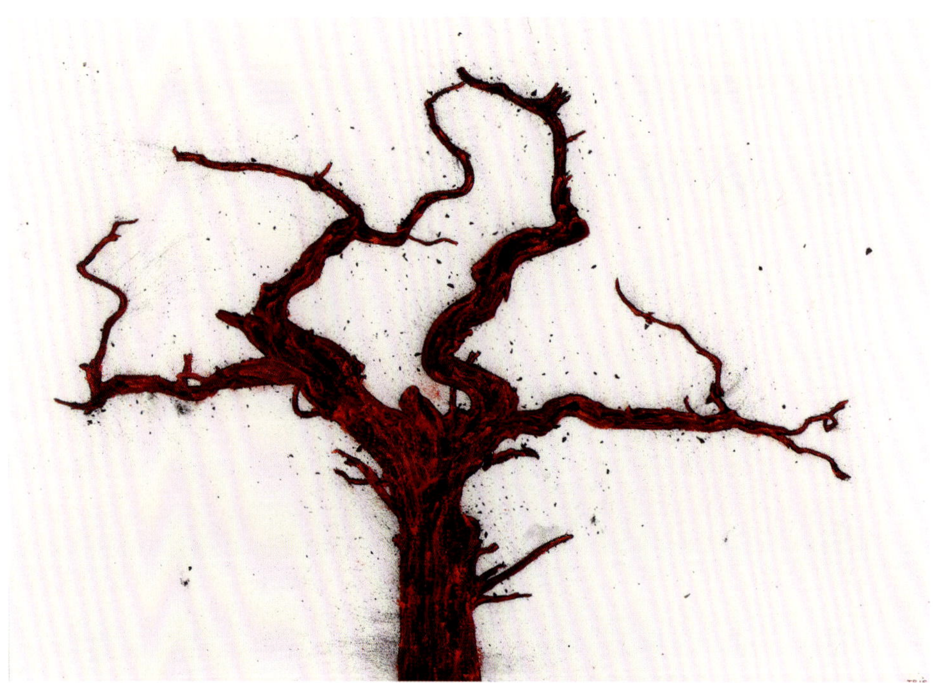

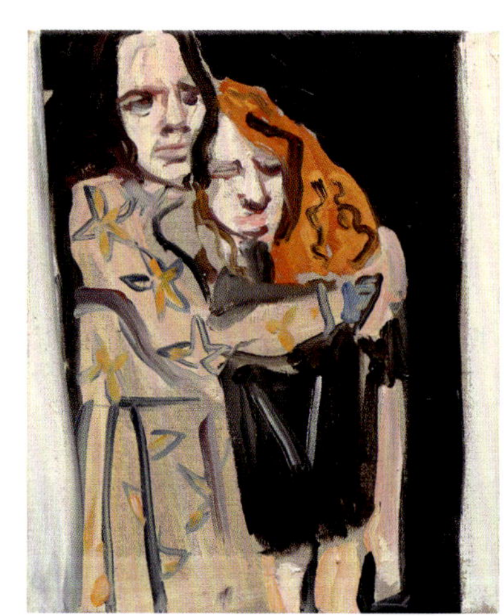

Eileen Cooper OBE RA
Indigo
Oil
137 × 106 cm

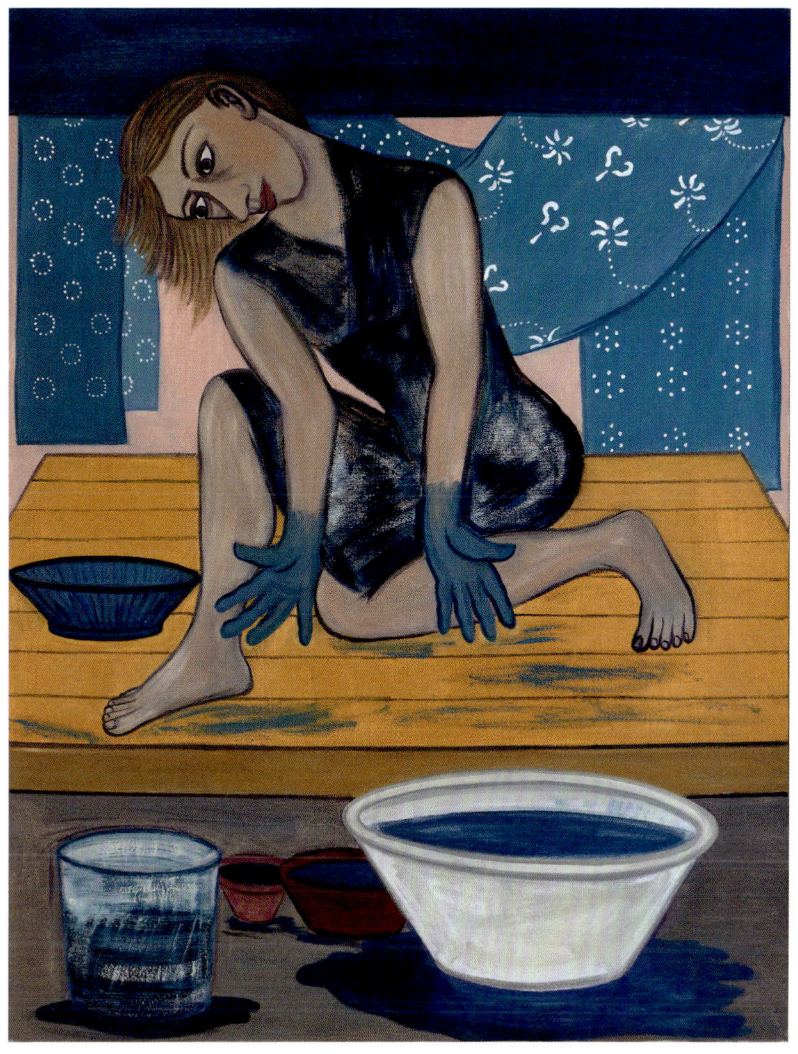

Cornelia Parker OBE RA
Glass and Its Shadows
Polymer photogravure etching
58 × 82 cm

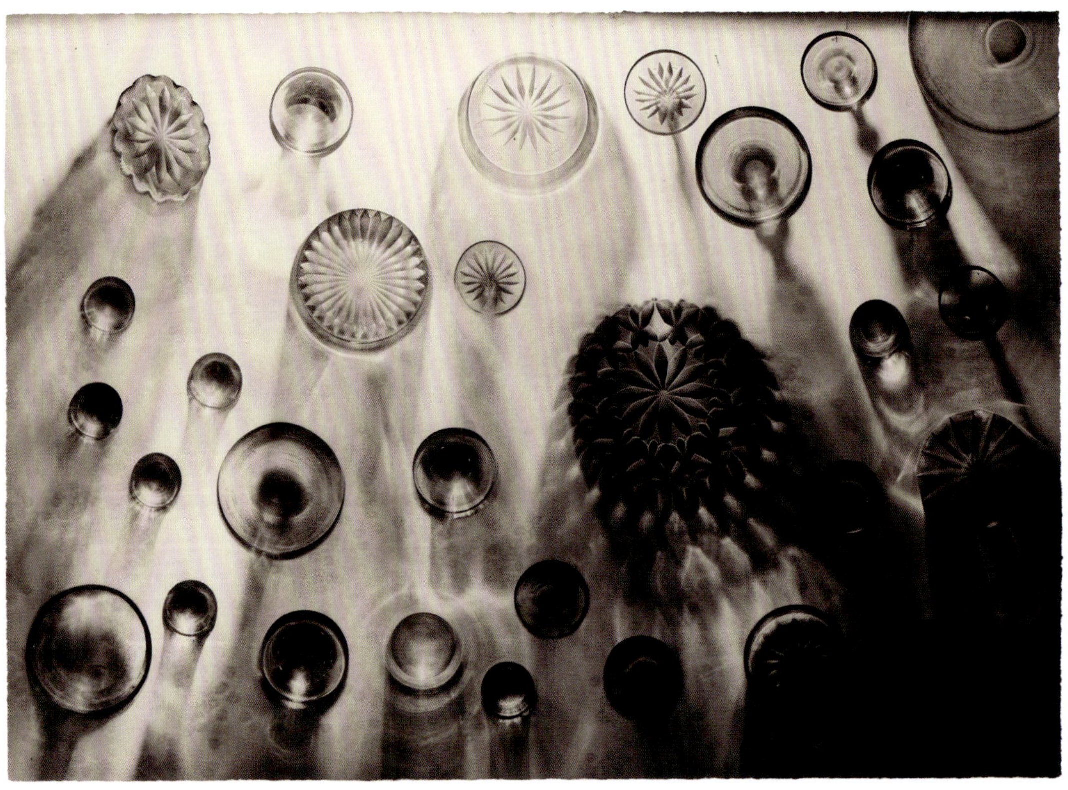

Tim Shaw RA
Head II
Bronze
H 118 cm

Michael Landy RA
Family Ruin 34
Watercolour
36 × 48 cm

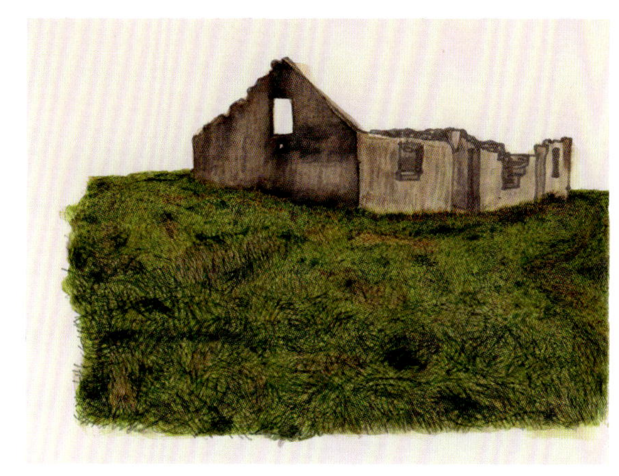

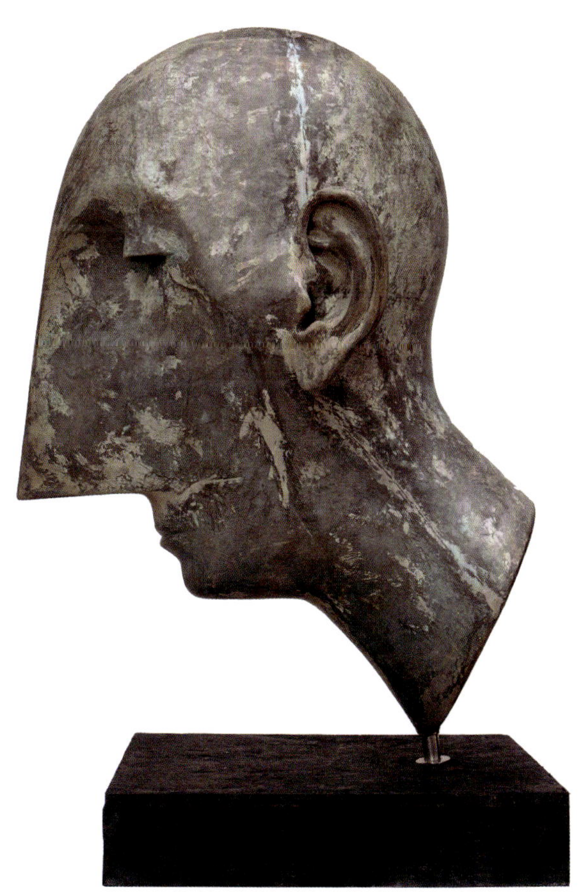

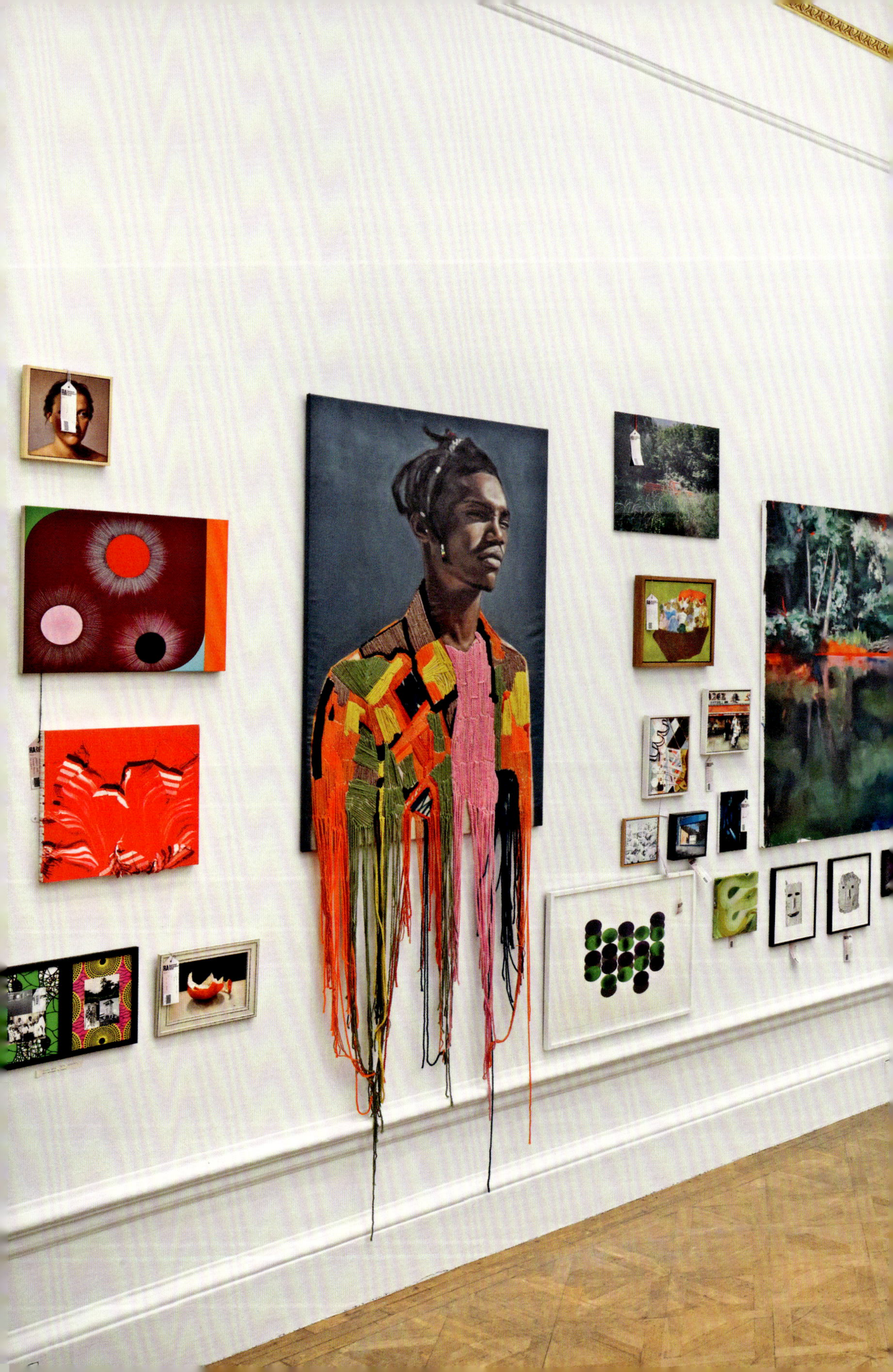

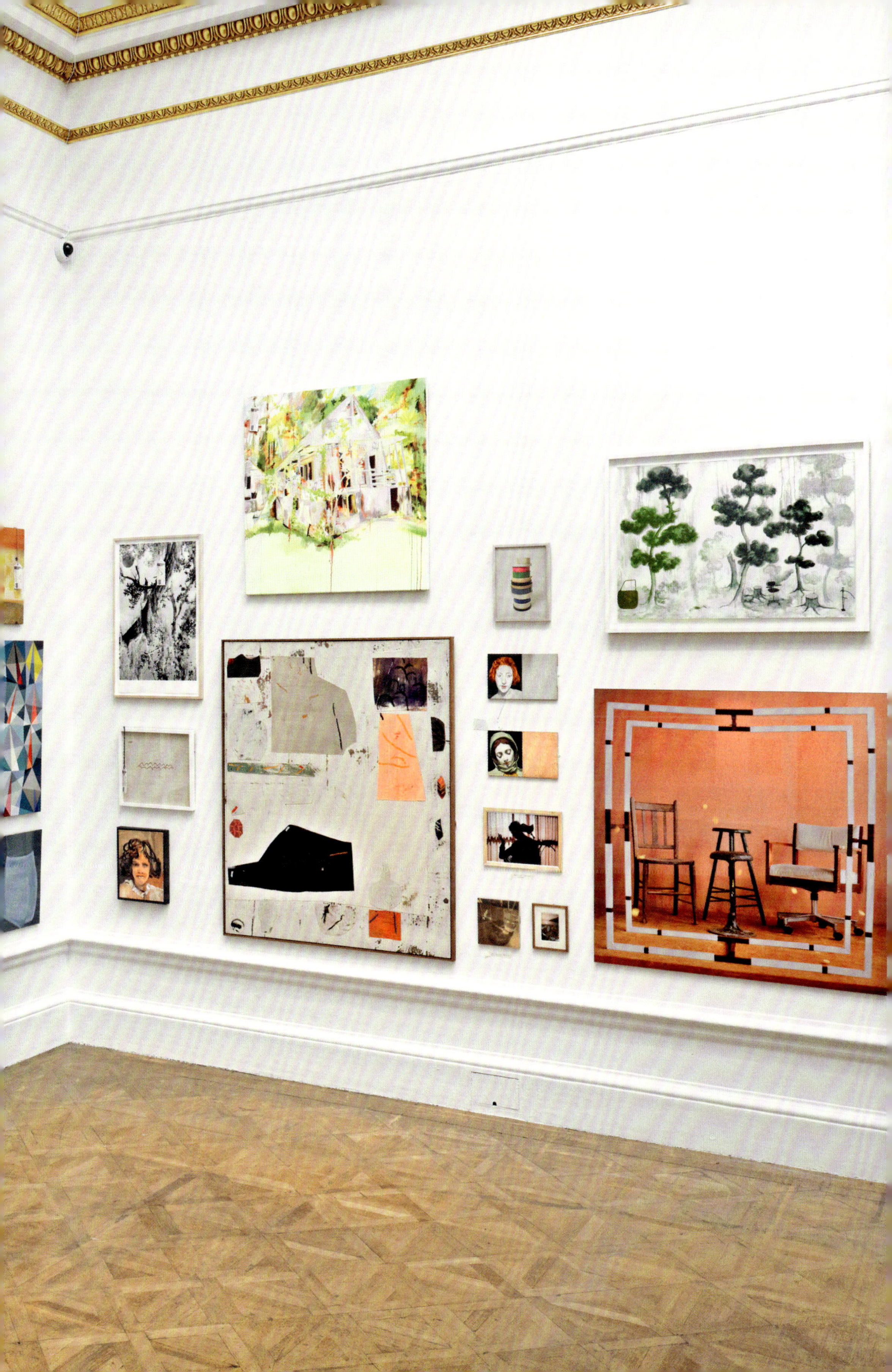

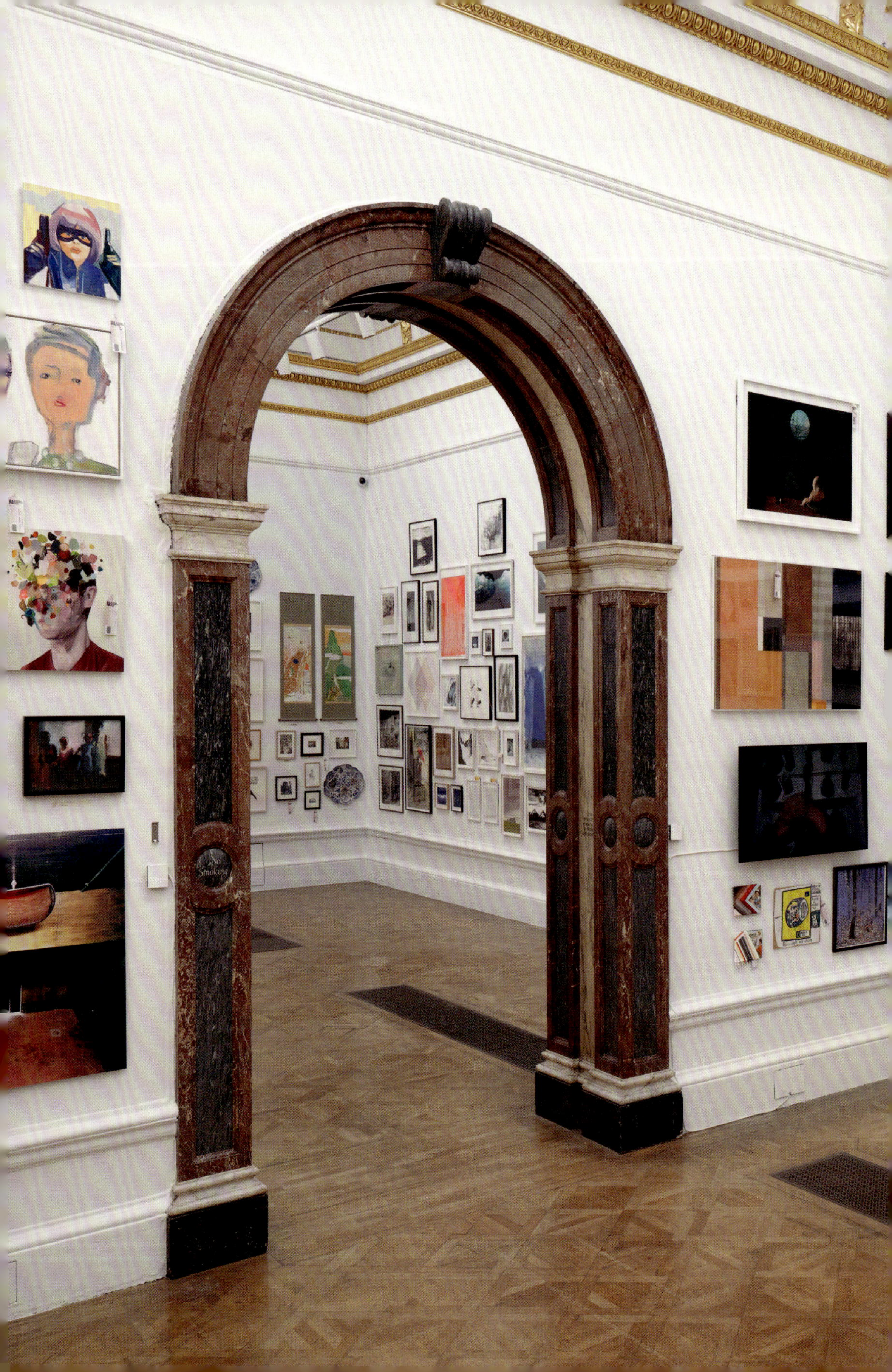
No
Smoking

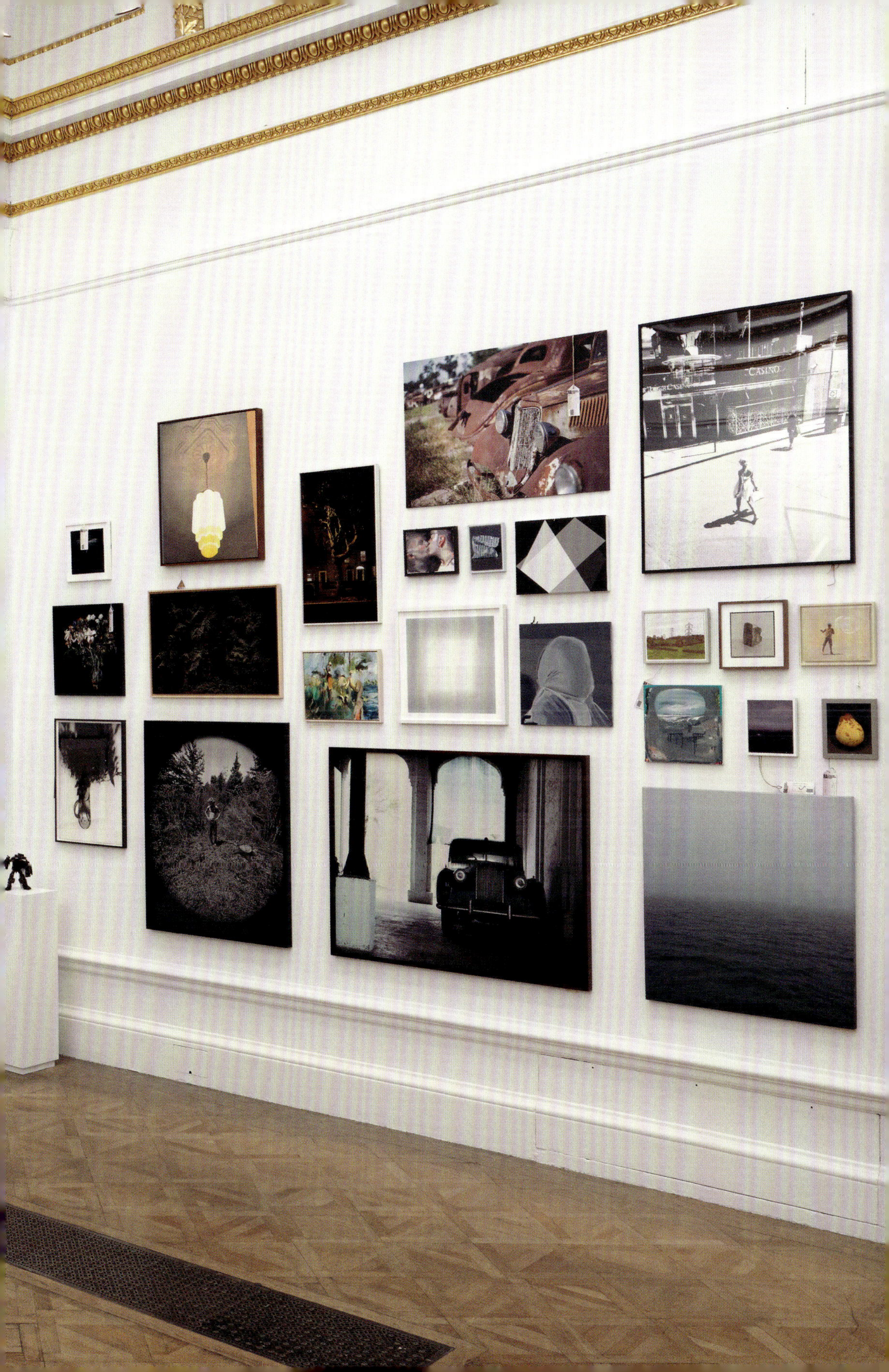
CASINO

Emma Stibbon RA
Drift
Intaglio print with hand colouring
38 × 53 cm

Prof Norman Ackroyd CBE RA
Harris from Lewis
Etching
18 × 35 cm

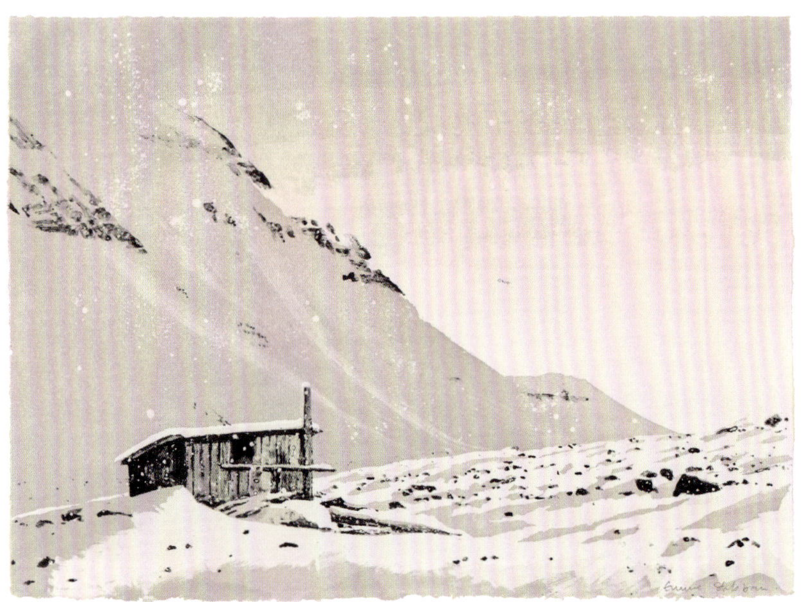

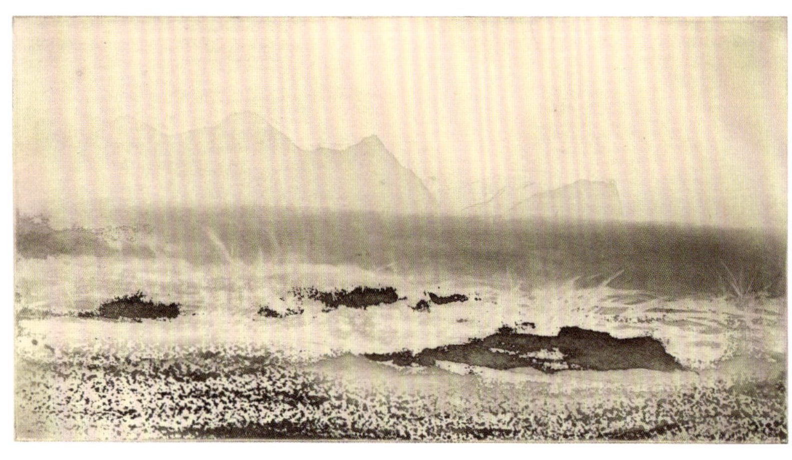

Prof Chris Orr MBE RA
The Boiling Pot – Y Pot Berwi
Engraving with hand colouring
88 × 74 cm

Peter Freeth RA
Pond Life
Aquatint
48 × 26 cm

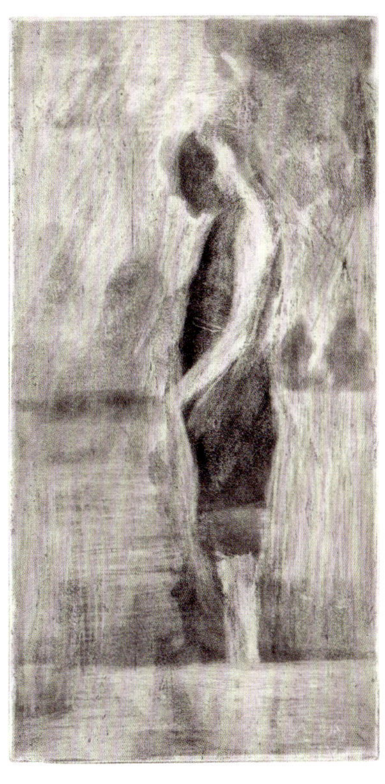

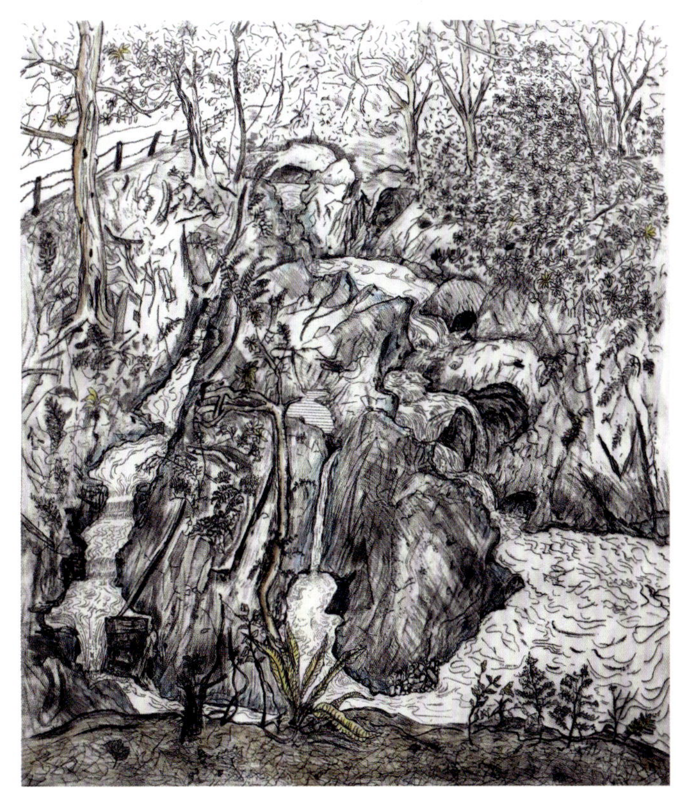

Dame Elizabeth Blackadder DBE RA
Fred
Etching
50 × 54 cm

Tom Phillips CBE RA
Homage to John Cage
Print with silkscreen
56 × 59 cm

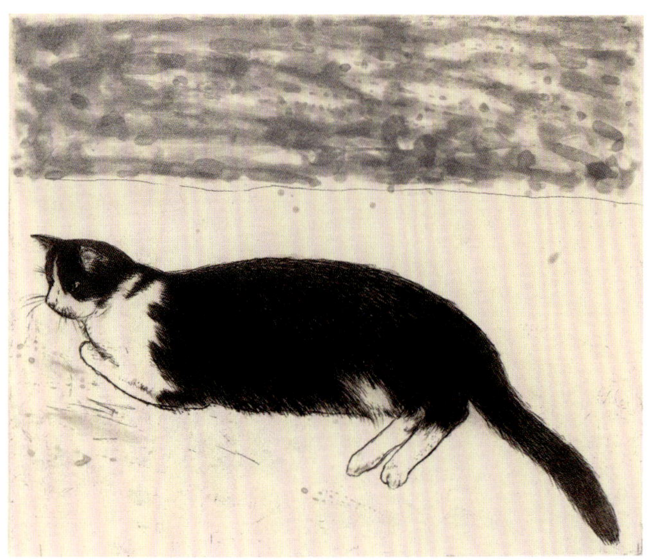

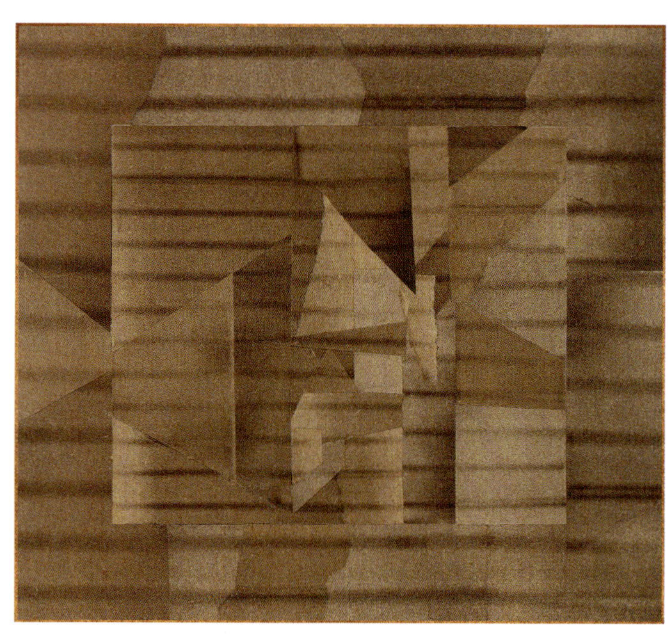

Jim Dine Hon RA
The Magic Sleeves
Woodcut and digital print
with hand colouring
107 × 158 cm

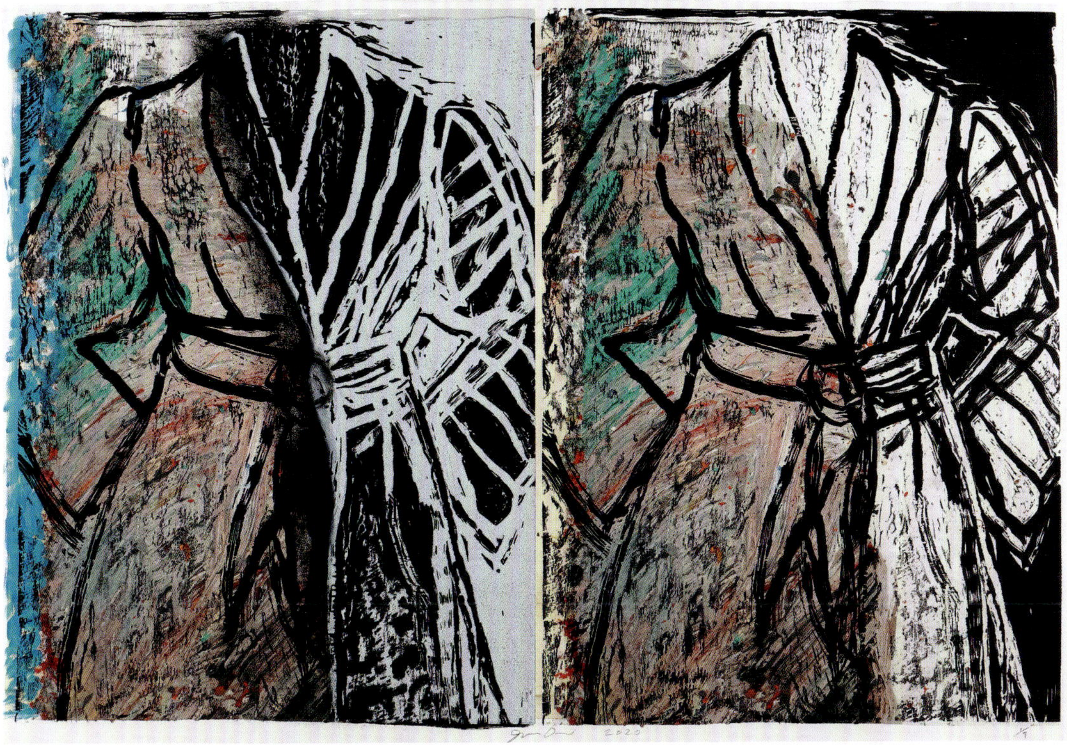

Anne Desmet RA
Oculi
Wood engraving, linocut and stencil
26 × 38 cm

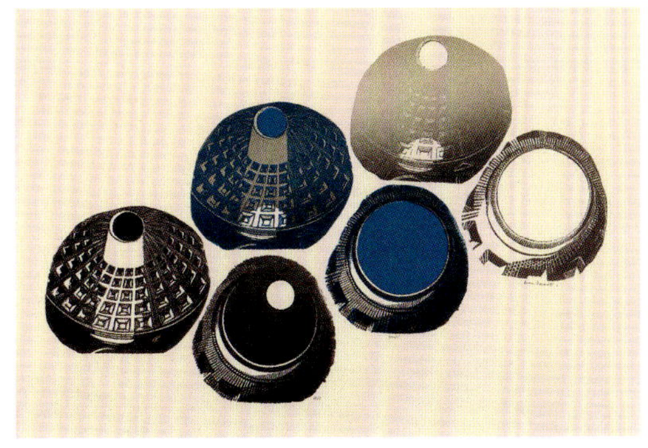

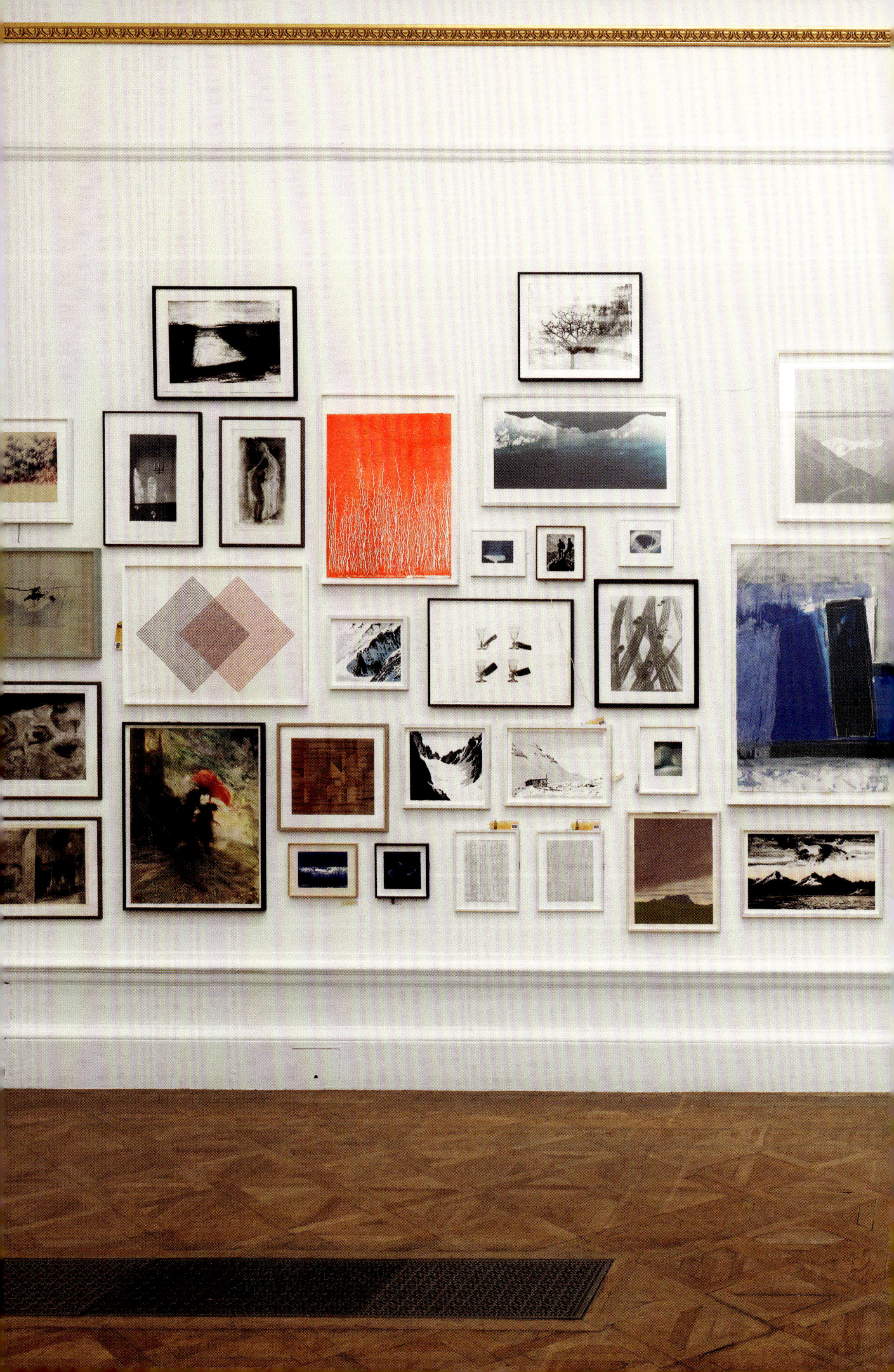

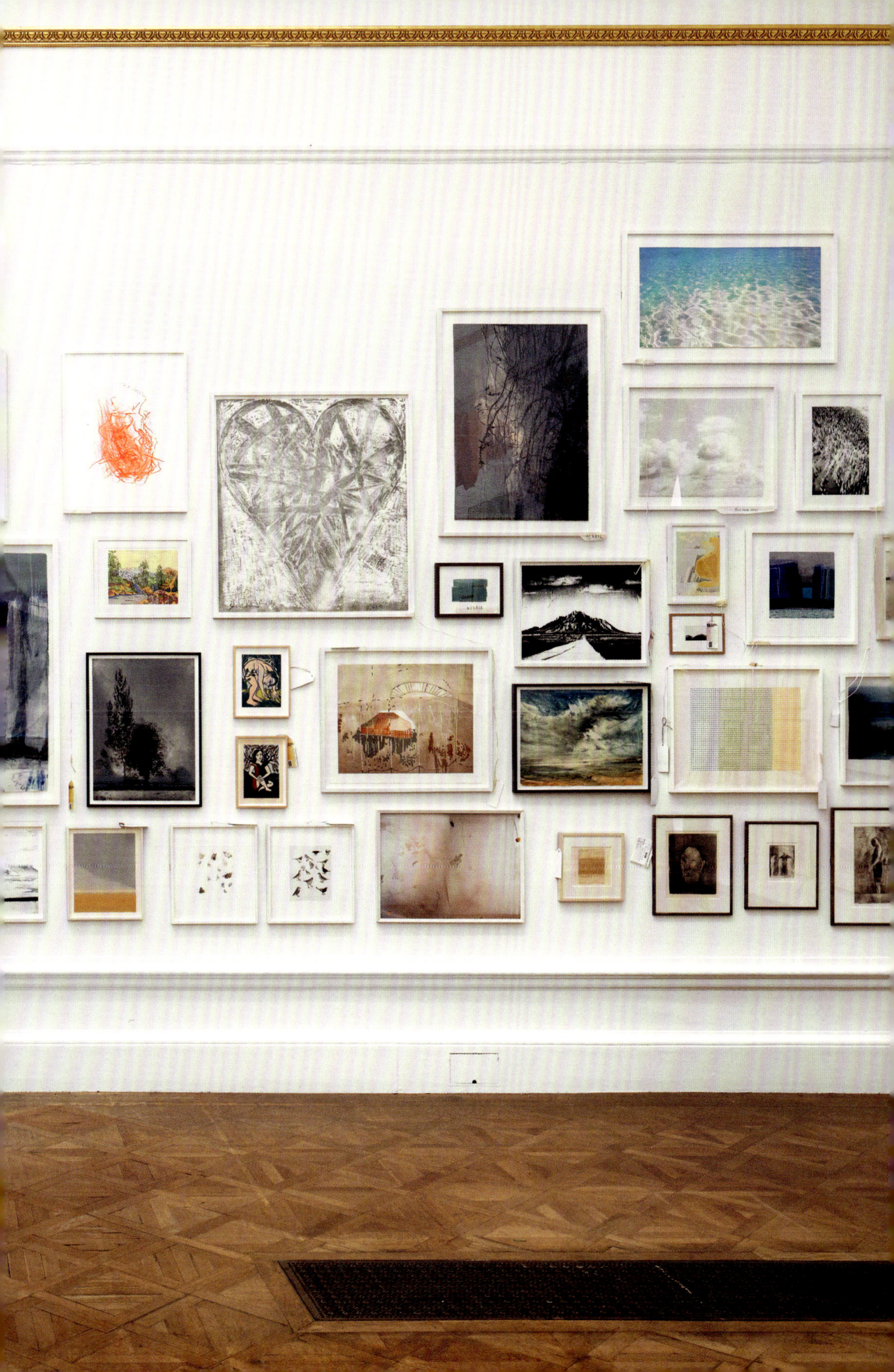

Níall McLaughlin Architects
Drawing Together: A Collective Drawing with 300 Participants on Zoom
Digital group drawing
59 × 84 cm

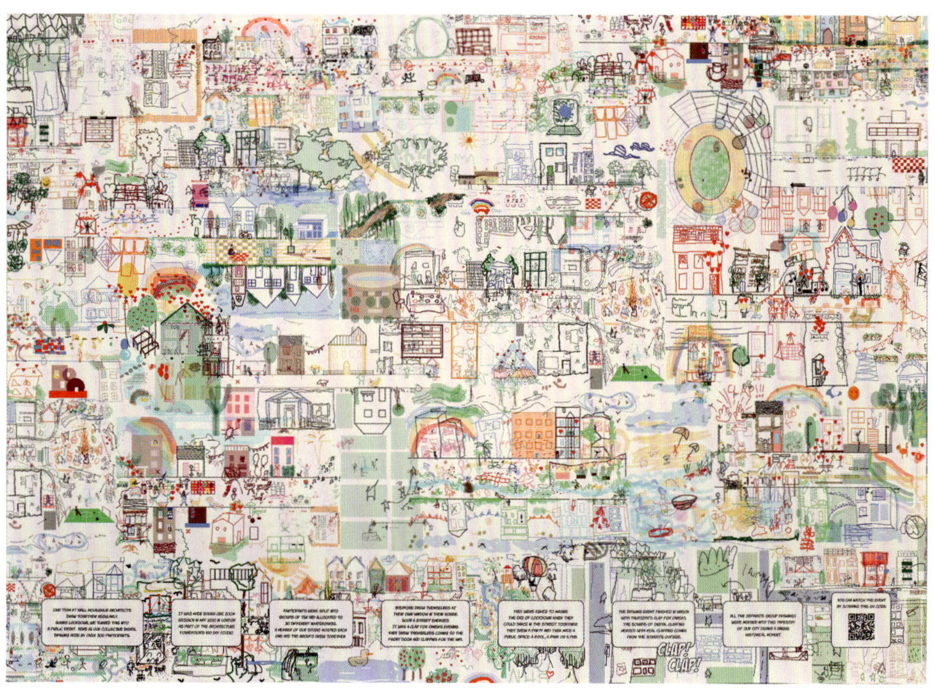

Prof Ian Ritchie CBE RA
Scary Cat
Etching
33 × 24 cm

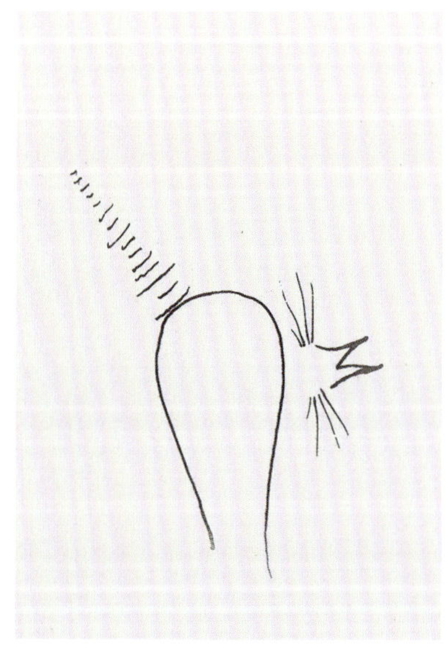

Prof Gordon Benson OBE RA
Cultural Substrate 2 – FT
Digital print and screenprint
84 × 59 cm

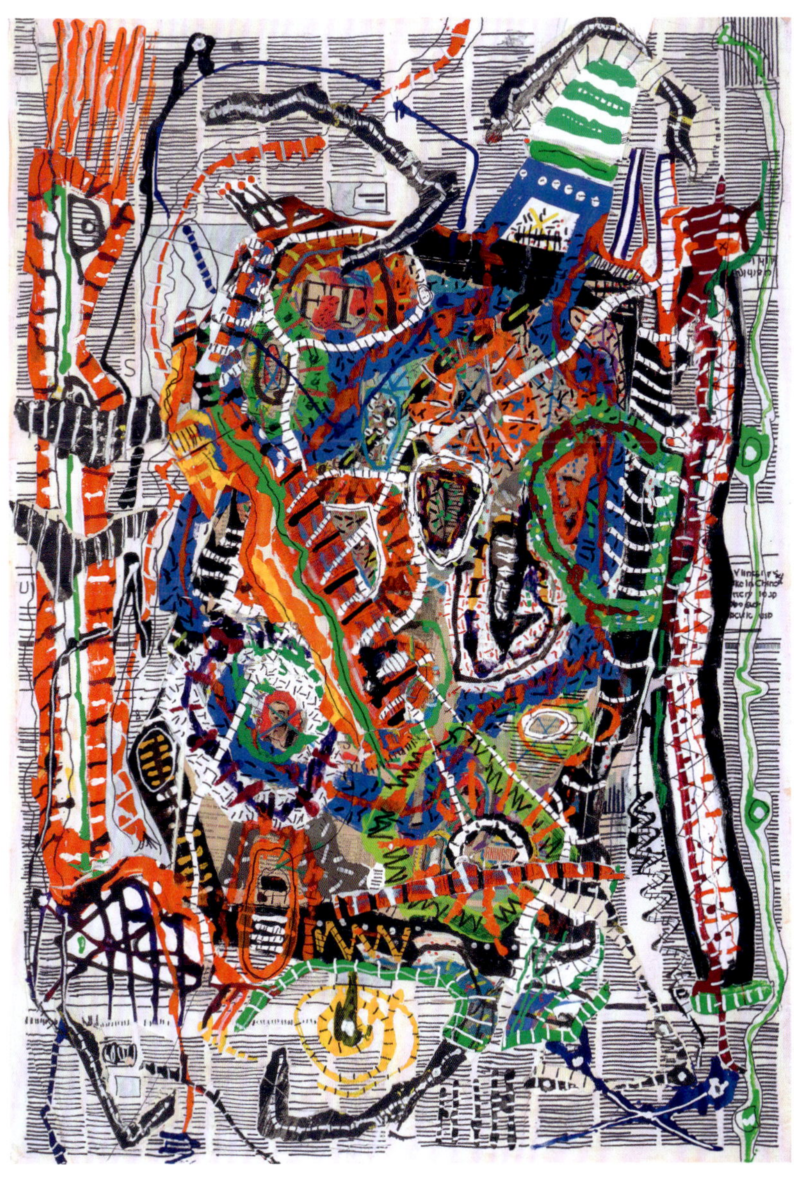

Thomas Heatherwick CBE RA
Eden, Singapore
Photographic print
125 × 100 cm

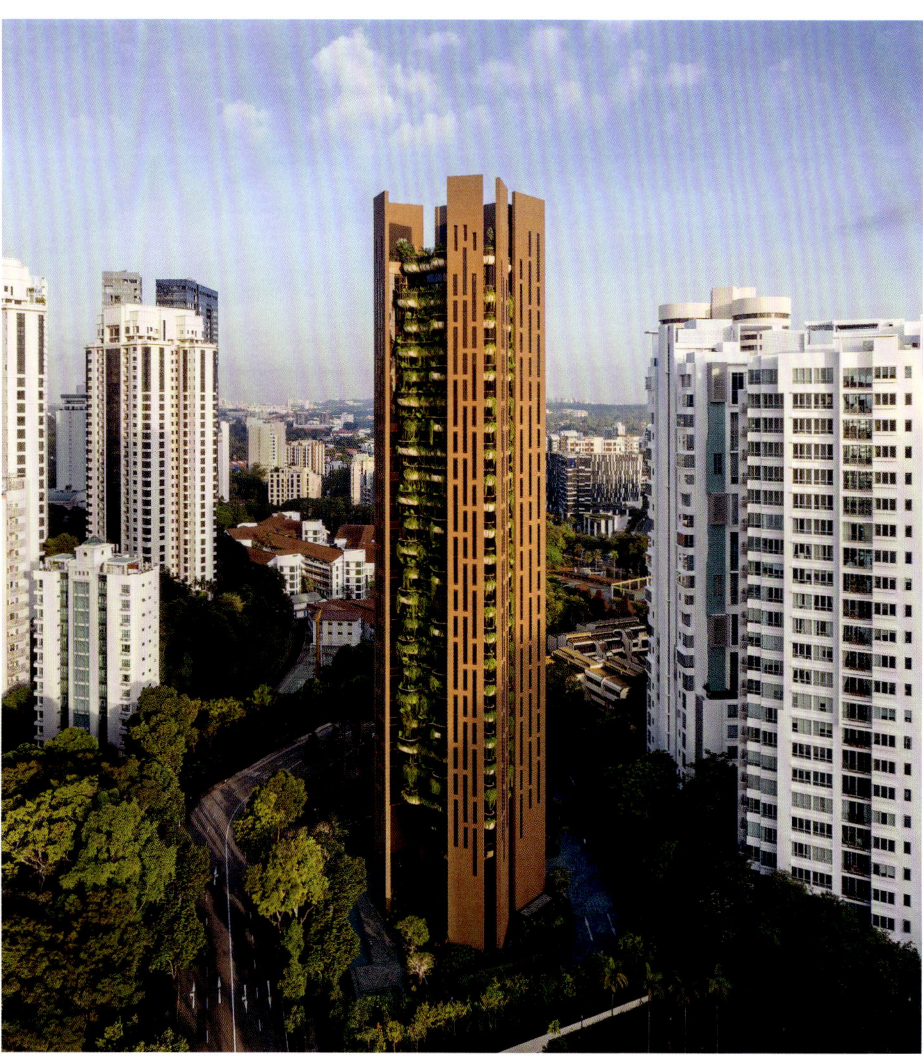

Eva Jiřičná CBE RA
Renaissance Castle Revitalisation (detail)
Digital print
84 × 59 cm

Sir Michael Hopkins CBE RA
Expo 2020 Thematic Districts
Mixed media
H 98 cm

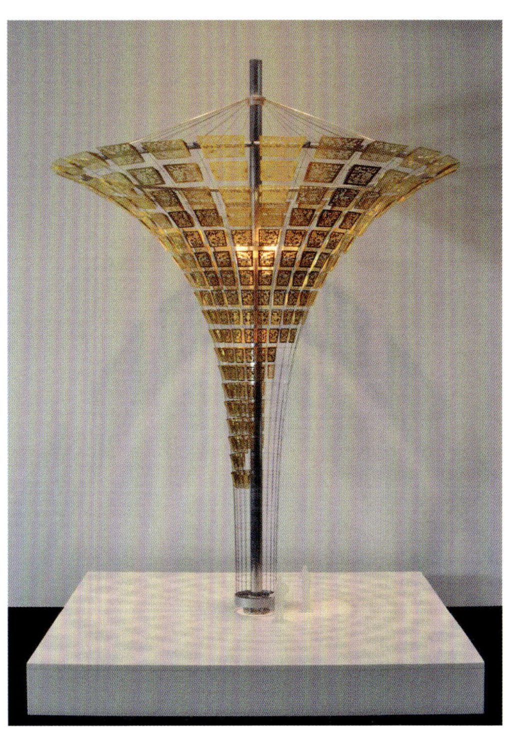

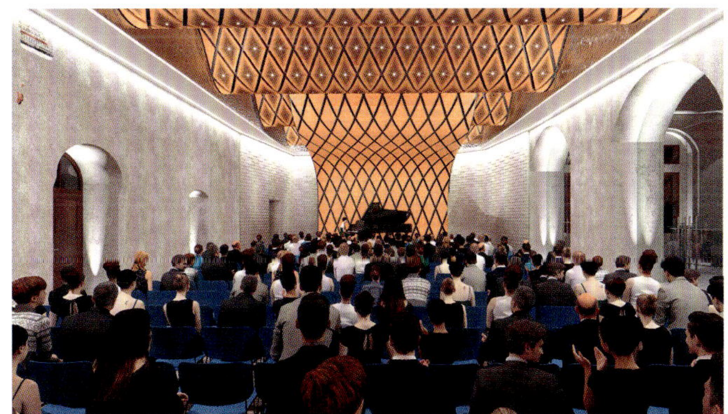

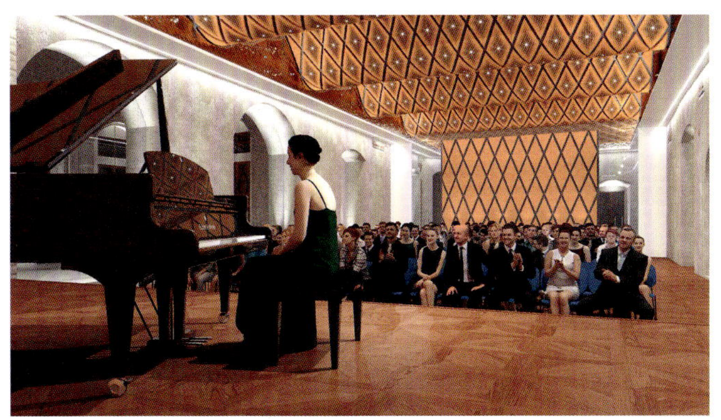

Louisa Hutton OBE RA and Matthias Sauerbruch (Sauerbruch Hutton)
Polychromatic Tower I
Print
52 × 42 cm

Sir David Chipperfield CBE RA
What Is Our Role? (detail)
Print
30 × 21 cm

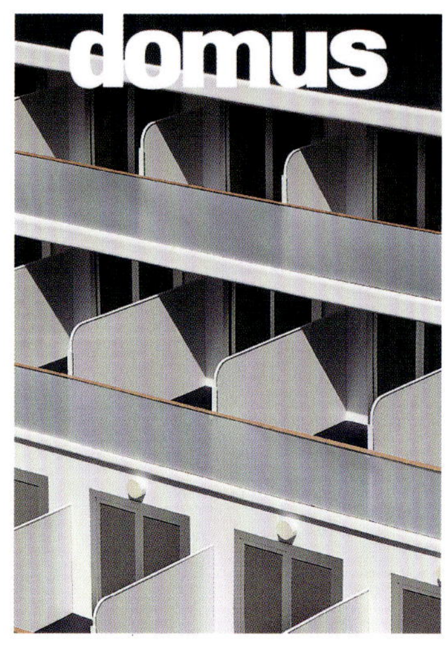

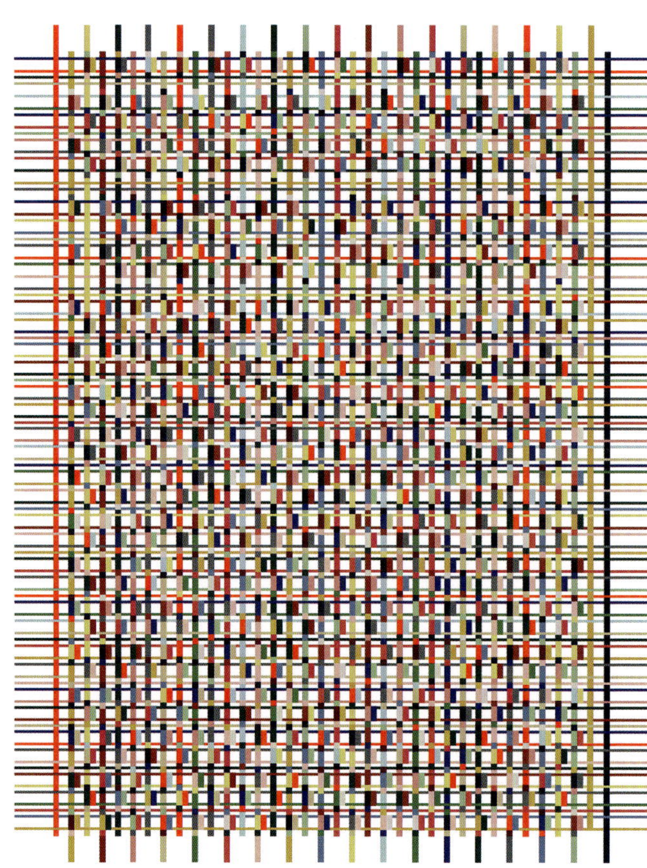

Prof Farshid Moussavi OBE RA
Transitions
Screenprint
62 × 62 cm

Lifschutz Davidson Sandilands
Illuminated River (Triptych)
Digital print
178 × 84 cm

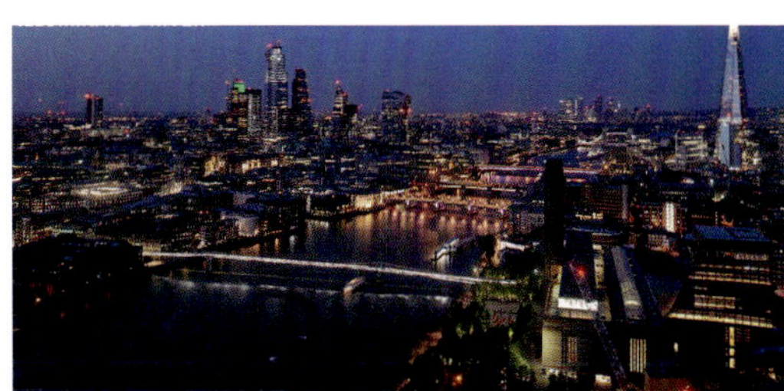

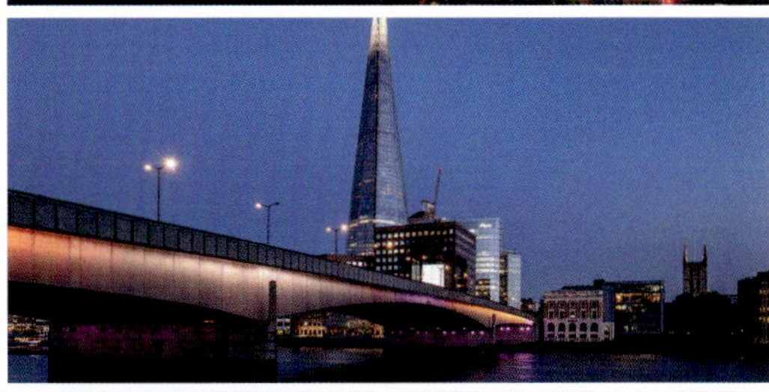

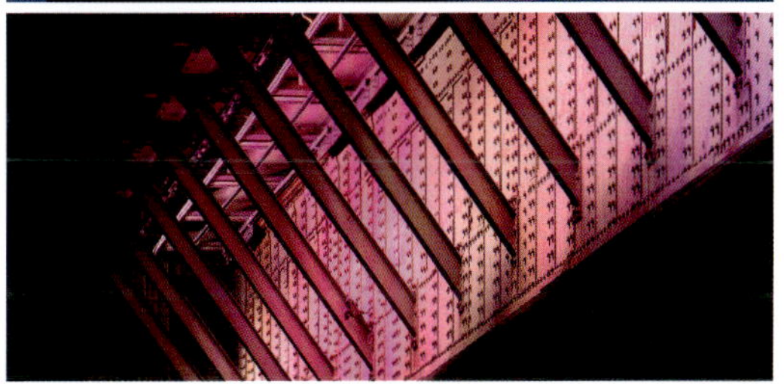

Caruso St John Architects
Swiss Life Arena
Giclée print
75 × 342 cm

Sir Nicholas Grimshaw CBE PPRA
Homebase Adaptive Reuse
Mixed media
H 32 cm

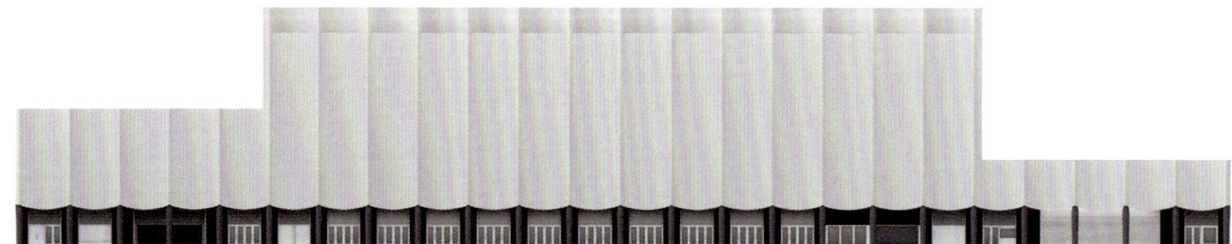

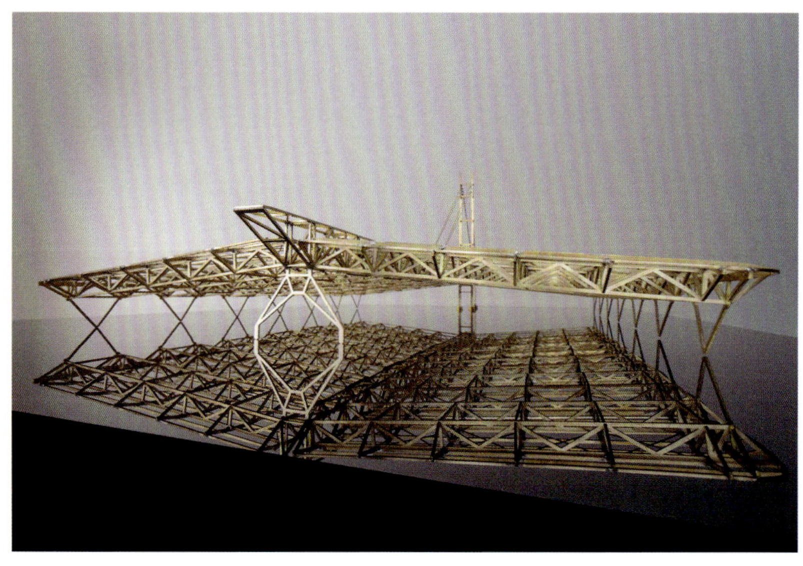

The late Edward Cullinan CBE RA
Twenty-first Century Townhouse
Ink
80 × 80 cm

Lord Foster of Thames Bank OM RA
Fred Olsen Offices, Vestby
Pen and pencil
84 × 178 cm

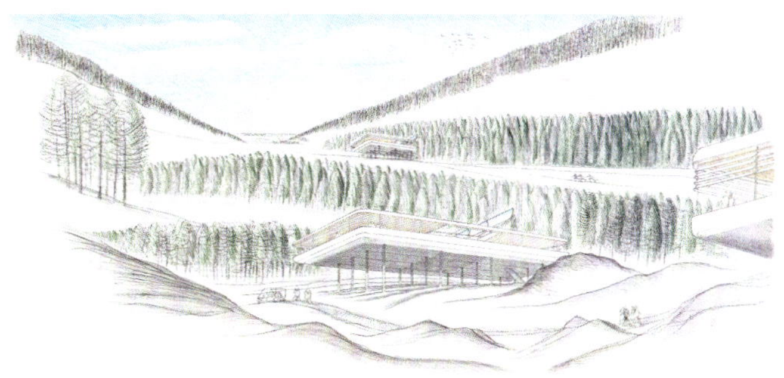

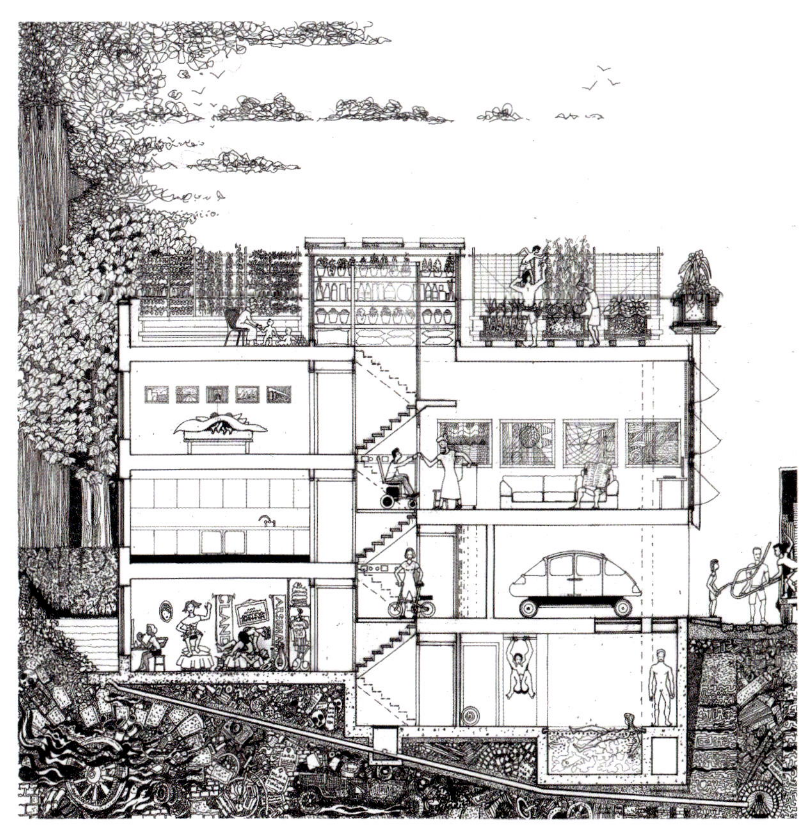

Stanton Williams
Bibliothèque Métropolitaine de L'Hôtel-Dieu Clermont-Ferrand, Auvergne, France
Mixed media
H 96 cm

Spencer de Grey CBE RA
Eco Resort Concepts, Coral Bloom and Forever Garden
Timber and card
H 42 cm

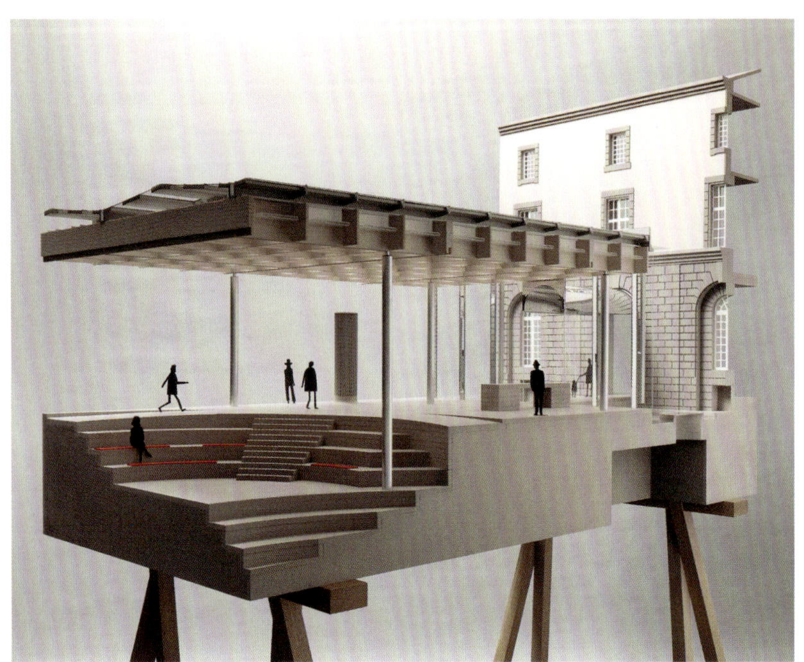

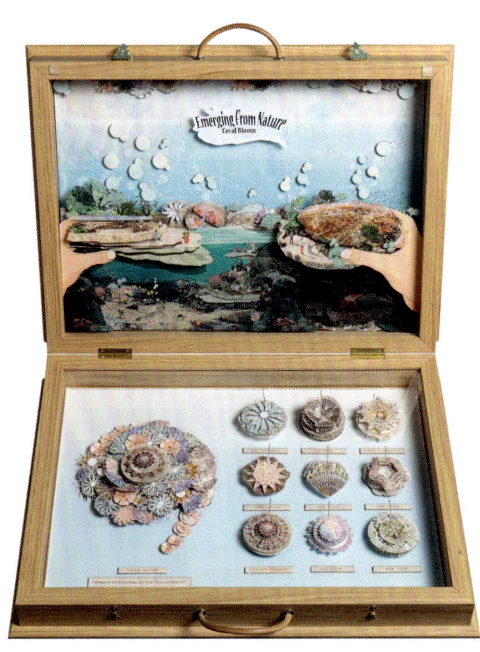

Prof Sir Peter Cook RA
The Citadel Up Close
Print from ink and watercolour
45 × 47 cm

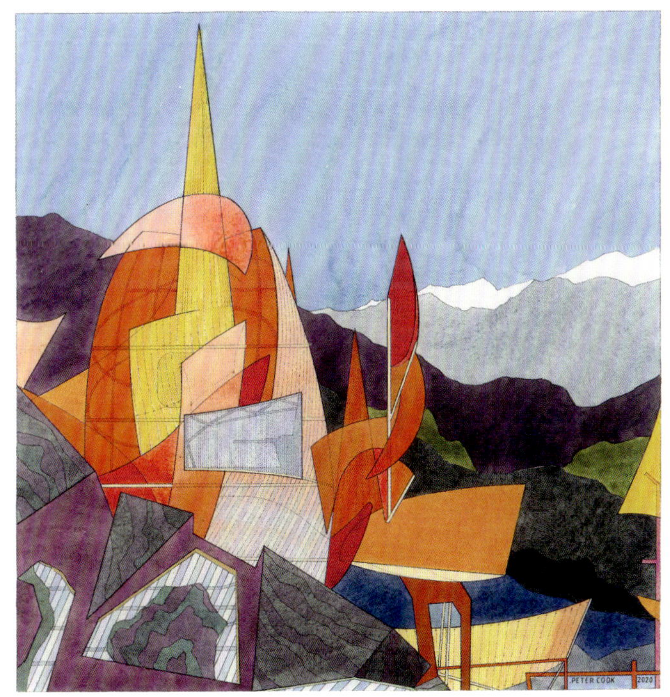

Lord Rogers of Riverside CH RA
Future Roads of Paris
Video

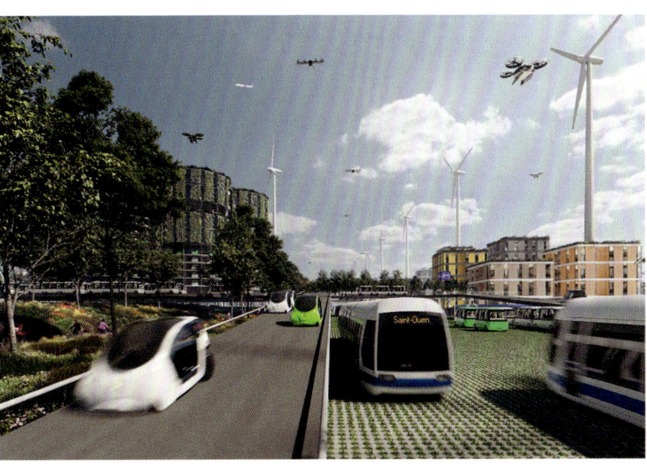

Eric Parry RA
Building Proposal for the University of Liverpool, School of Architecture
Pen and ink
34 × 53 cm

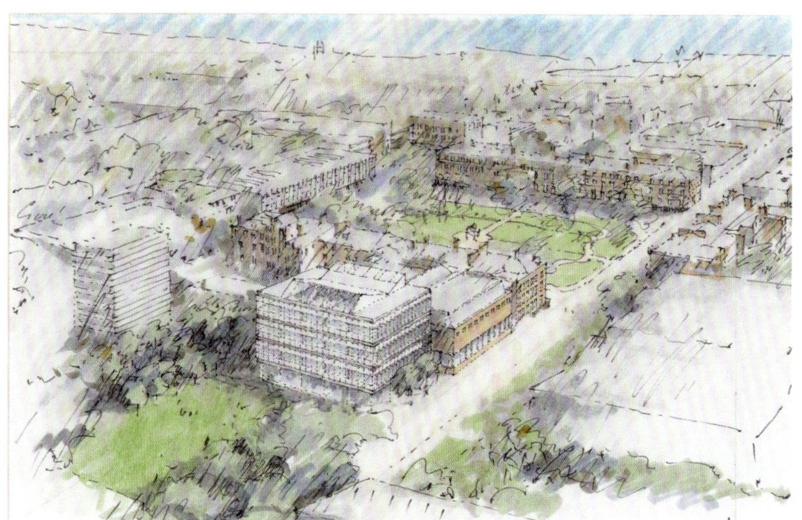

The late Paul Koralek CBE RA
Techniquest
Pen
21 × 30 cm

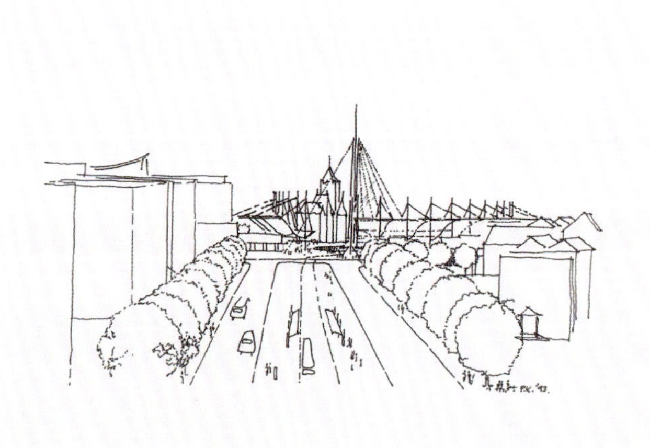

WilkinsonEyre
Biodomes
Mixed media
25 × 75 cm

Renzo Piano Building Workshop
Stavros Niarchos Foundation Cultural Centre
Digital print
266 × 272 cm

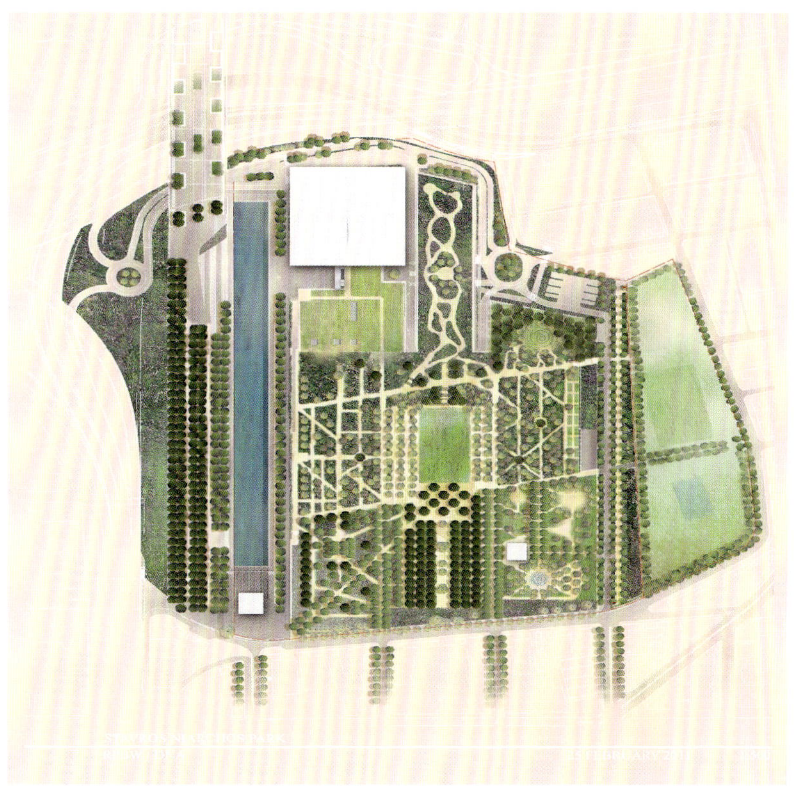

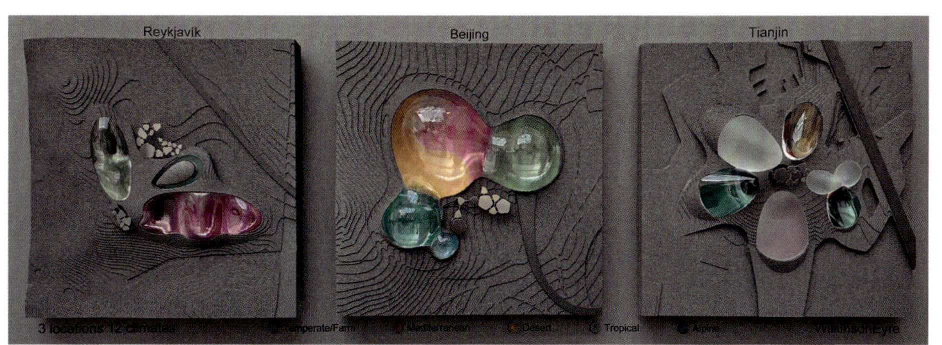

Rose Wylie OBE RA
Clothes I Wore #18
Mixed media
122 × 164 cm

Grayson Perry CBE RA
The American Dream
Etching
110 × 240 cm

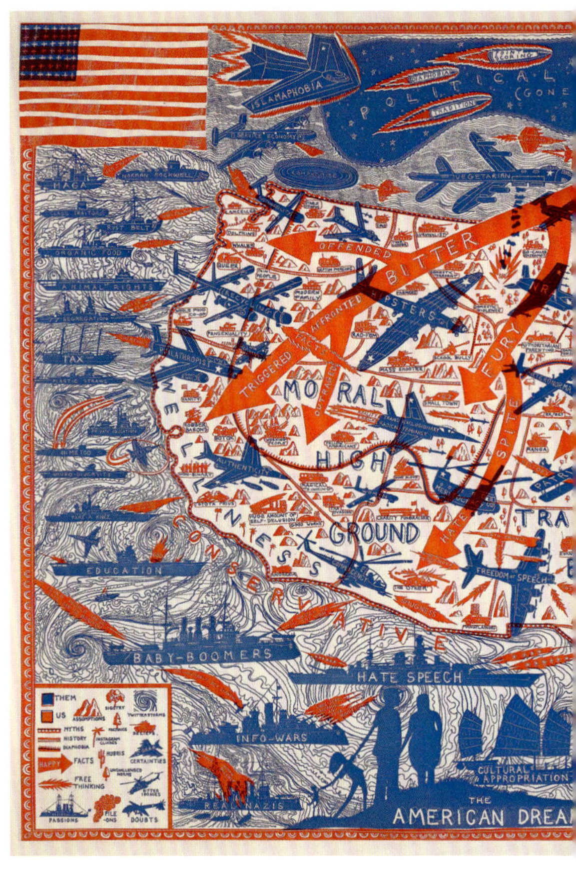

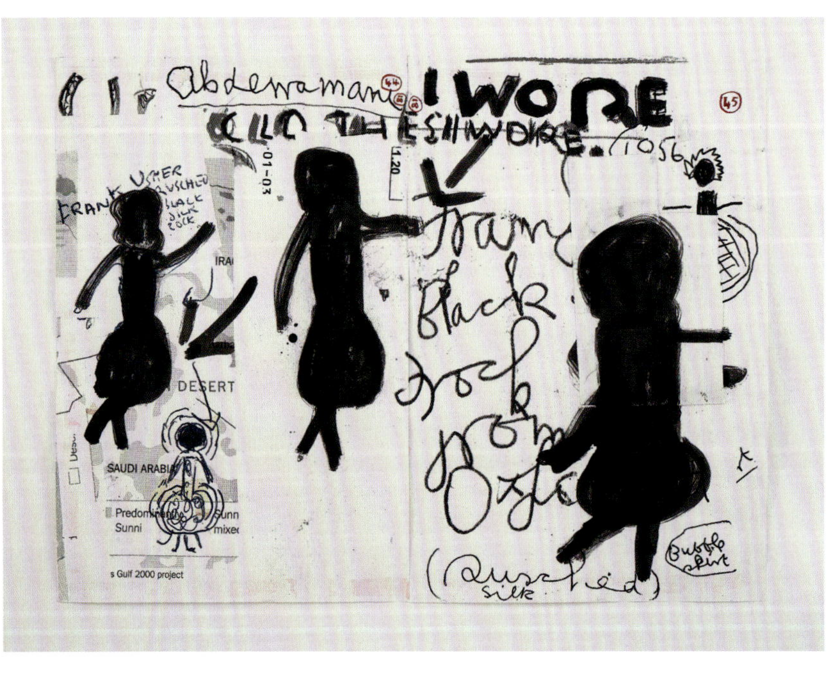

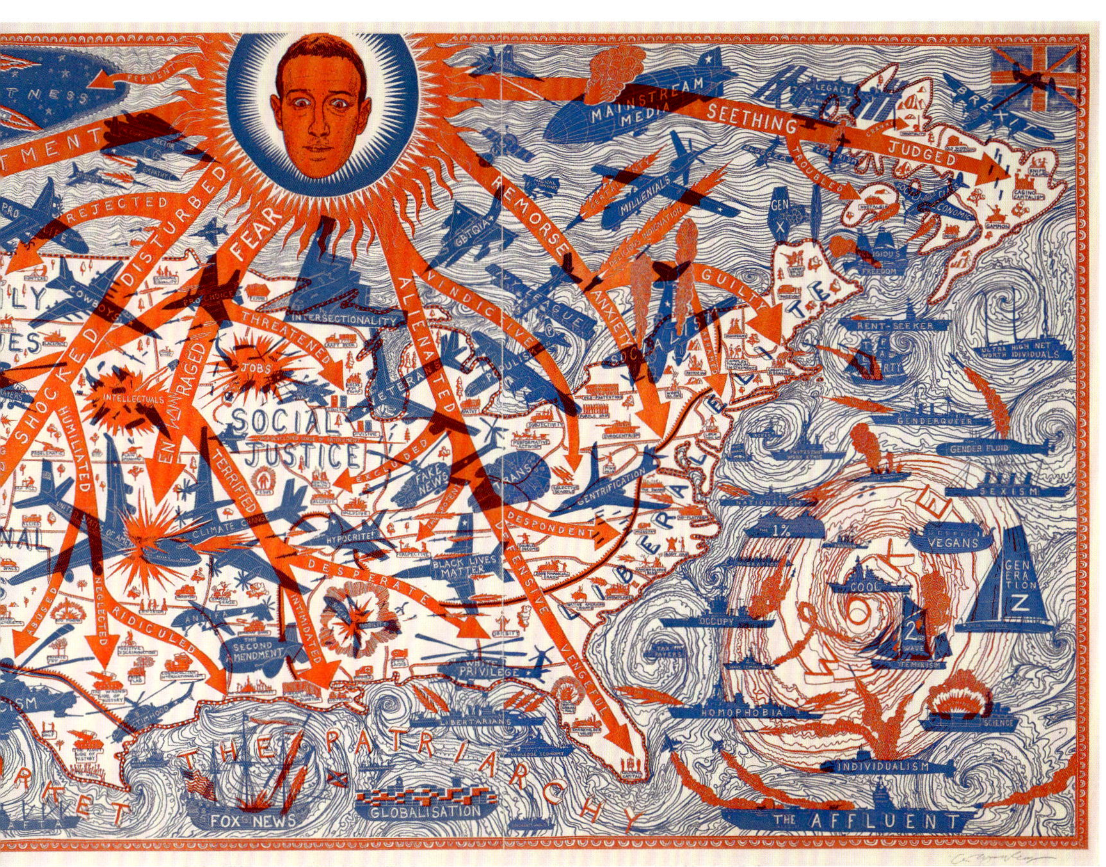

FERVENT
MAINSTREAM MEDIA
SEETHING
JUDGED
BREXIT
REJECTED
DISTURBED
FEAR
REMORSE
MILLENIALS
GEN X
ALIENATED
VINDICTIVE
ANXIETY
GUILTY
THREATENED
INTERSECTIONALITY
SHOCKED
ENRAGED
JOBS
INTELLECTUALS
SOCIAL JUSTICE
HUMILIATED
TERRIFIED
EXCLUDED
FAKE NEWS
GENTRIFICATION
DESPONDENT
LIBERAL ELITE
RENT-SEEKER
ULTRA HIGH NET WORTH IDIVIDUALS
GENDERQUEER
GENDER FLUID
SEXISM
NATIONALISM
1%
VEGANS
GENERATION Z
COOL
WOKE
OCCUPY
CLIMATE CHANGE
HYPOCRITE
BLACK LIVES MATTER
DESPERATE
DEFENSIVE
VENGEFUL
ABUSED
NEGLECTED
RIDICULED
INTIMIDATED
THE SECOND AMENDMENT
PRIVILEGE
LIBERTARIANS
HOMOPHOBIA
SCIENCE
INDIVIDUALISM
THE PATRIARCHY
FOX NEWS
GLOBALISATION
THE AFFLUENT

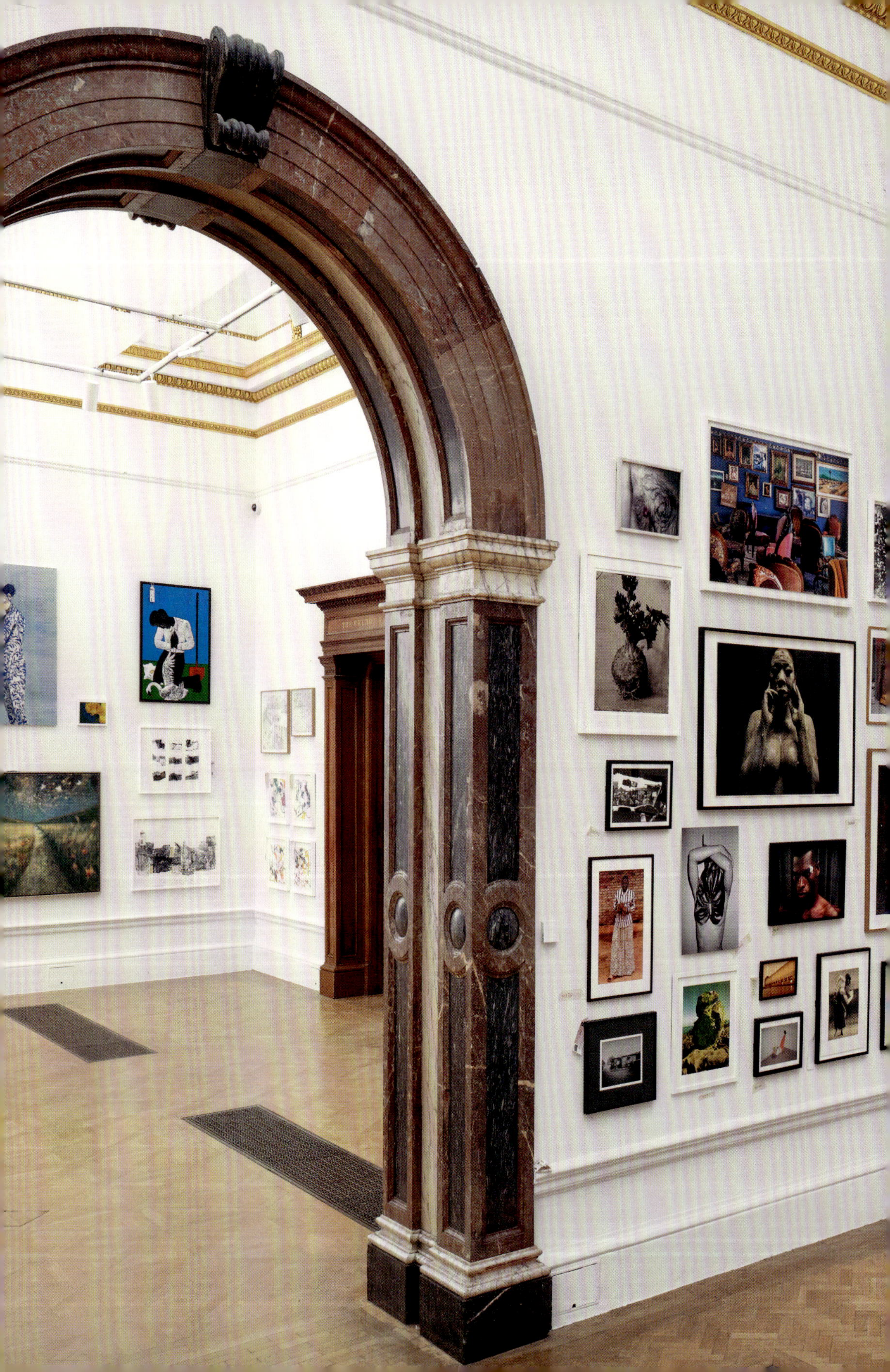

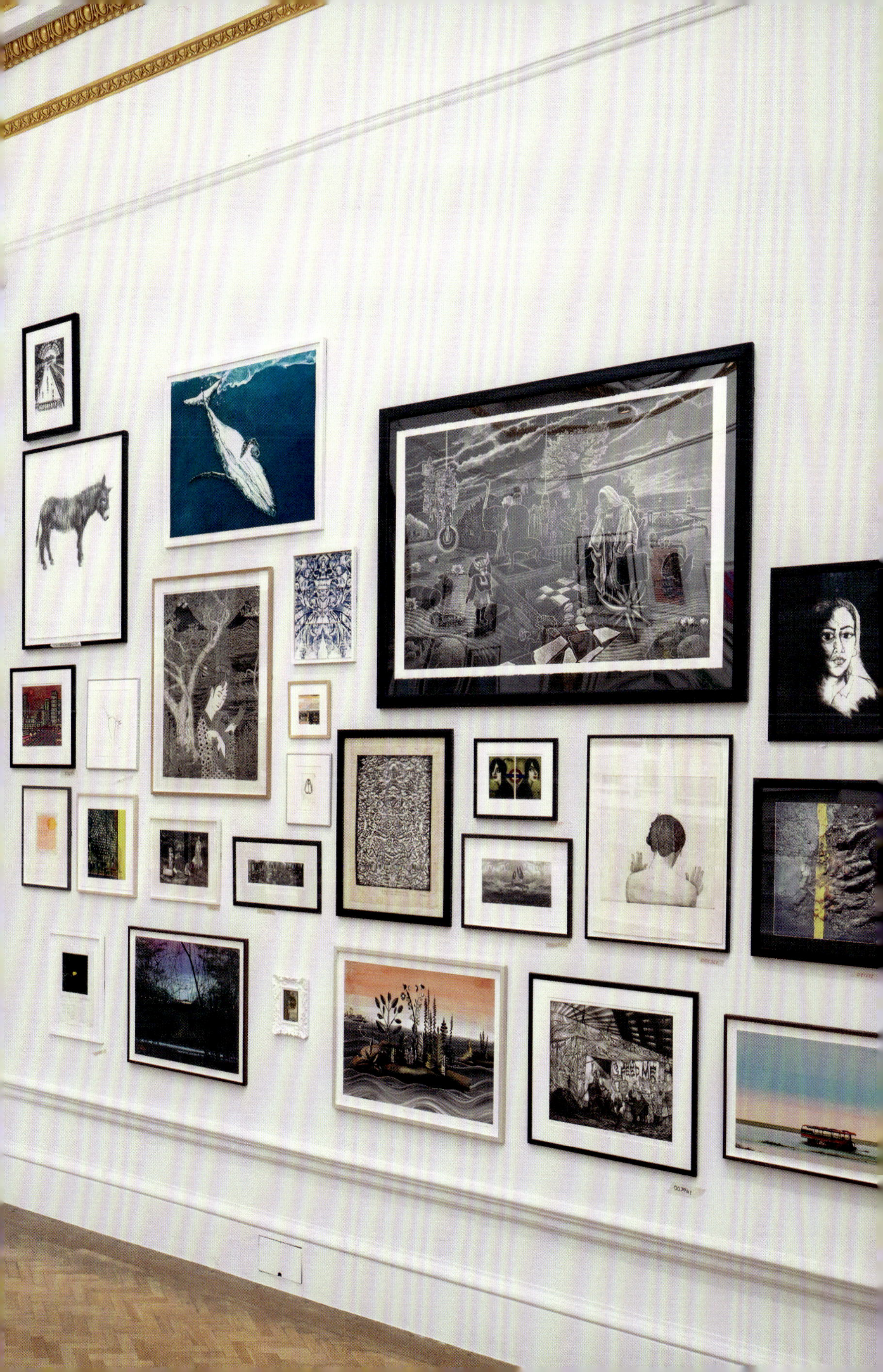
FEED ME

Peter Randall-Page RA
Evolution XIV
Ink
51 × 83 cm

Fiona Robinson
Chopin Polonaise
Mixed media
76 × 56 cm

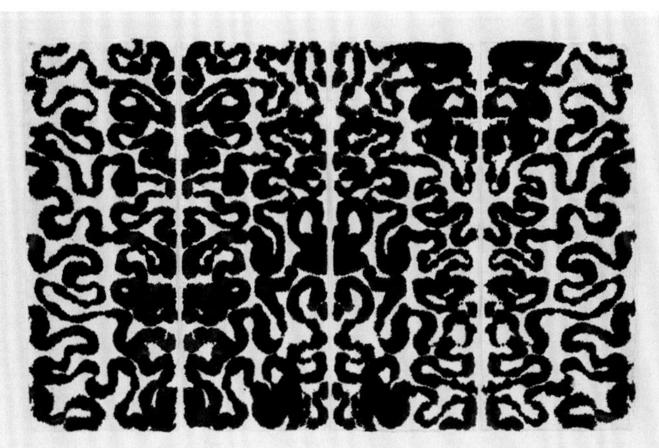

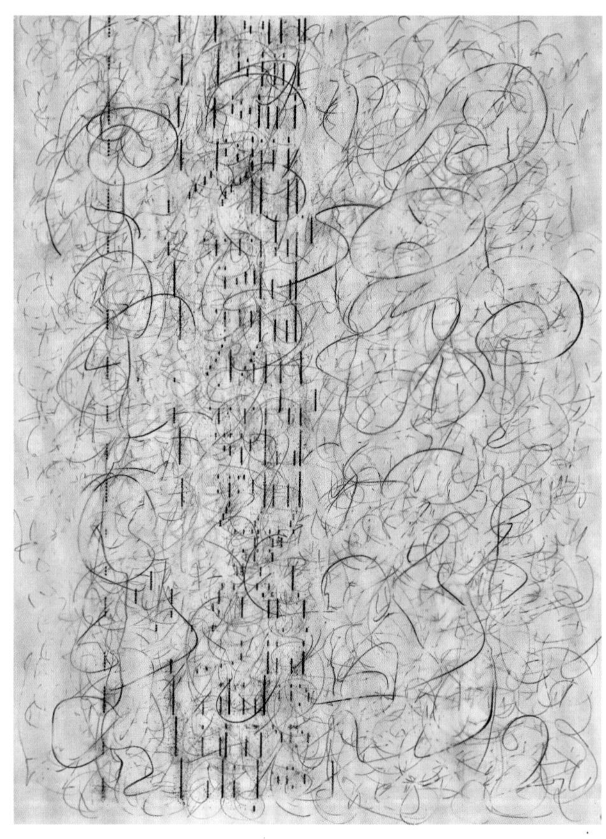

Georg Baselitz Hon RA
Frank Auerbach (F.AU.)
Etching and aquatint
86 × 65 cm

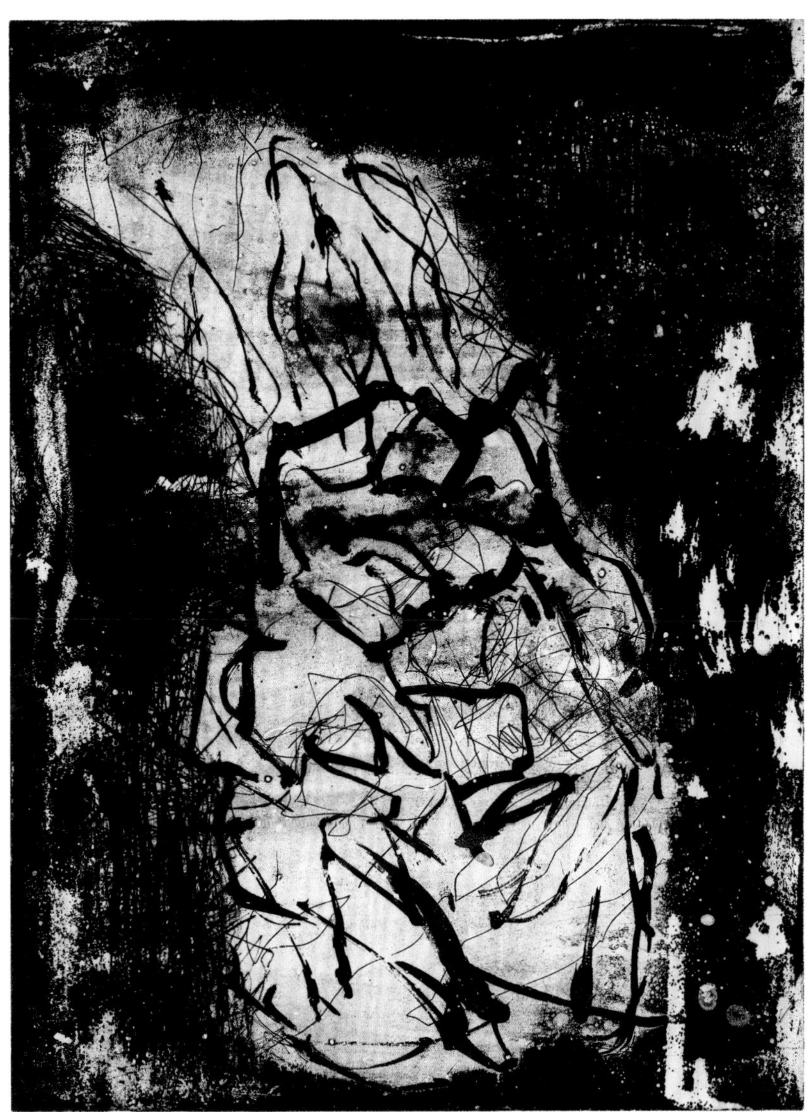

Dr Barbara Rae CBE RA
Ice Passage – Ilulissat
Carborundum print
66 × 54 cm

Rebecca Salter PRA
Untitled AR30
Mixed media
180 × 130 cm

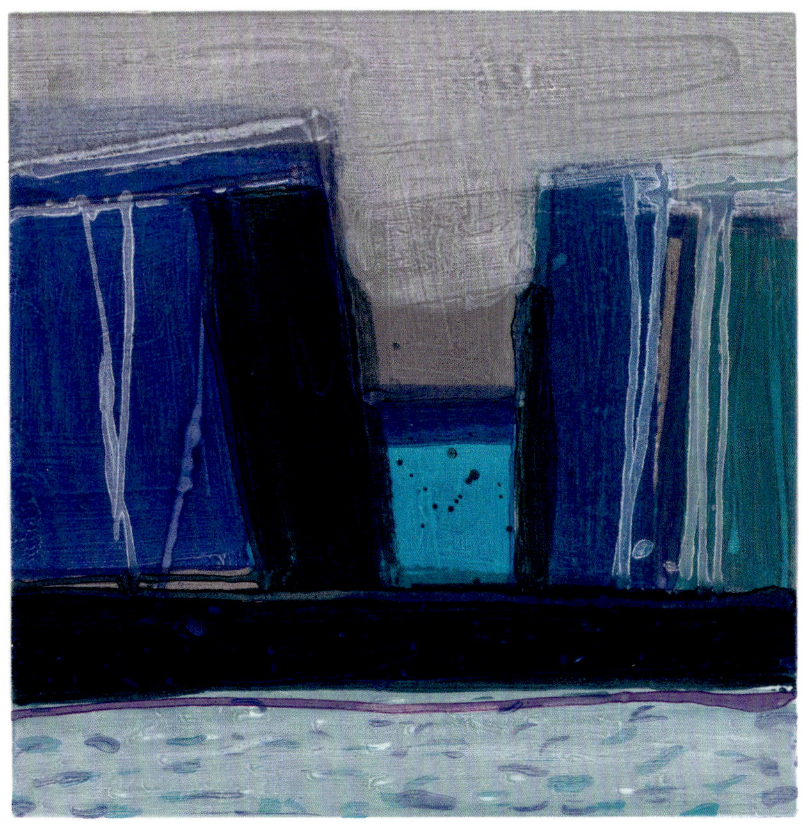

Dr David Tindle RA
Garden Arena, Noon
Acrylic and tempera
50 × 70 cm

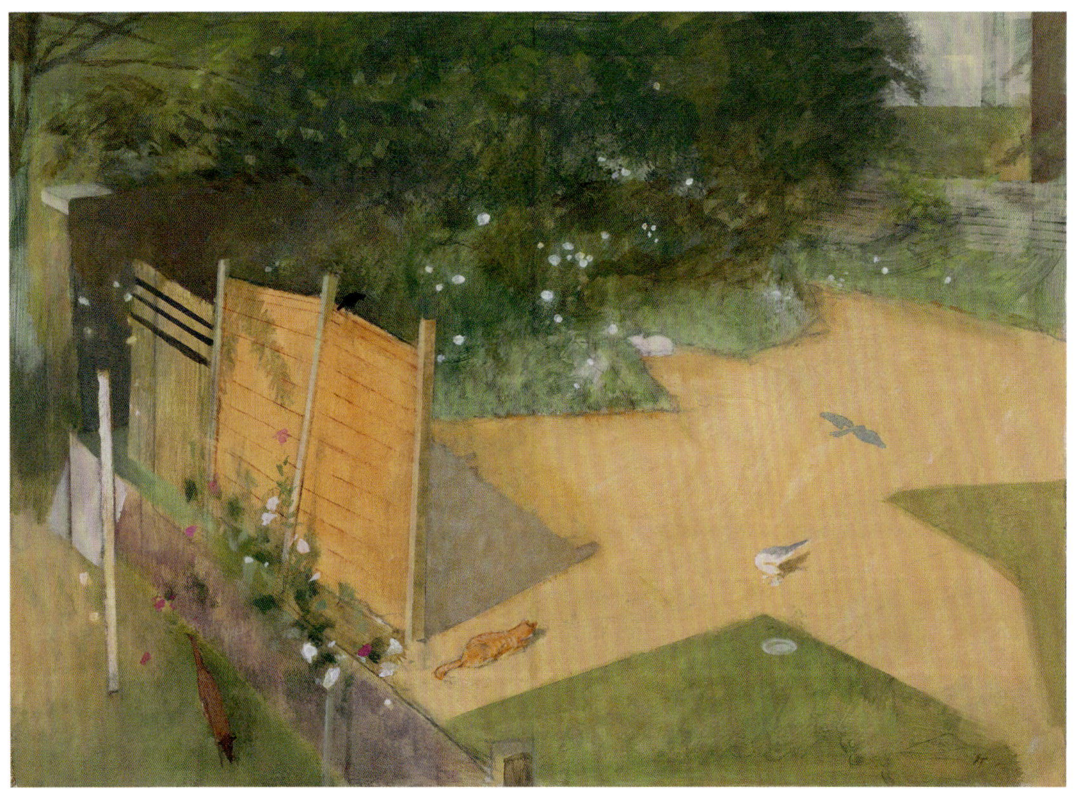

Prof Trevor Dannatt OBE RA
Andros, Après Midi
Watercolour
35 × 28 cm

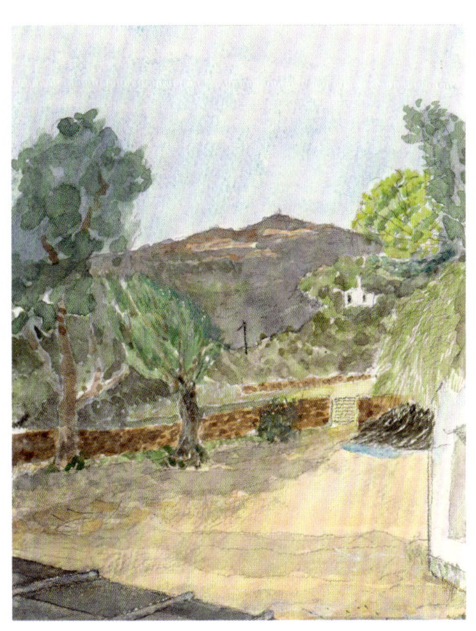

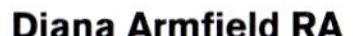

Diana Armfield RA
The Magnificent Head
Pastel
40 × 29 cm

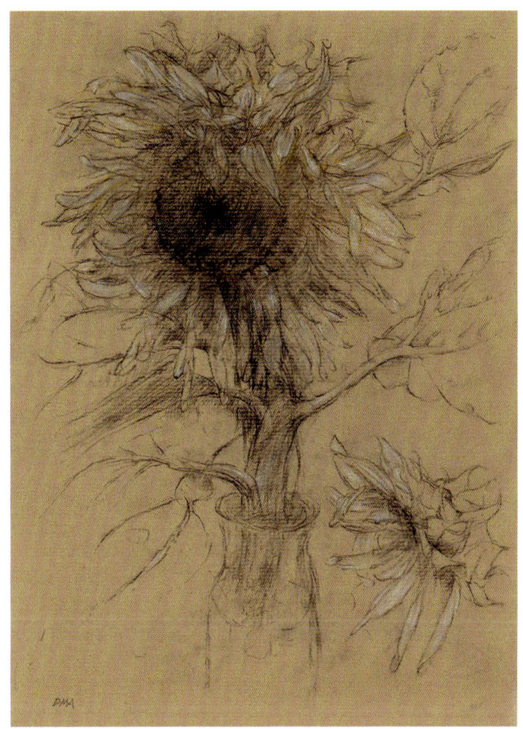

Fiona Rae RA
Abstract 21 (Drawing)
Gouache and watercolour
42 × 56 cm

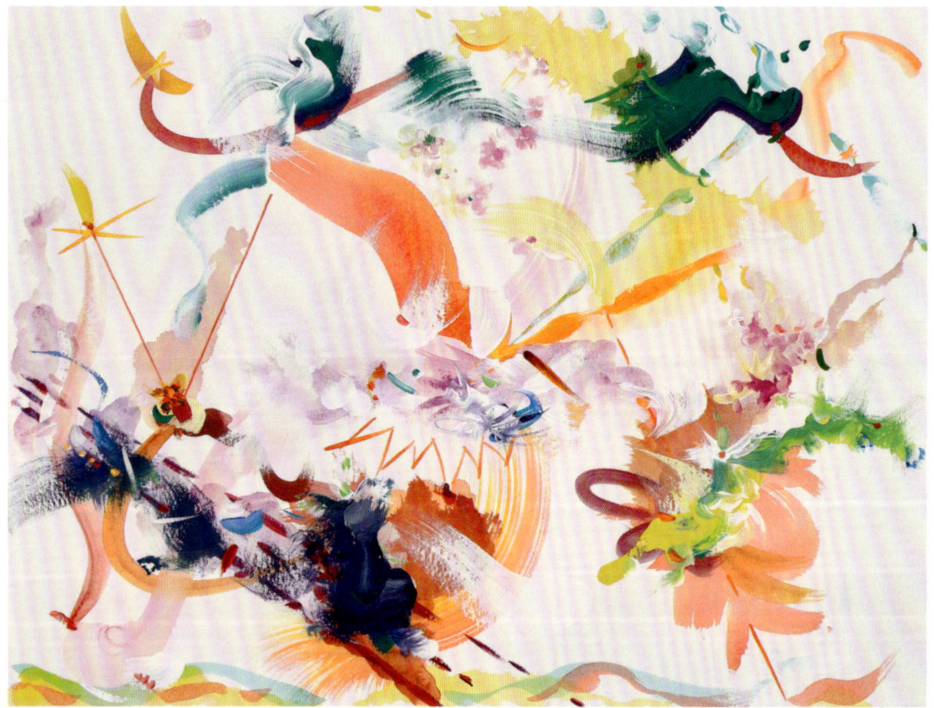

Joyce Cairns

Cher Ami and Martinpuch

Oil

152 × 152 cm

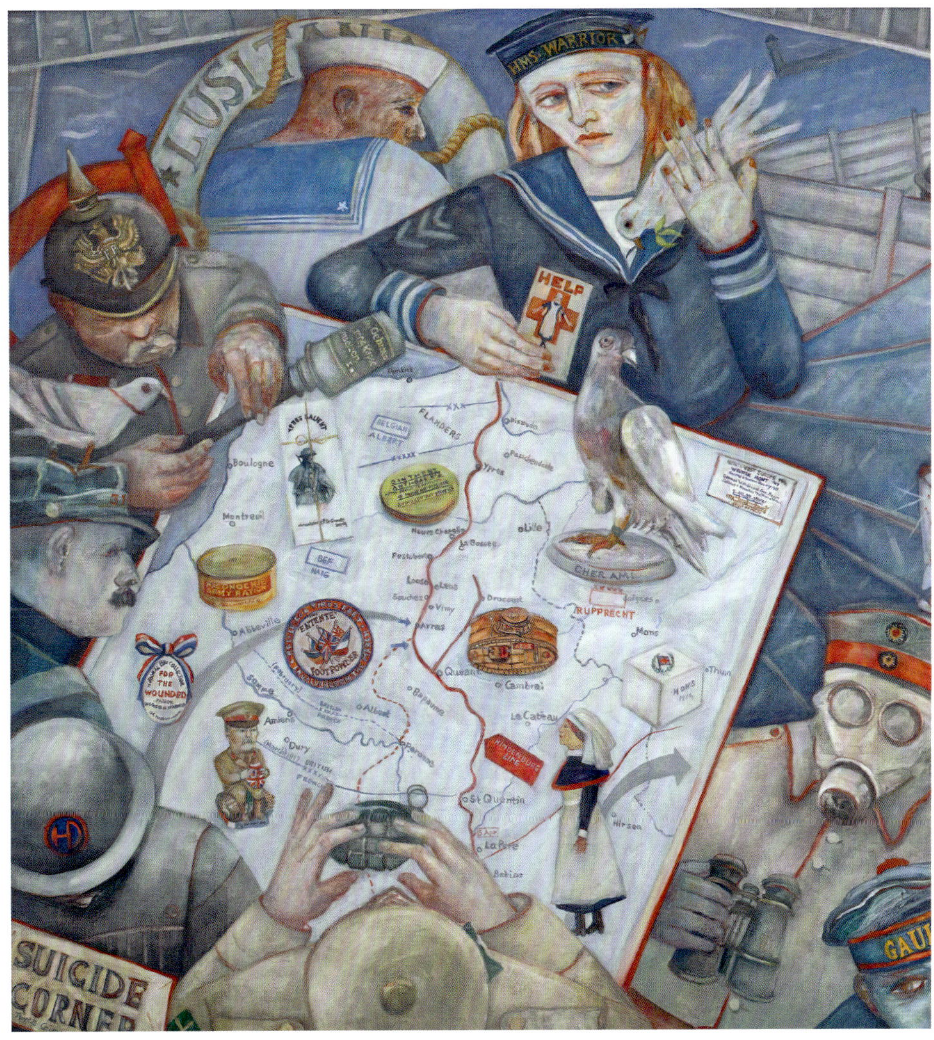

Olwyn Bowey RA
Garden Shed
Oil
120 × 91 cm

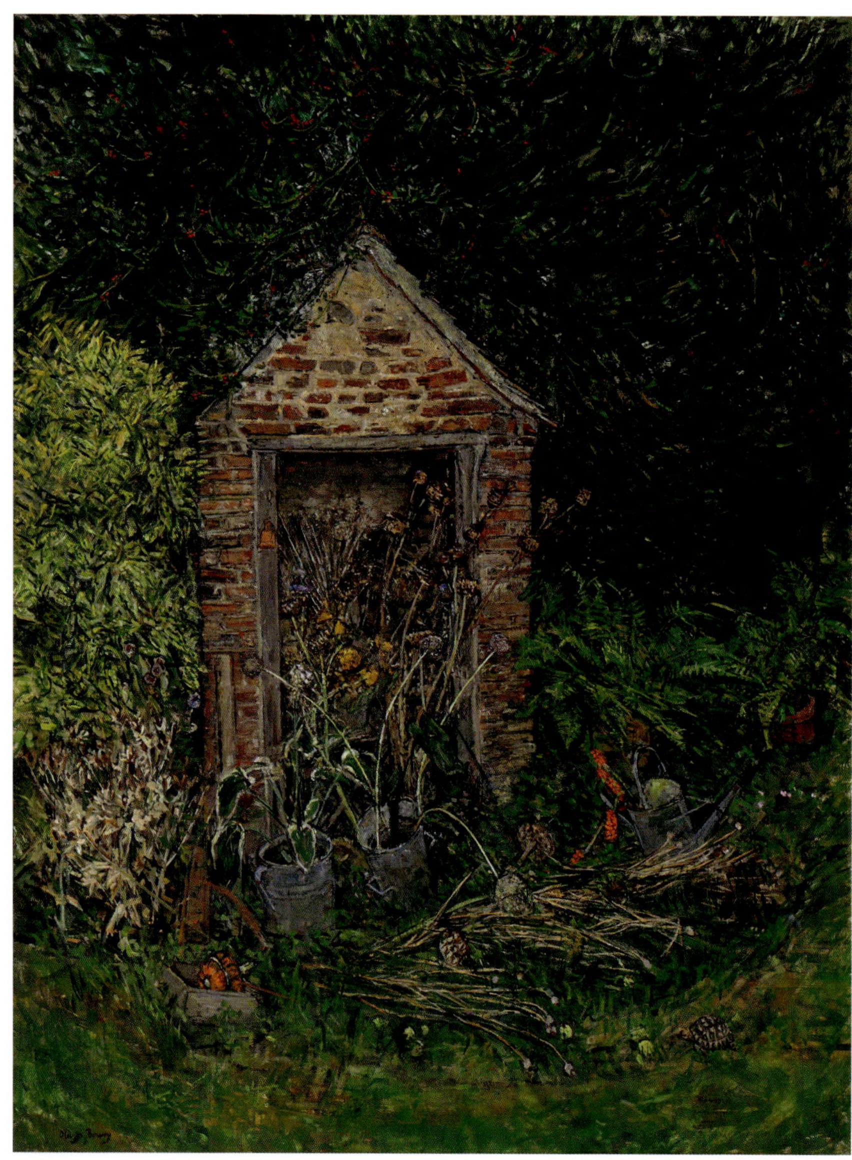

Anthony Eyton RA
Brixton Road Spring
Oil
120 × 85 cm

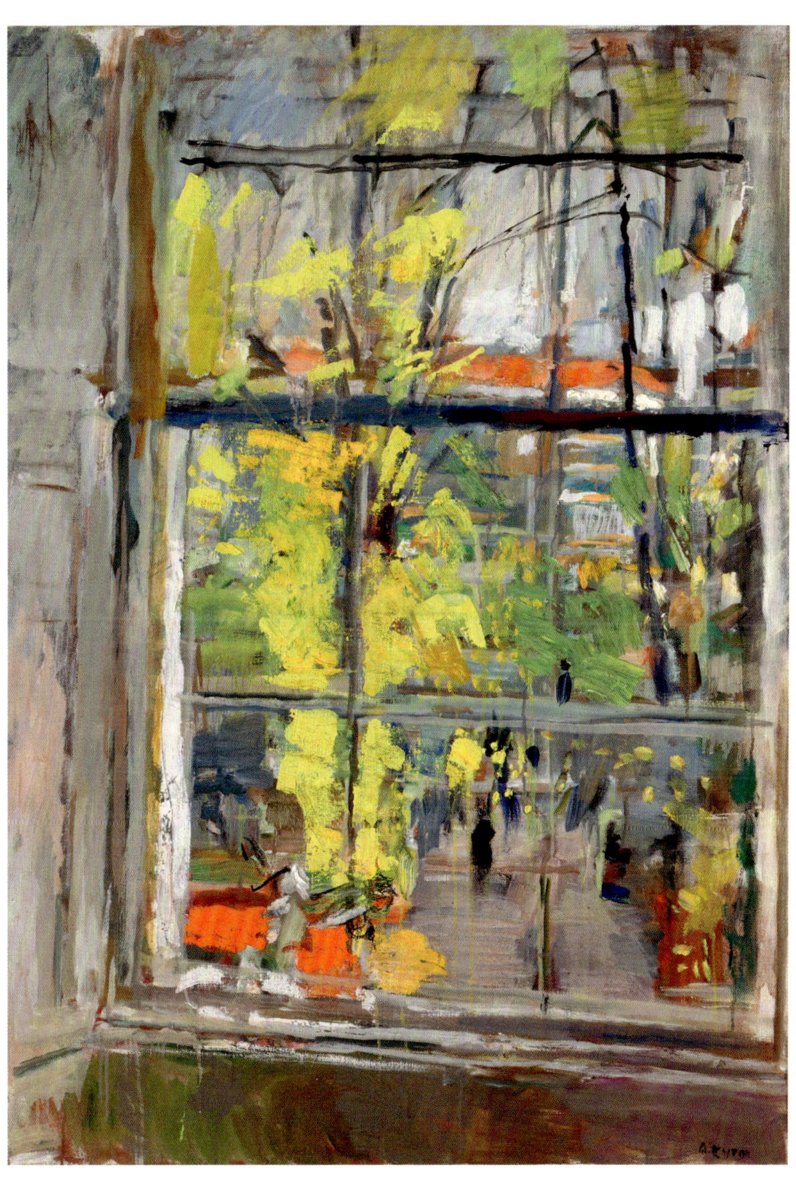

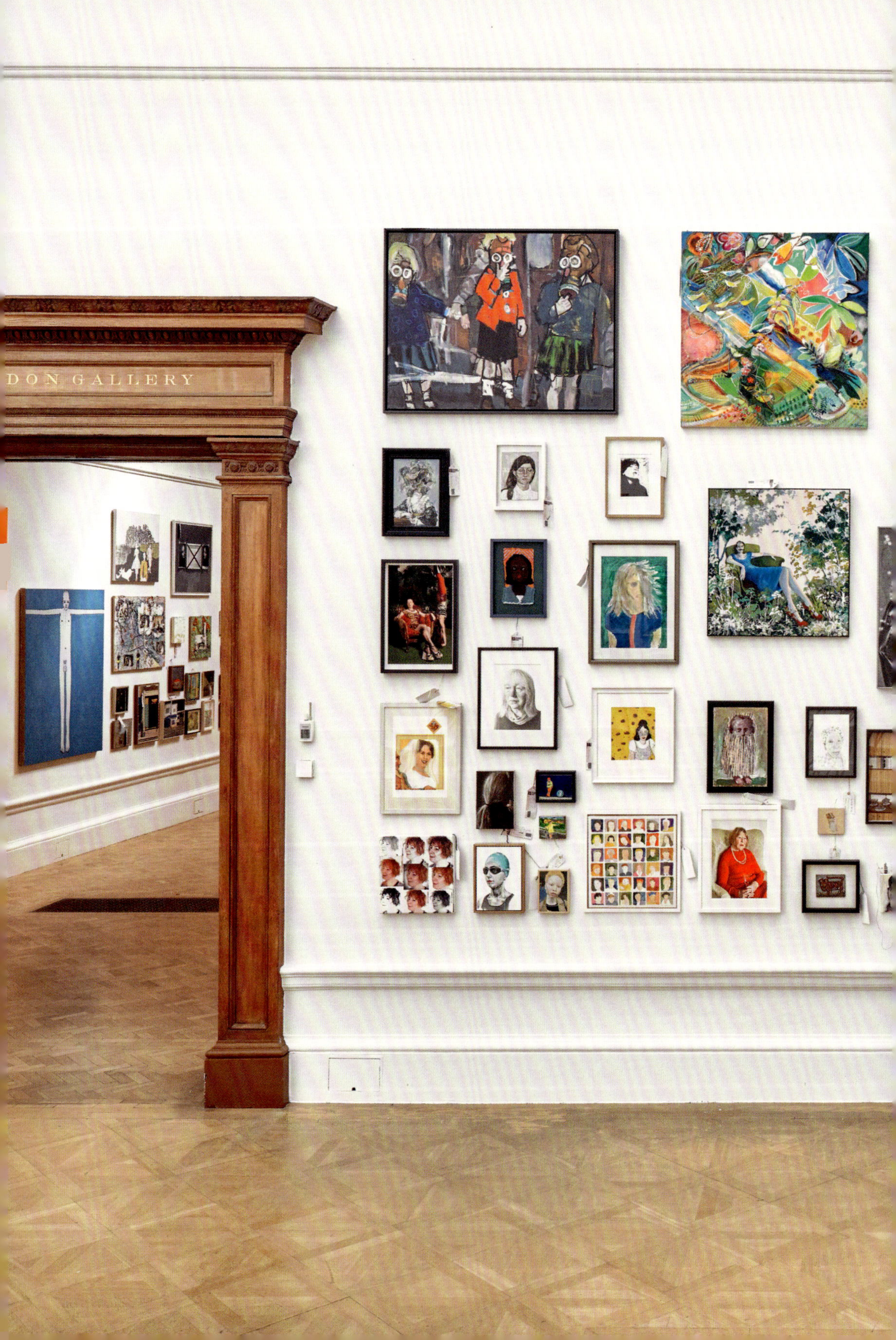
DON GALLERY

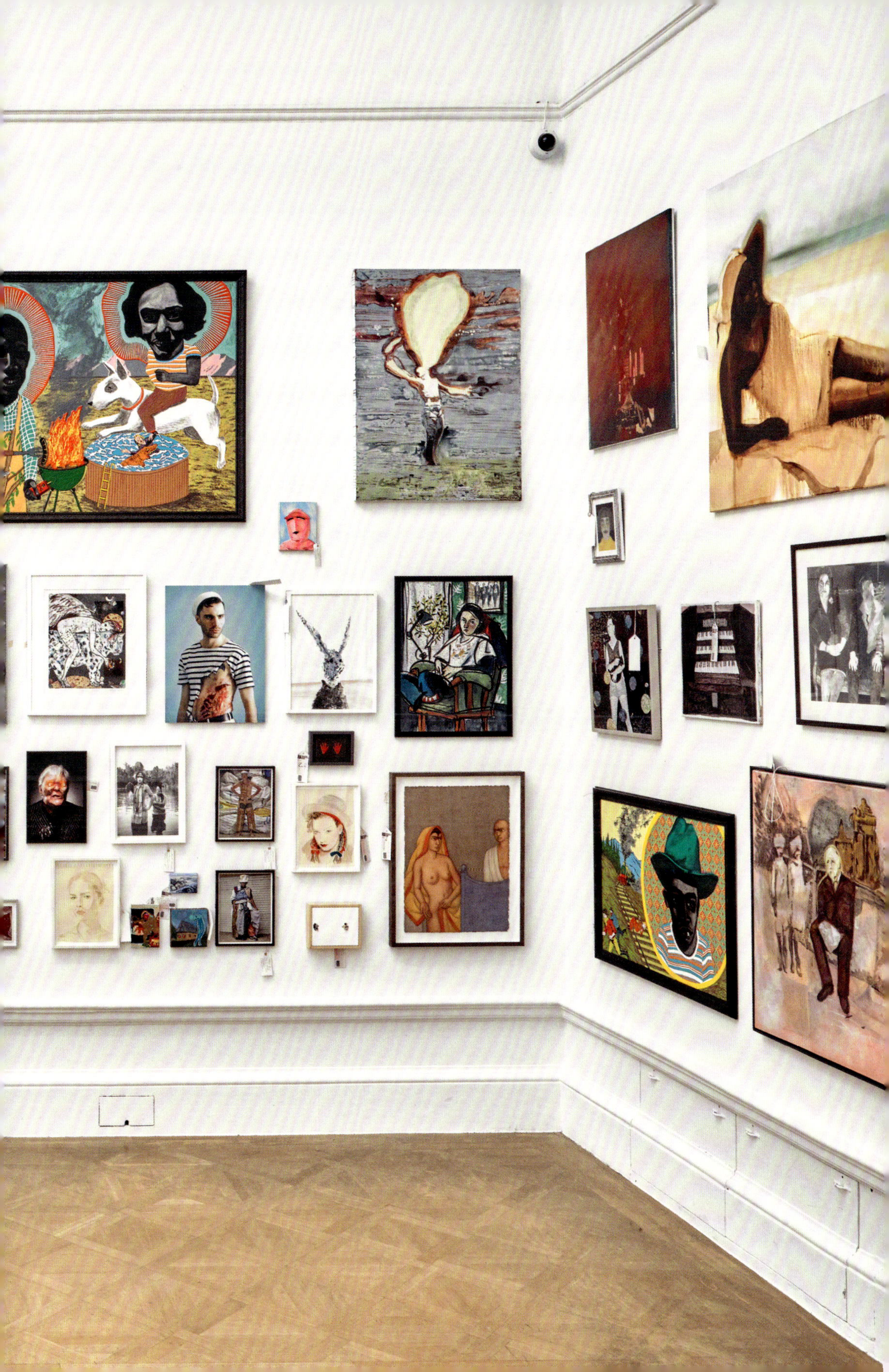

Prof David Mach RA
Roll
Screenprint
32 × 42 cm

Neil Jeffries RA
John Keats Reading
Aluminium and oil
H 69 cm

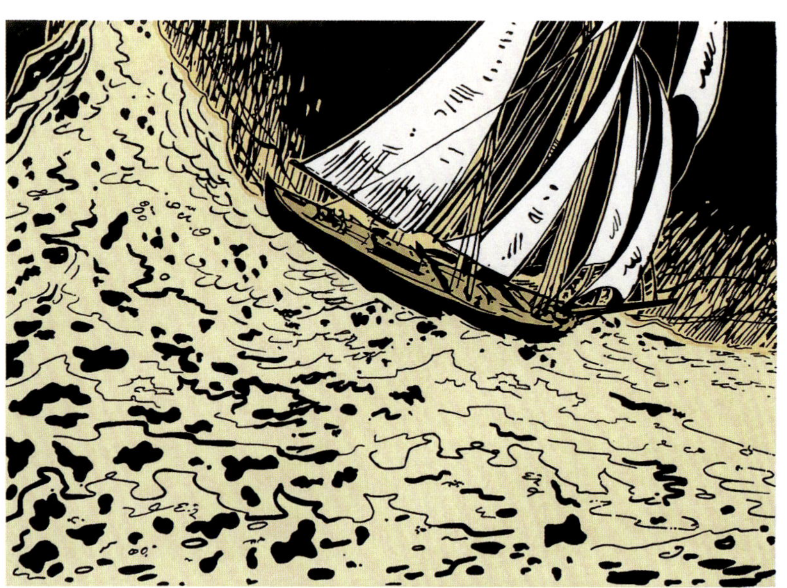

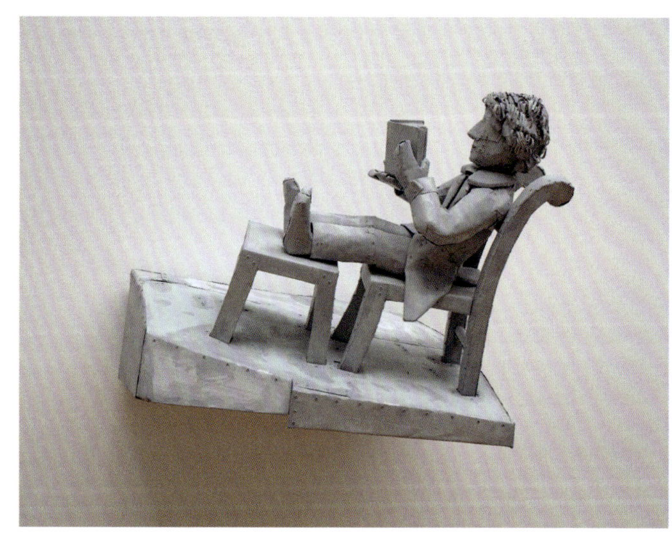

Bob and Roberta Smith OBE RA
There Is Still Art, There Is Still Hope
Signwriters' paint
61 × 61 cm

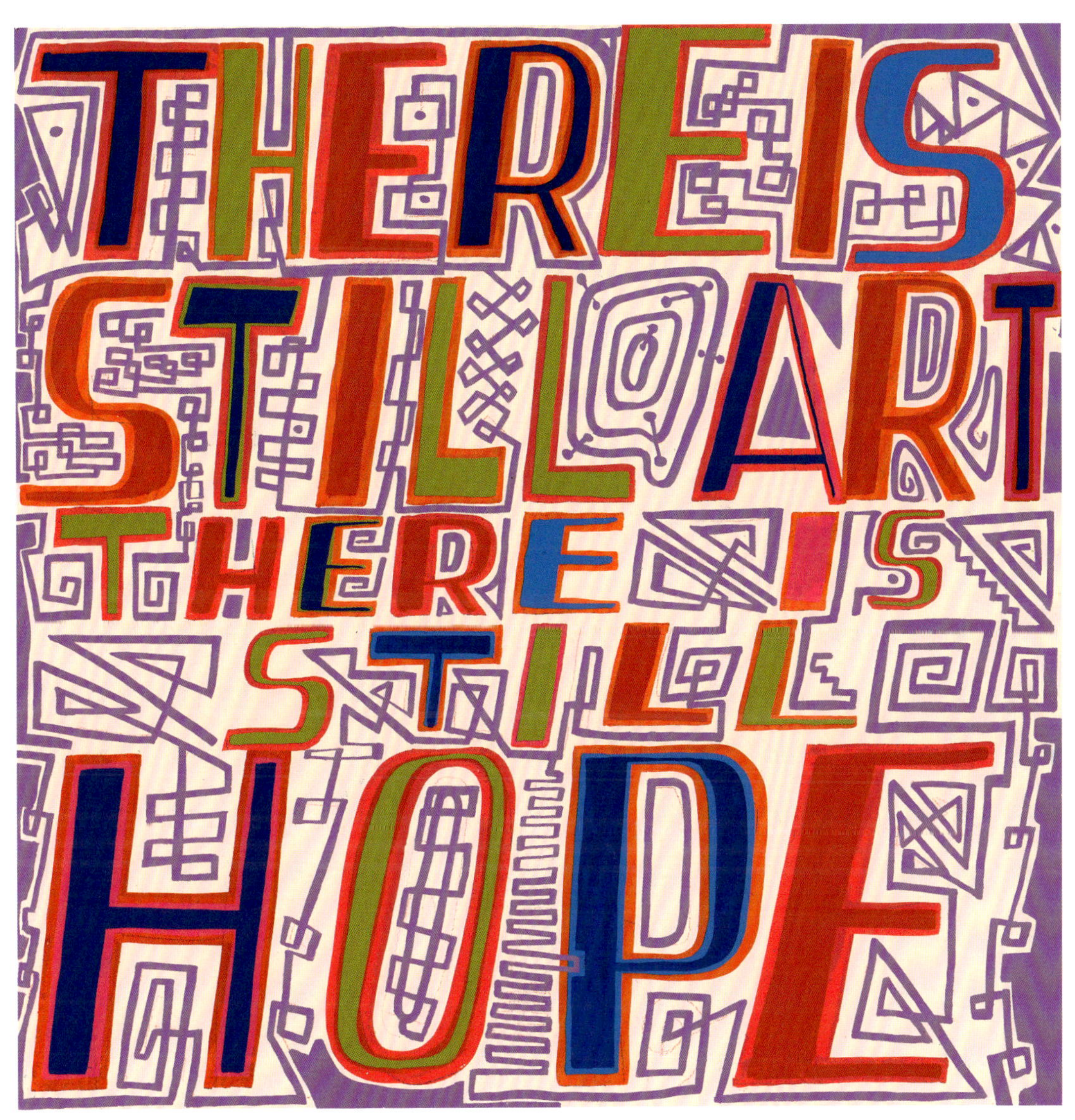

David Austen
Blue Boy
Oil and charcoal
167 × 152 cm

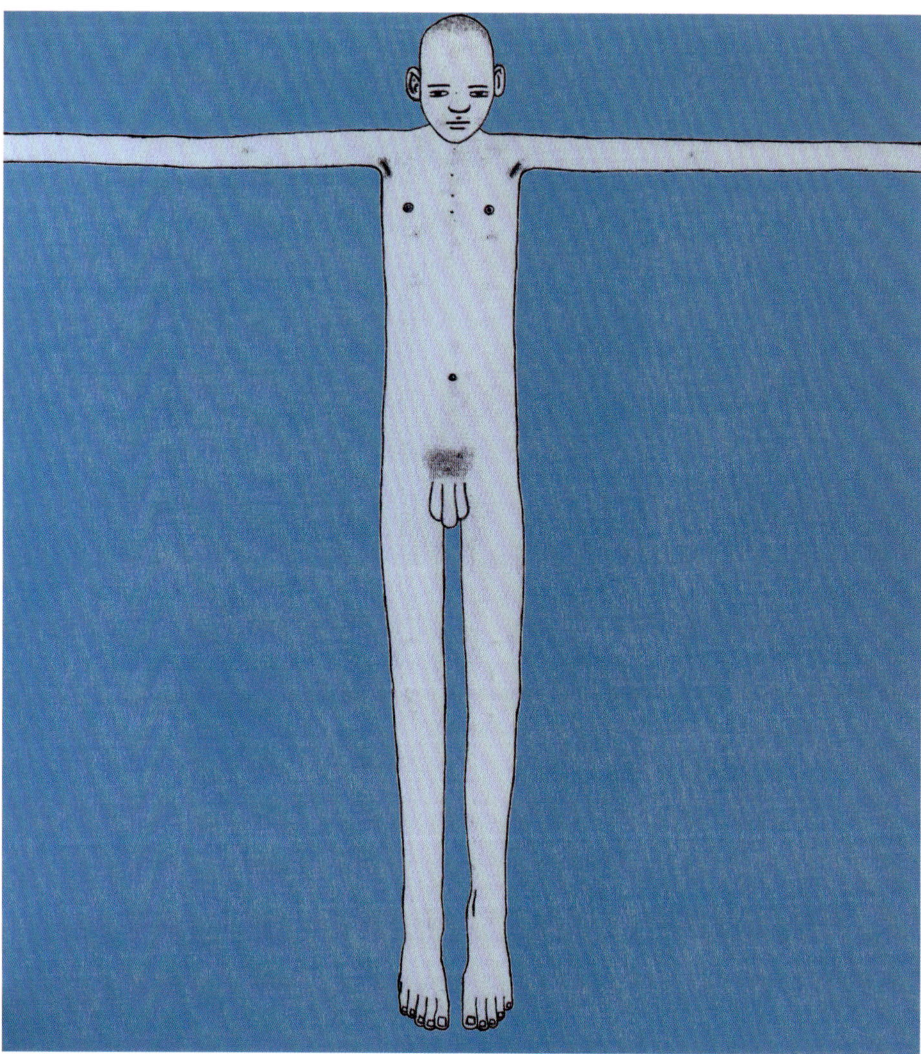

Stephen Chambers RA
Snail Love (Catalani) 6
Oil
30 × 26 cm

Prof Brian Catling RA
Split Dish and Tide Pool
Mixed media
36 × 36 cm

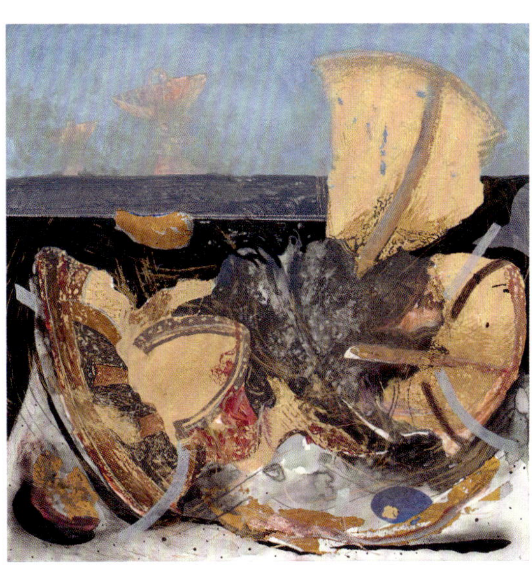

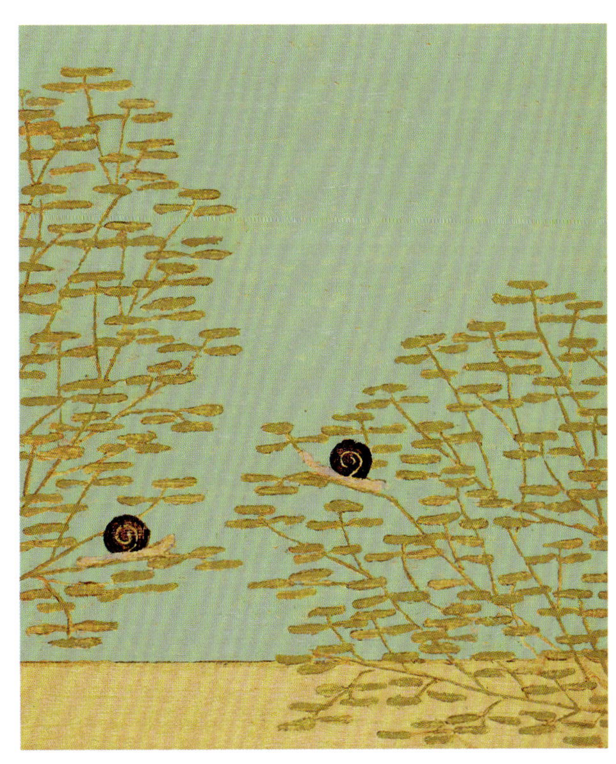

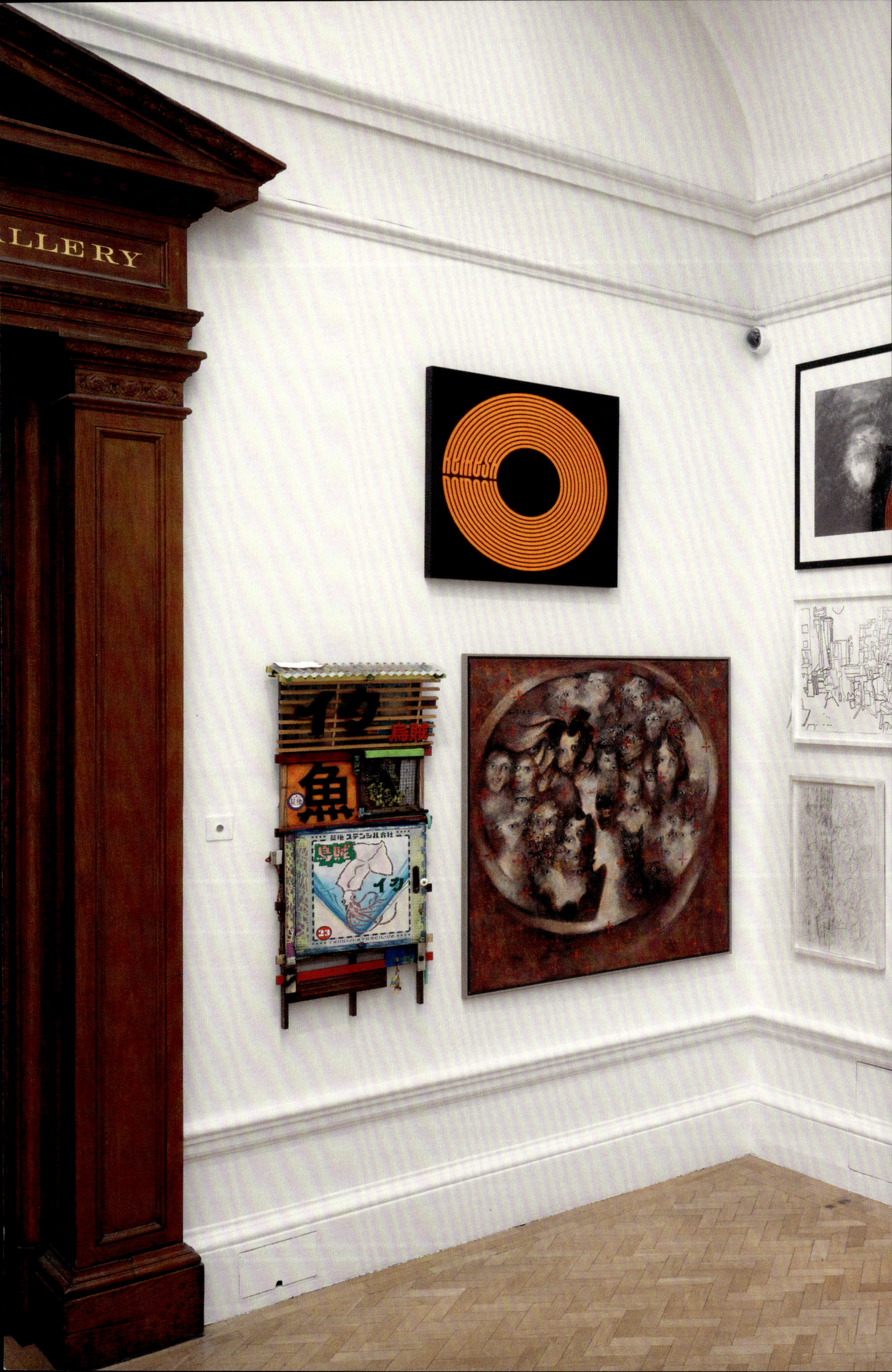
ALLERY
イカ
烏賊
魚

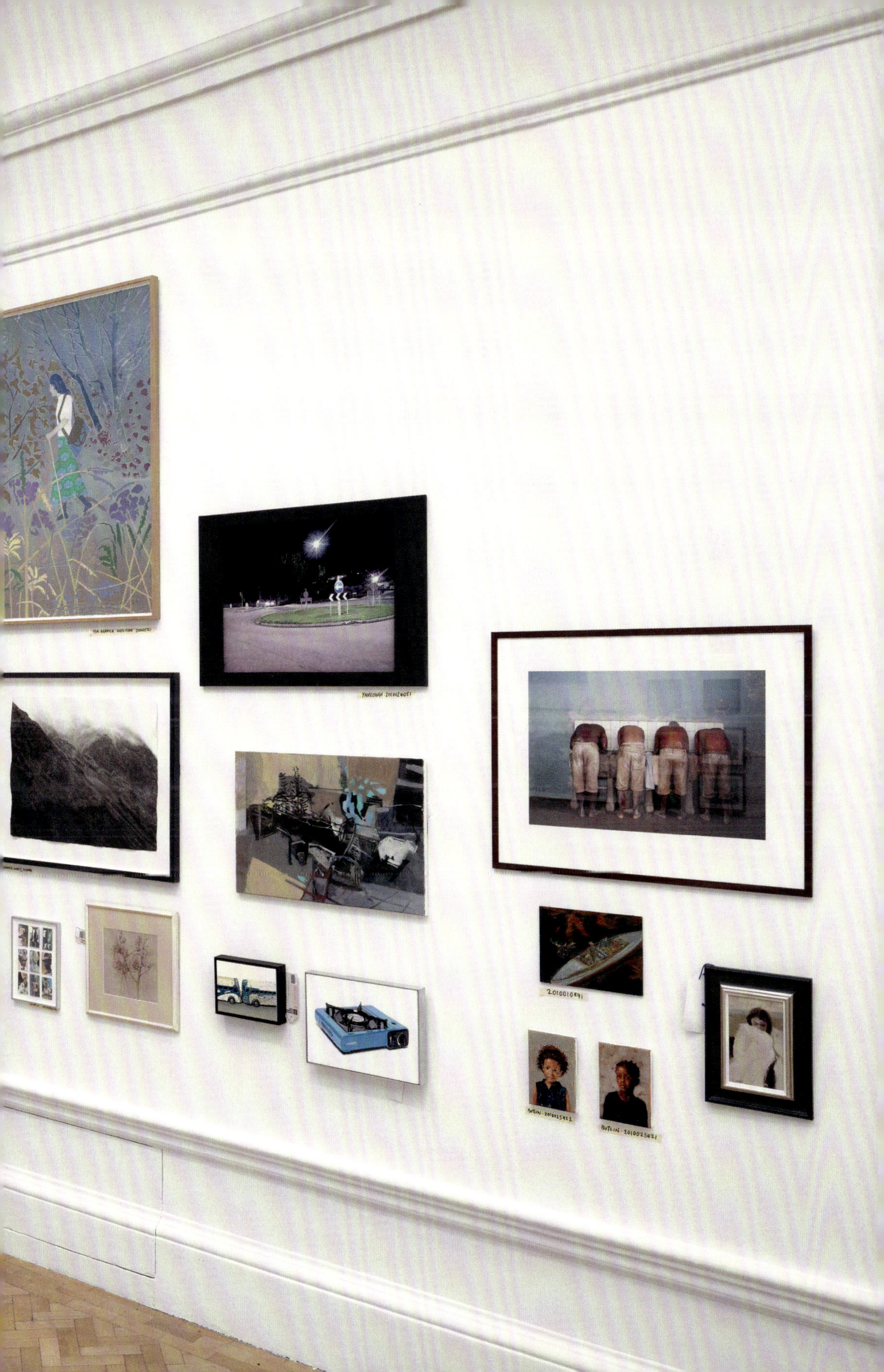

Dr Jennifer Dickson RA
Zen Gardens: Four (Water)
Inkjet print
43 × 56 cm

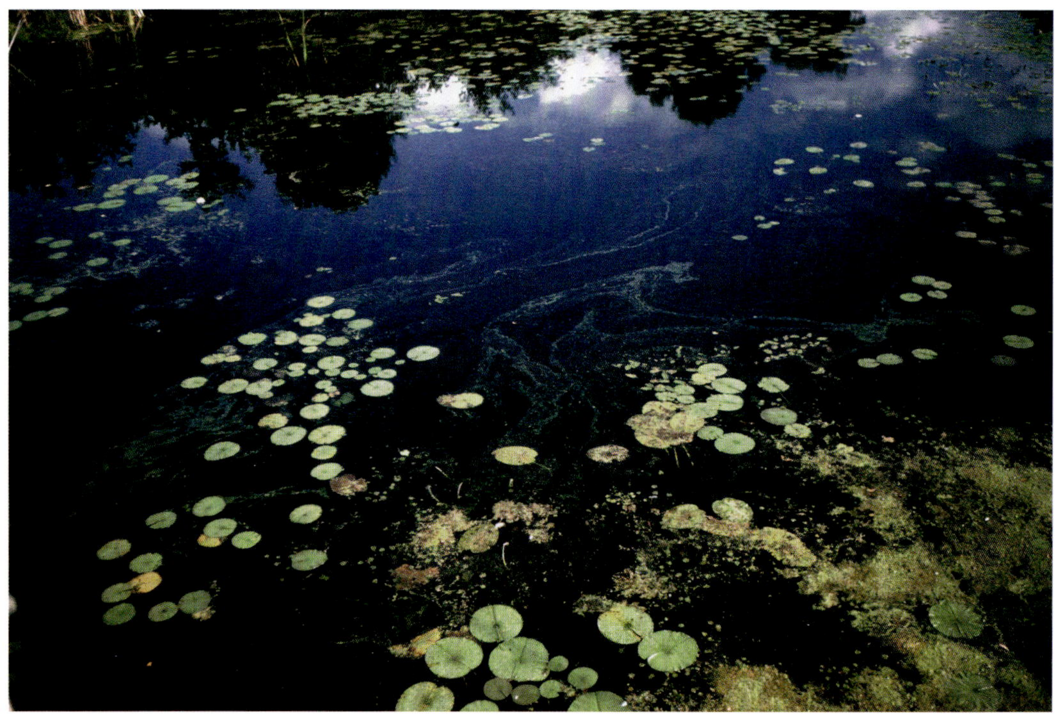

David Remfry MBE RA
Pink Specs
Oil
24 × 19 cm

Kenneth Draper RA
Sacred Stones
Pencil
36 × 36 cm

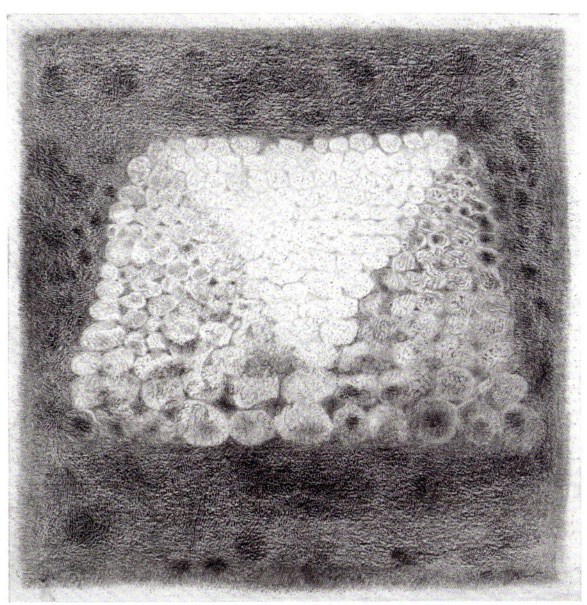

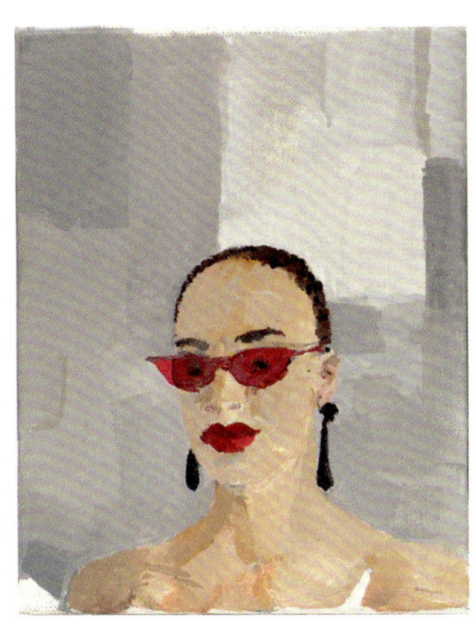

Ann Christopher RA
Holding Lines
Mixed media
H 240 cm

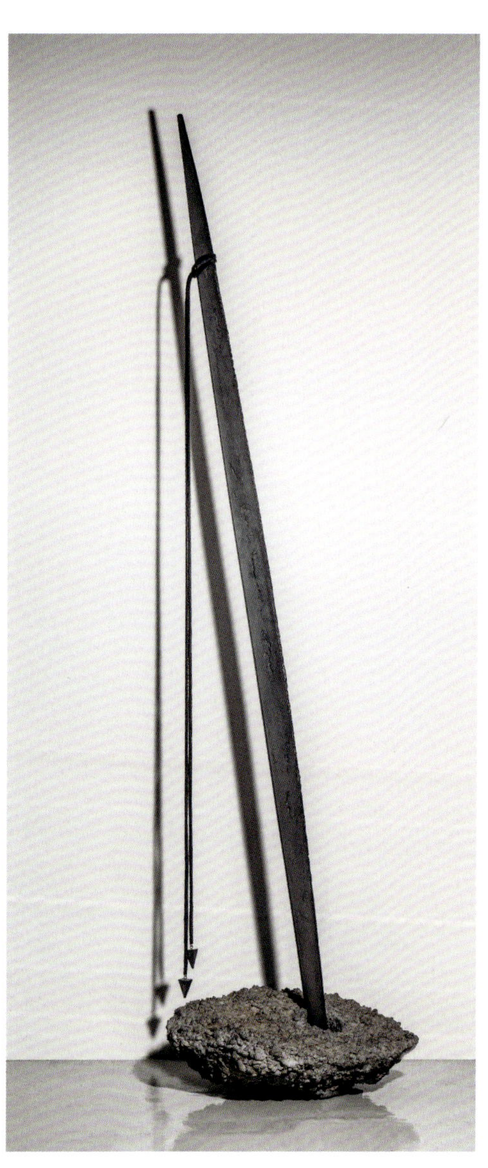

Richard Wilson RA
Block of Silence
Mixed media
H 24 cm

Rana Begum RA
No. 1002
Paint and aluminium
45 × 40 cm

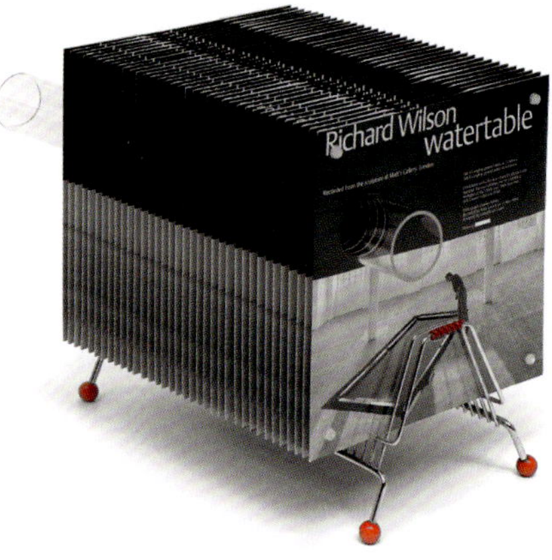

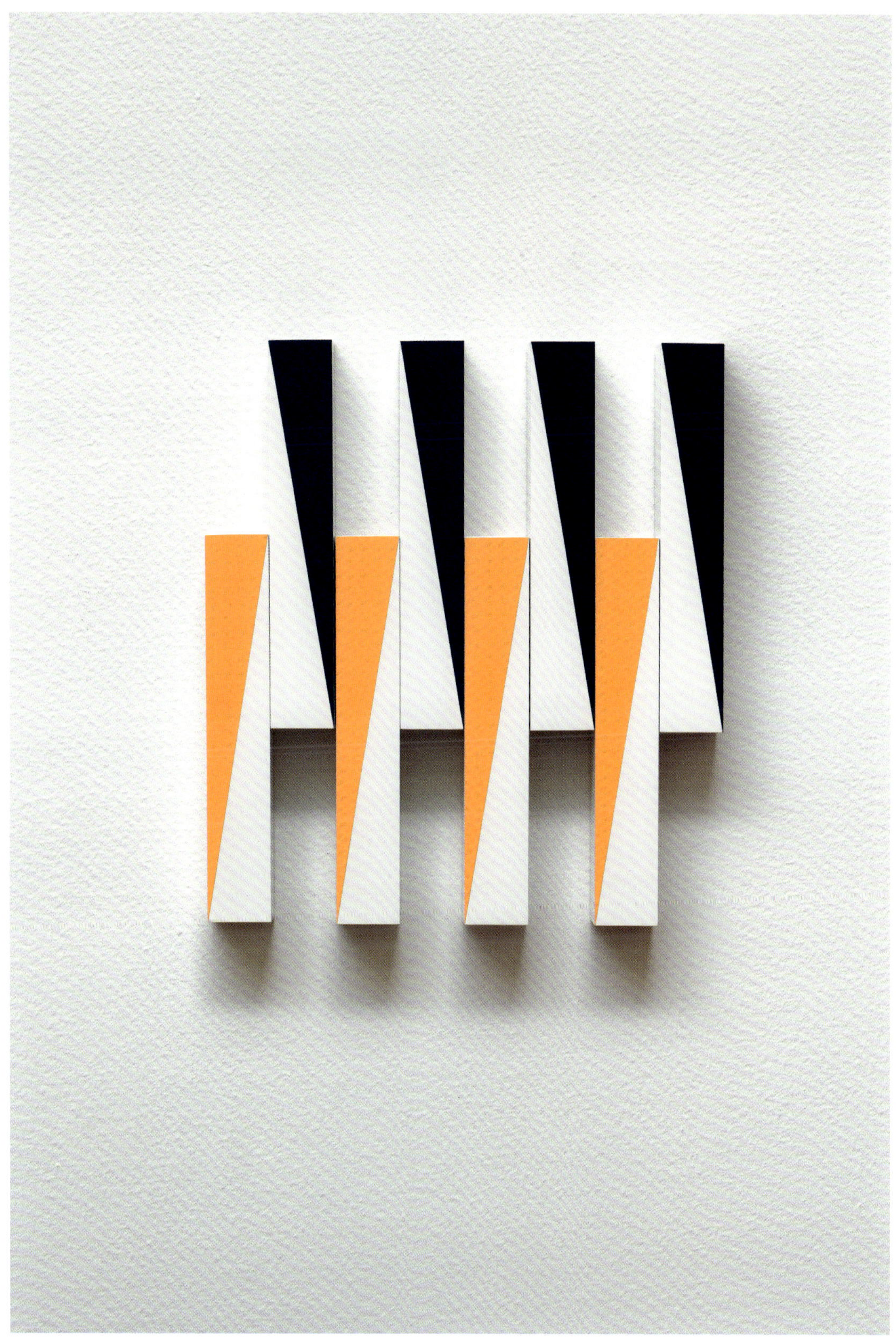

Ron Arad RA
Oh Lord, Won't You Buy Me?
Steel, rubber and paint
290 × 550 cm

Prof Dhruva Mistry CBE RA
Doodledom
Painted steel
H 34 cm

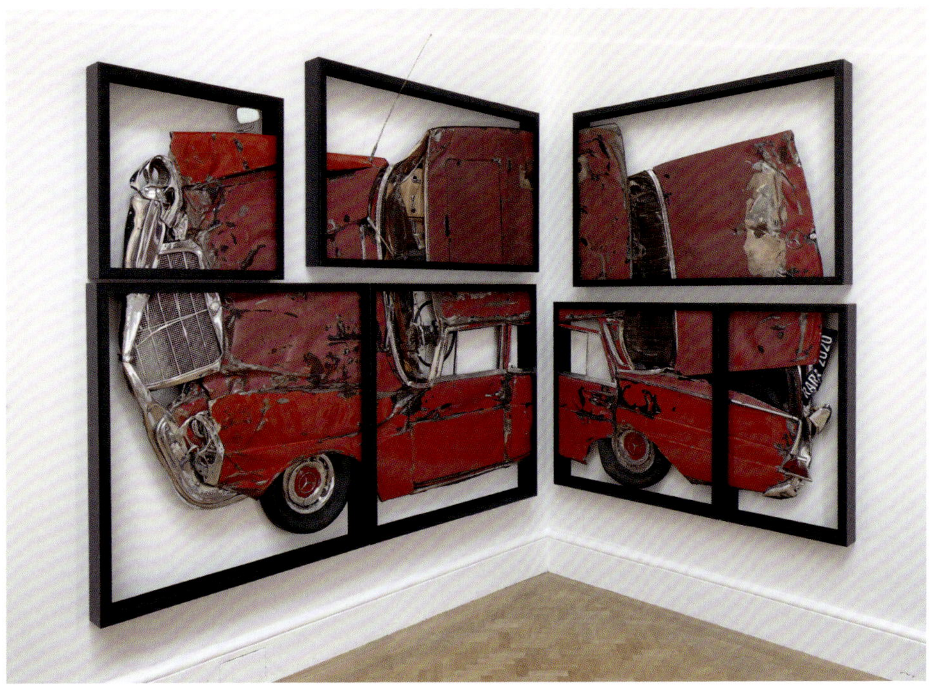

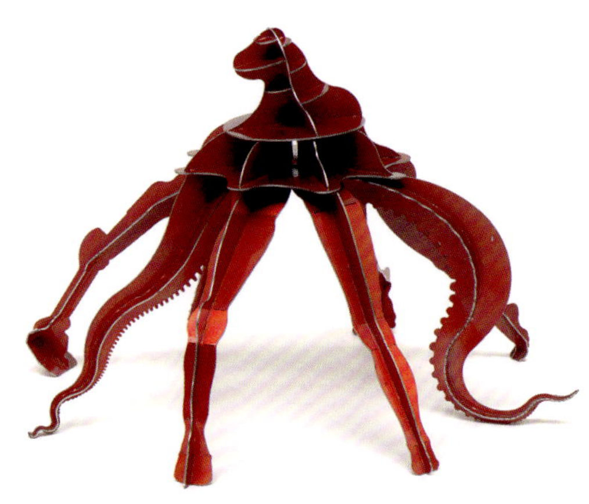

David Nash OBE RA
Red Column
Bronze
H 77 cm

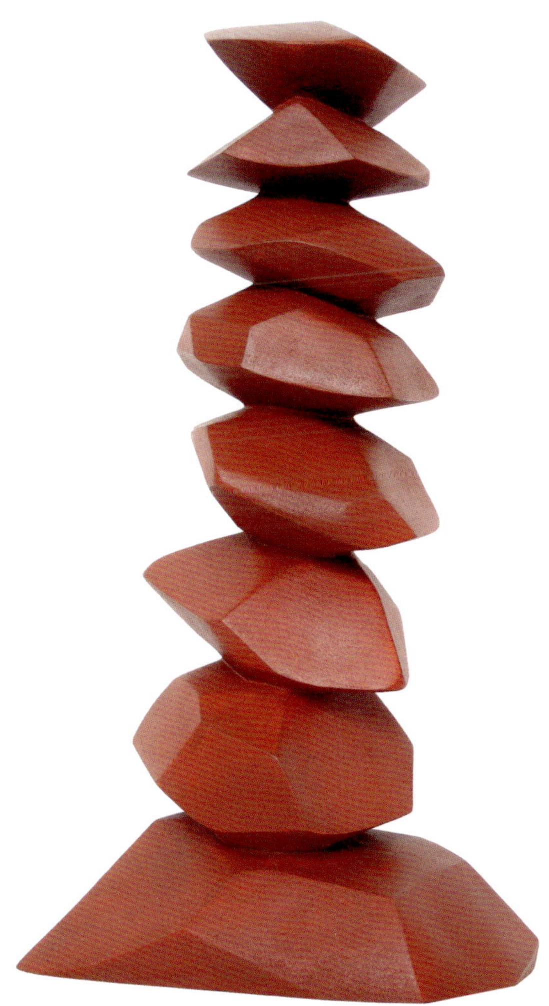

John Smith
Twice
Video

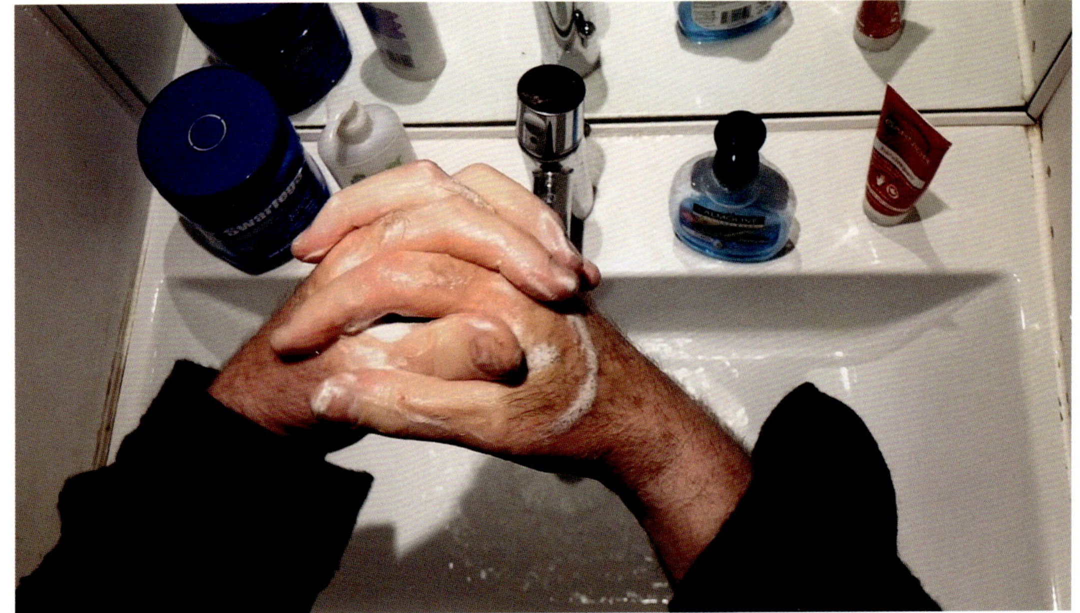

Prof Alison Wilding OBE RA
Shrubs 3
Oak and brass
H 51 cm

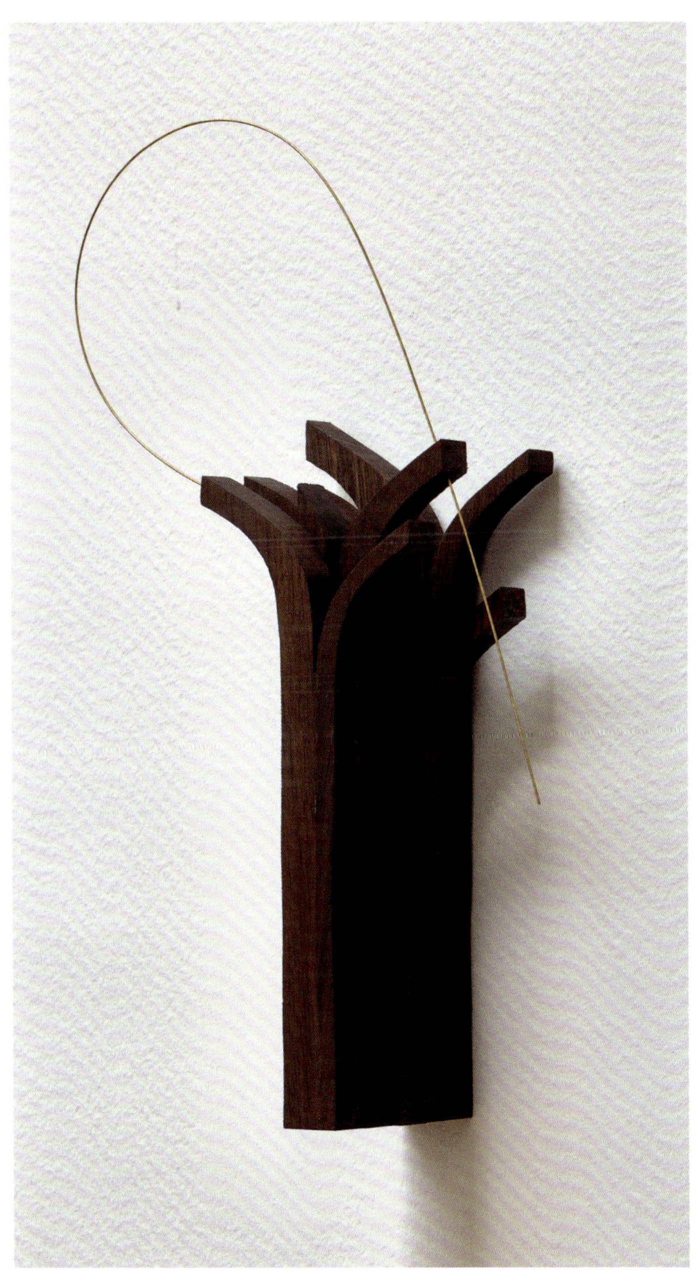

John Maine RA
Epicentre 2
Acrylic
151 × 112 cm

Prof Phillip King CBE PPRA
Wave
PVC and wood
H 40 cm

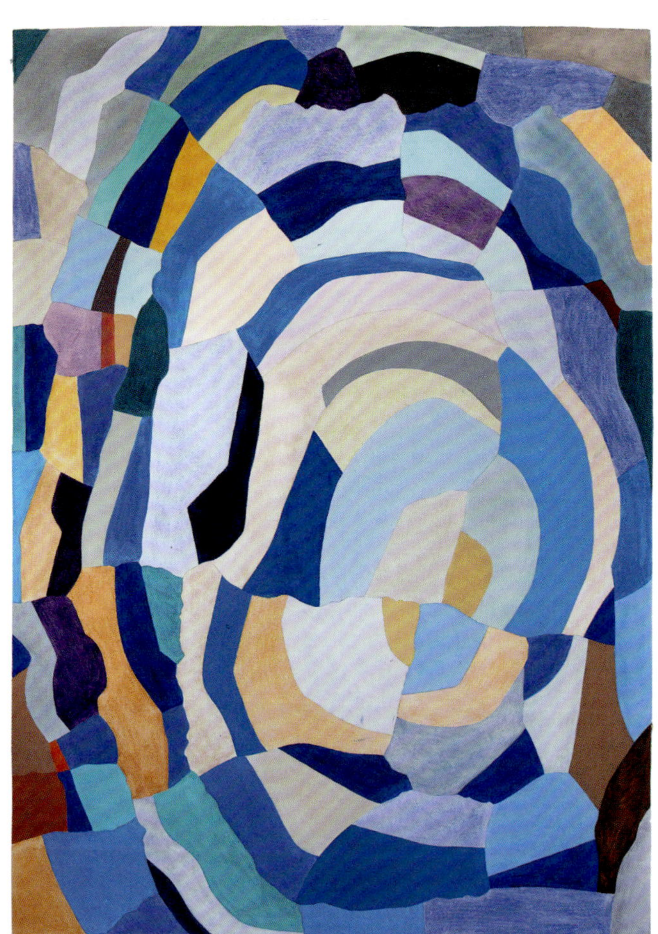

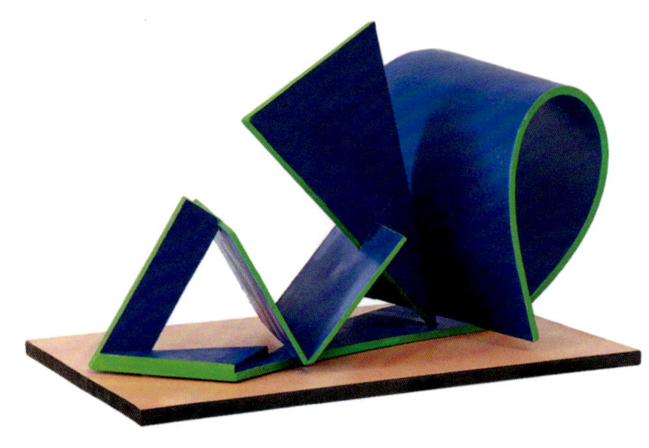

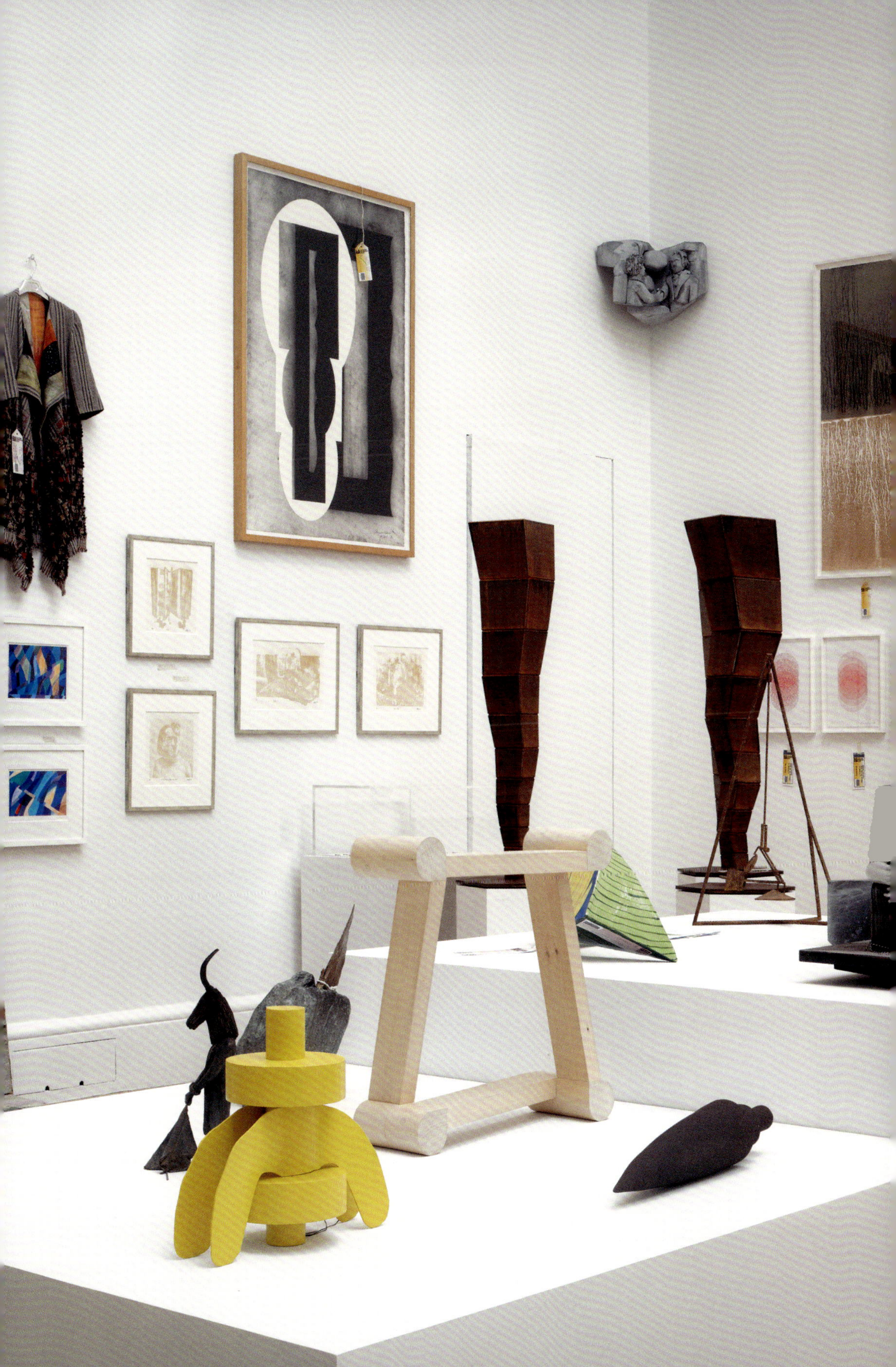

Prof Bryan Kneale MBE RA
Pendulum Maquette
Bronze
H 59 cm

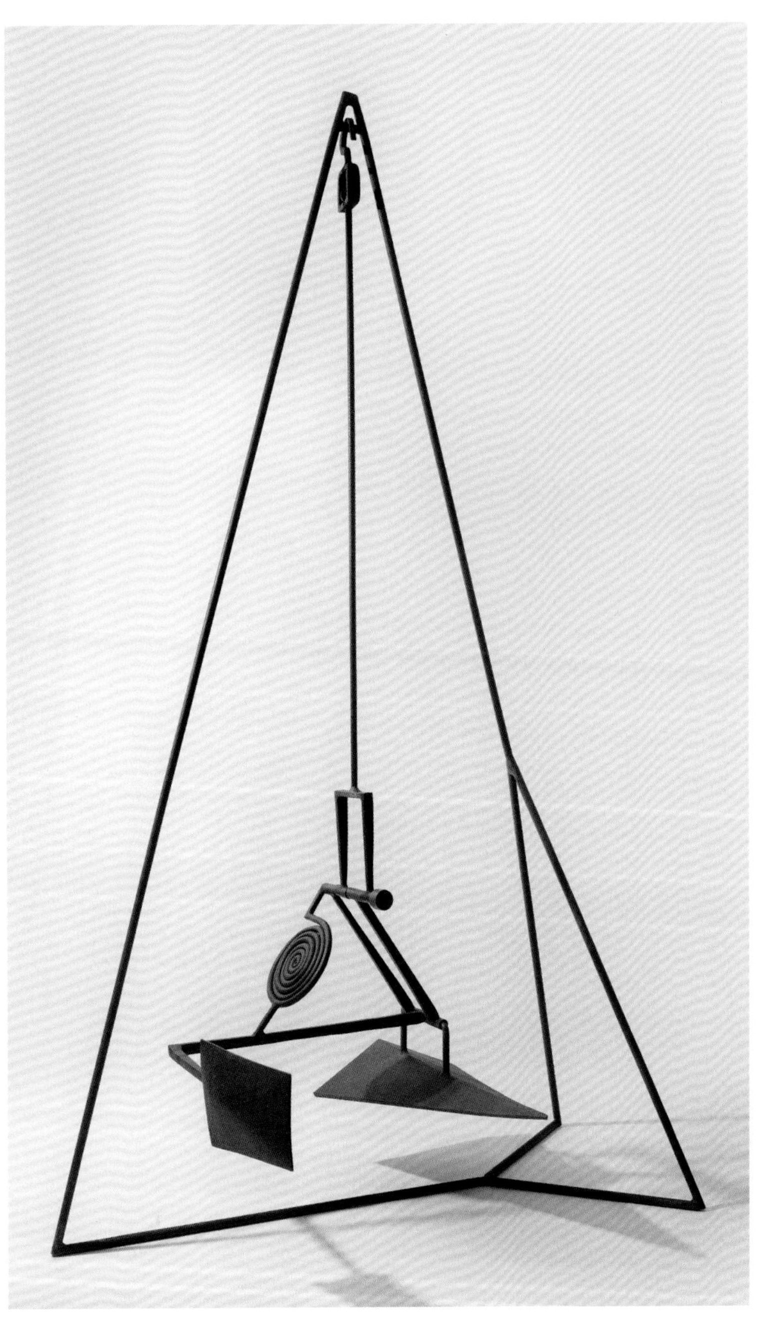

Conrad Shawcross RA
Catastrophe Sequence (Solid)
Steel
H 123 cm

Tracey Emin CBE RA
Take Me Home
Bronze
H 12 cm

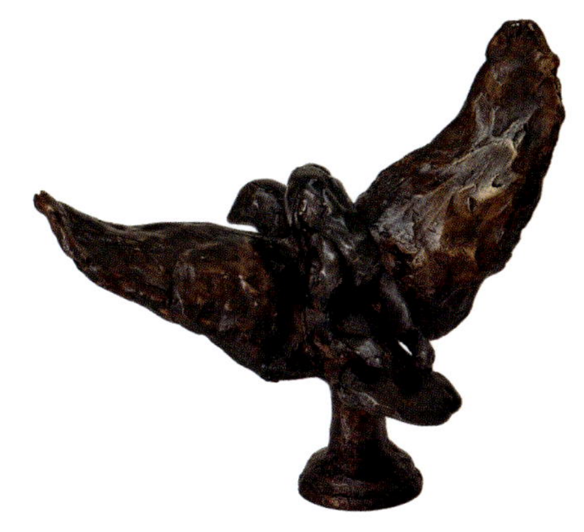

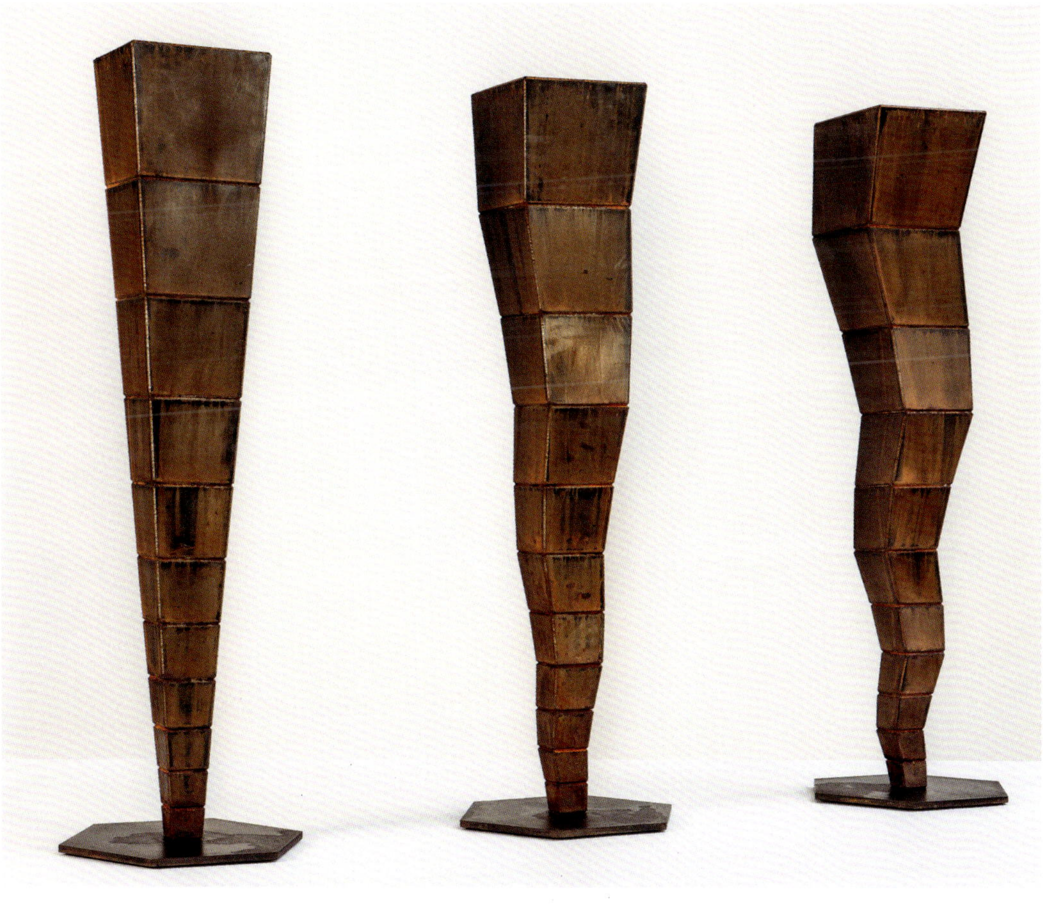

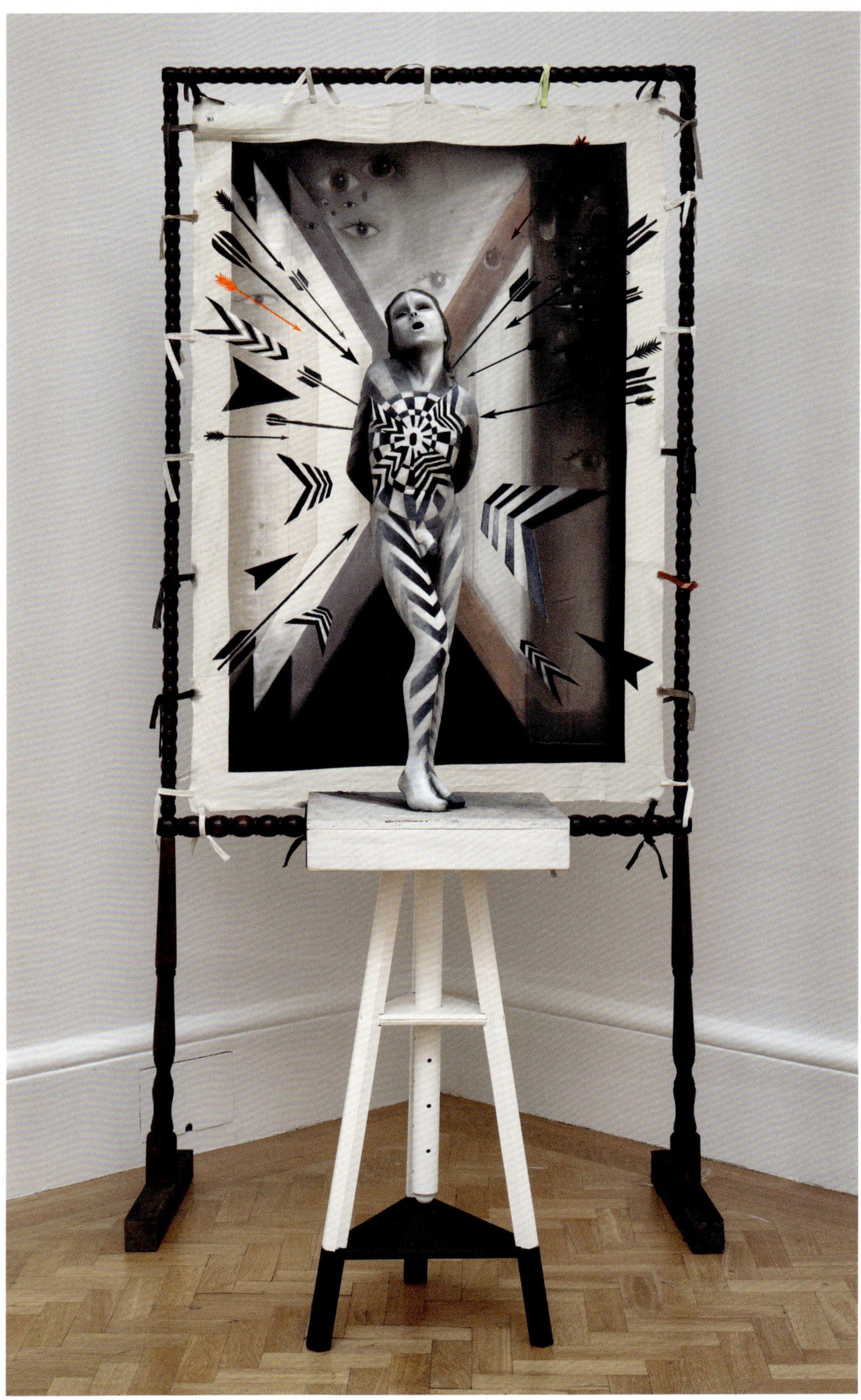

Cathie Pilkington RA
Dazzle
Mixed media
H 238 cm

Prof Michael Sandle RA
Helmut Bieler-Wendt Performing
Ink and acrylic
148 × 98 cm

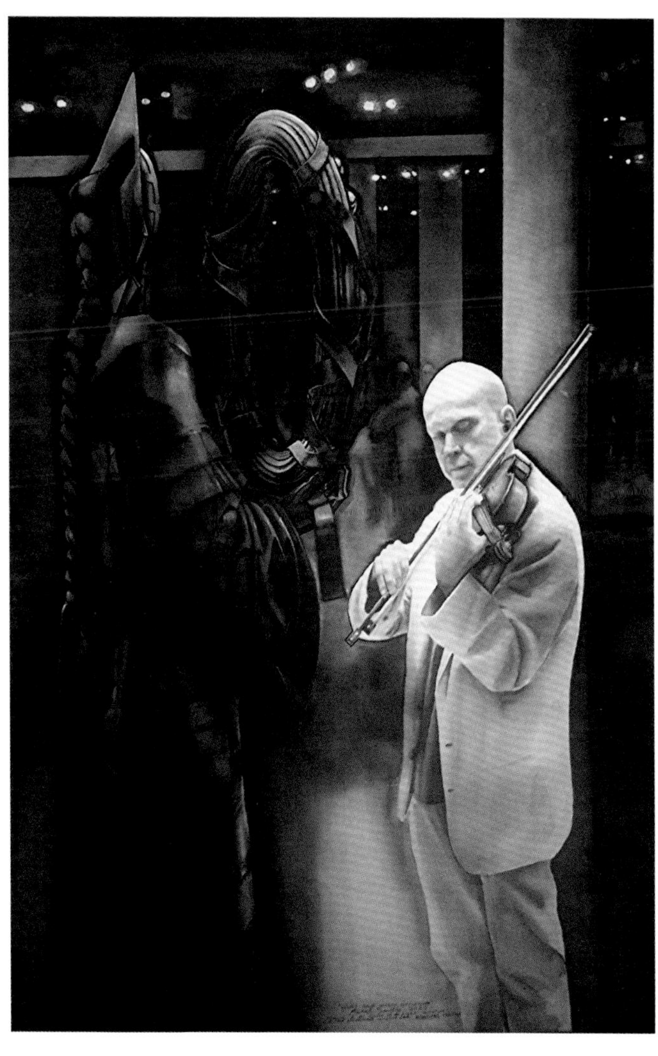

Richard Deacon CBE RA
Square Cut #1
Ceramic
96 × 68 cm

Stephen Cox RA
Return to the Hunt in the Forest
Brick and wood
H 292 cm

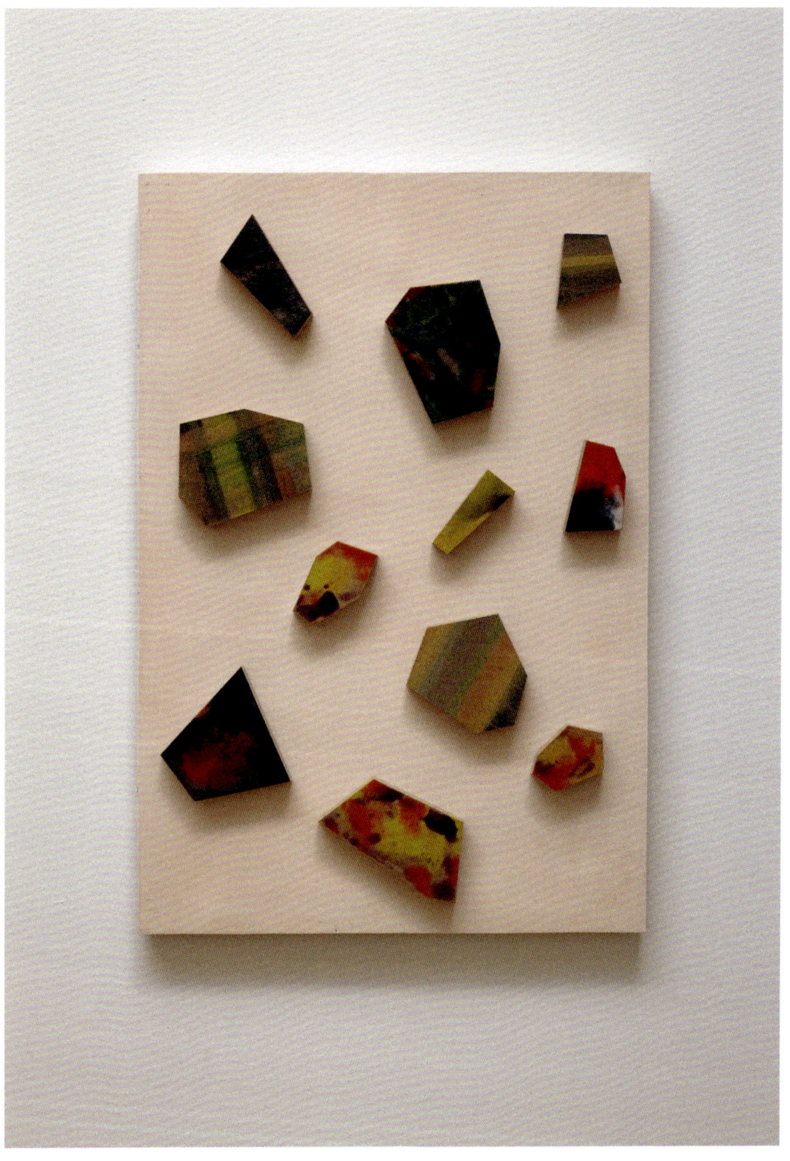

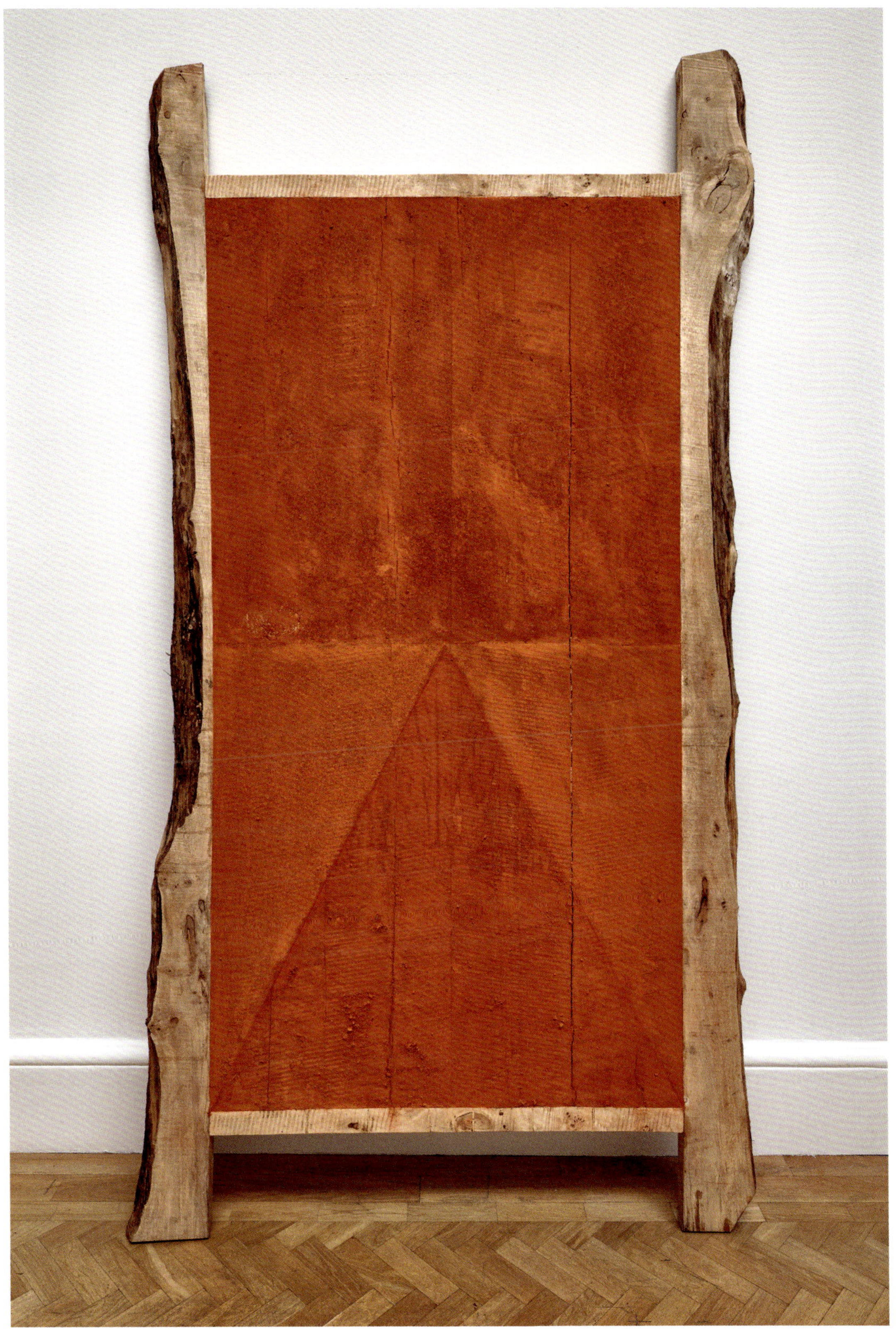

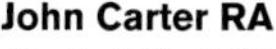

Nigel Hall RA
Drawing 753
Gouache and charcoal
153 × 102 cm

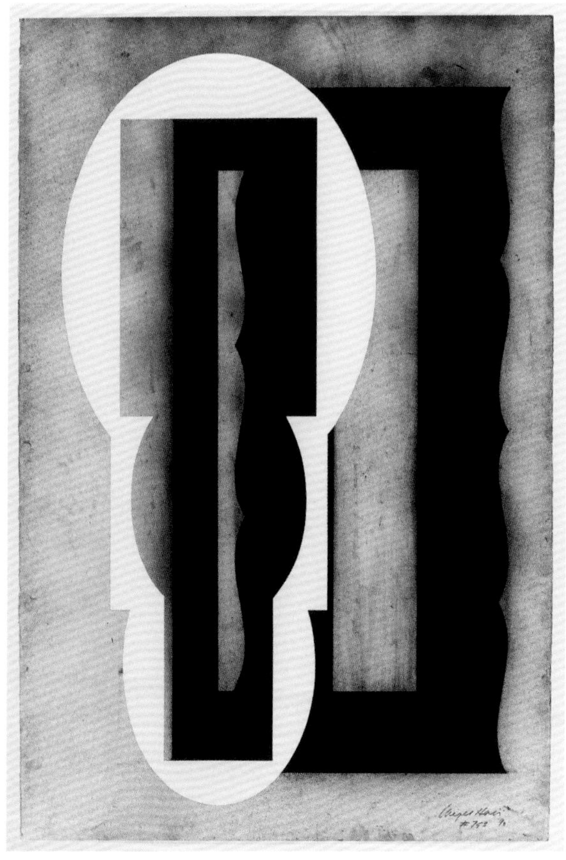

John Carter RA
Vertical Shaft (From One Side to the Other)
Mixed media
65 × 40 cm

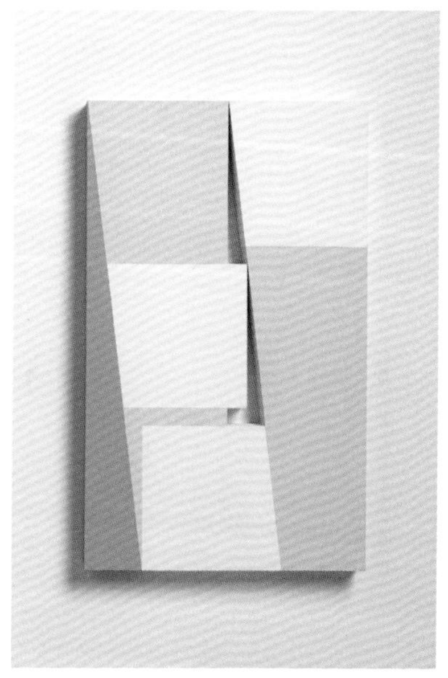

Sir Richard Long CBE RA
Ebb and Flow
Screenprint
148 × 59 cm

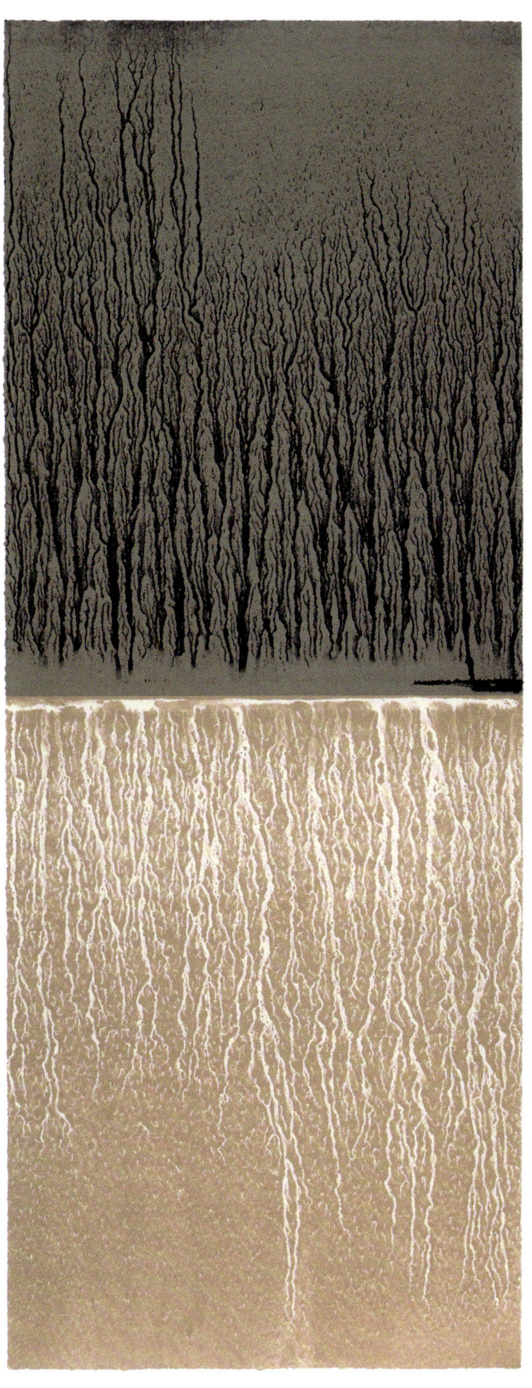

Lisa Milroy RA
White on Black
Oil
158 × 119 cm

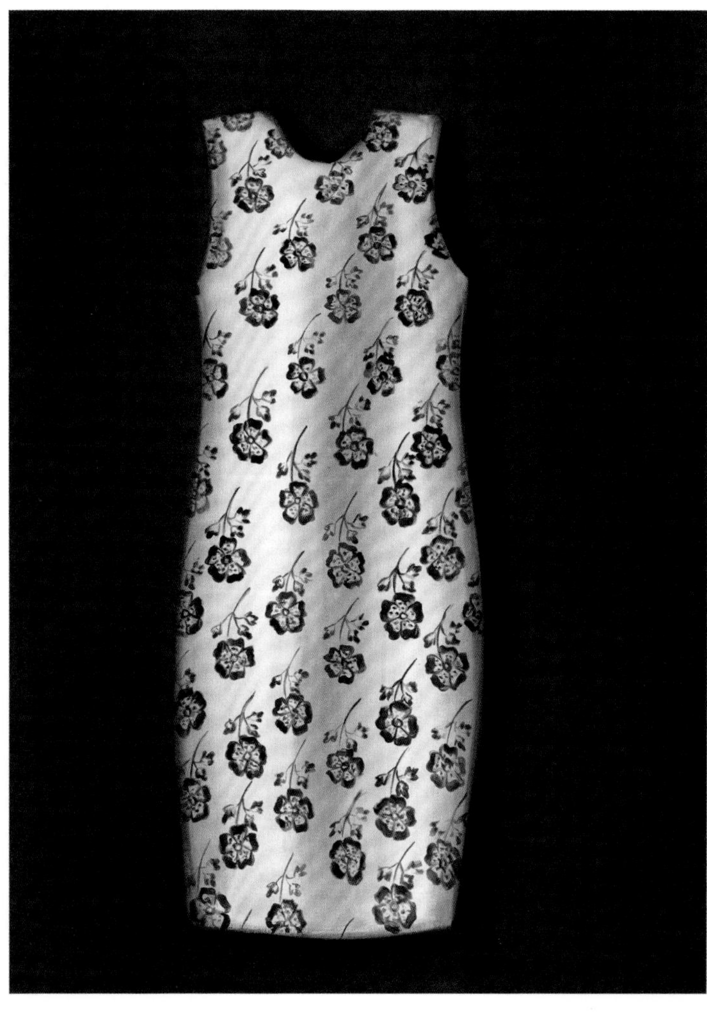

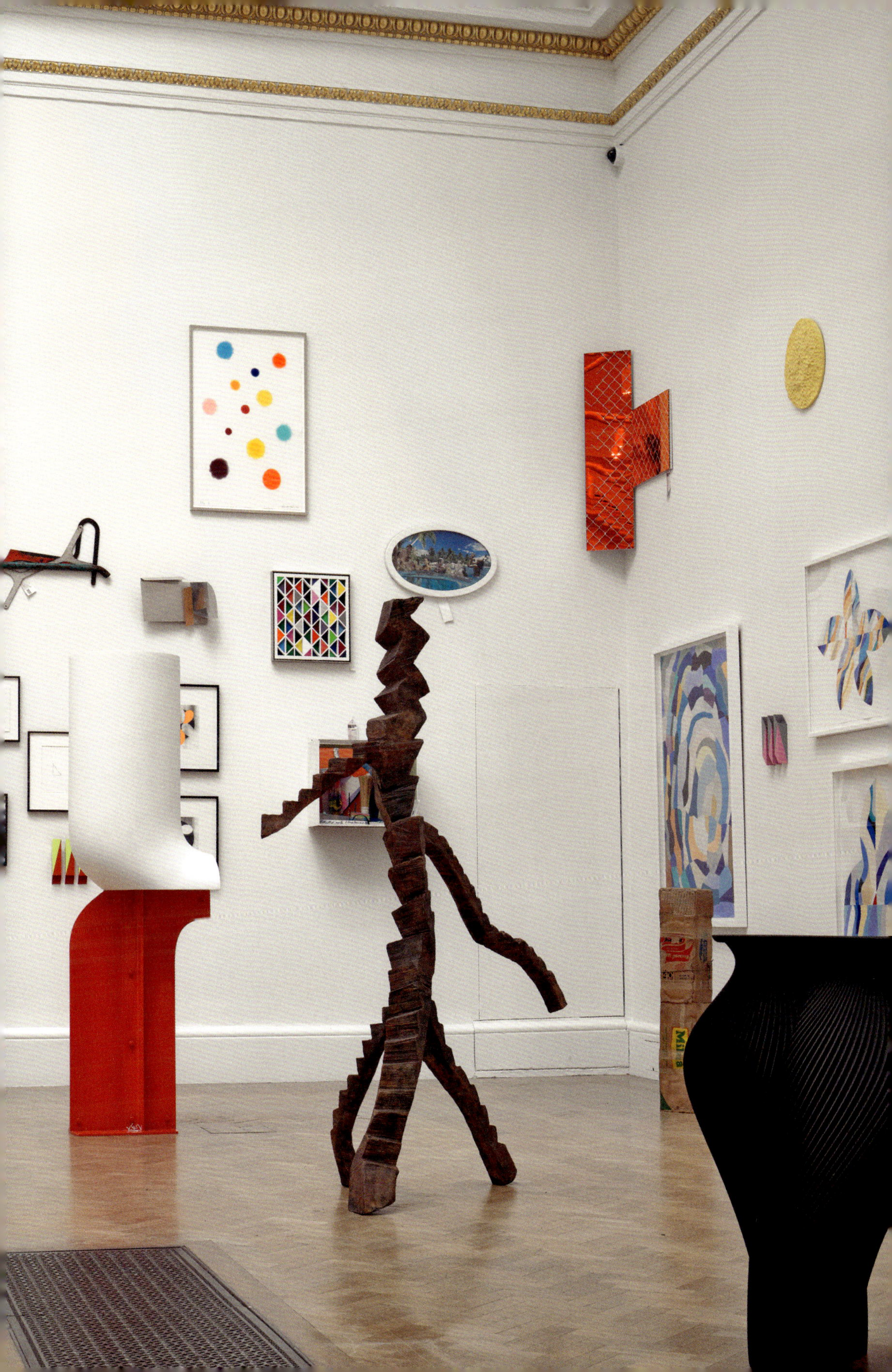

Ai Weiwei Hon RA
Porcelain Vase (Ruins)
Porcelain
H 52 cm

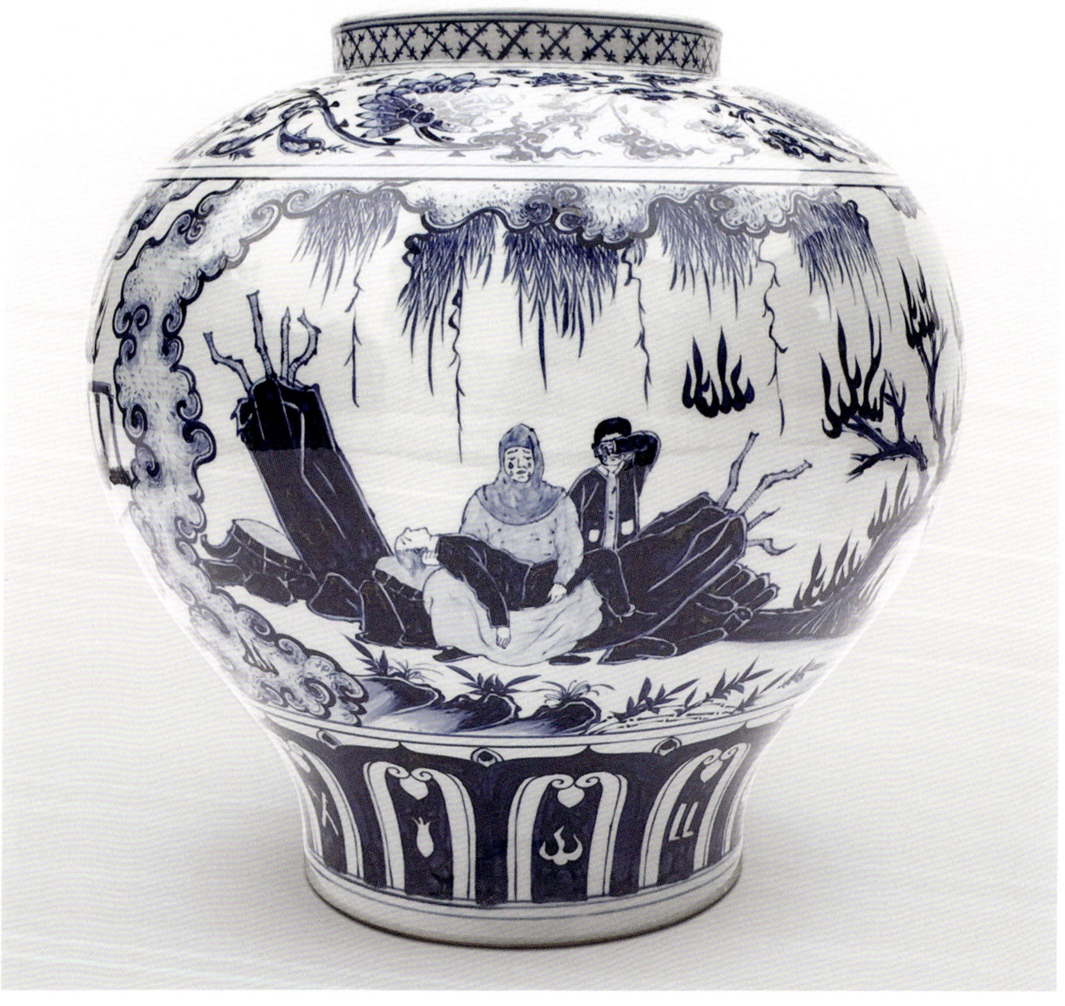

Paul Scott
Cumbrian Blue(s), Palestine, Gaza 2014 (Triptych) (detail)
Mixed media
H 22 cm

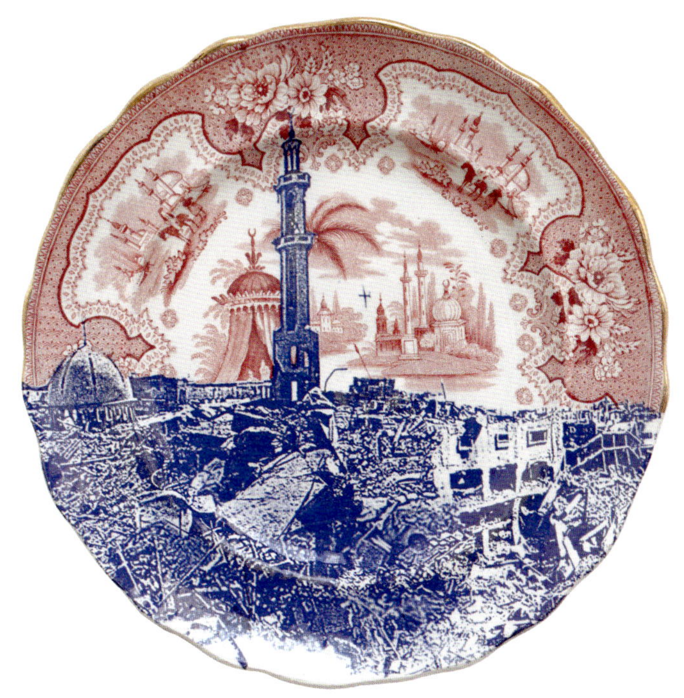

Wolfgang Tillmans RA
Sicily Morning
Inkjet print
138 × 206 cm

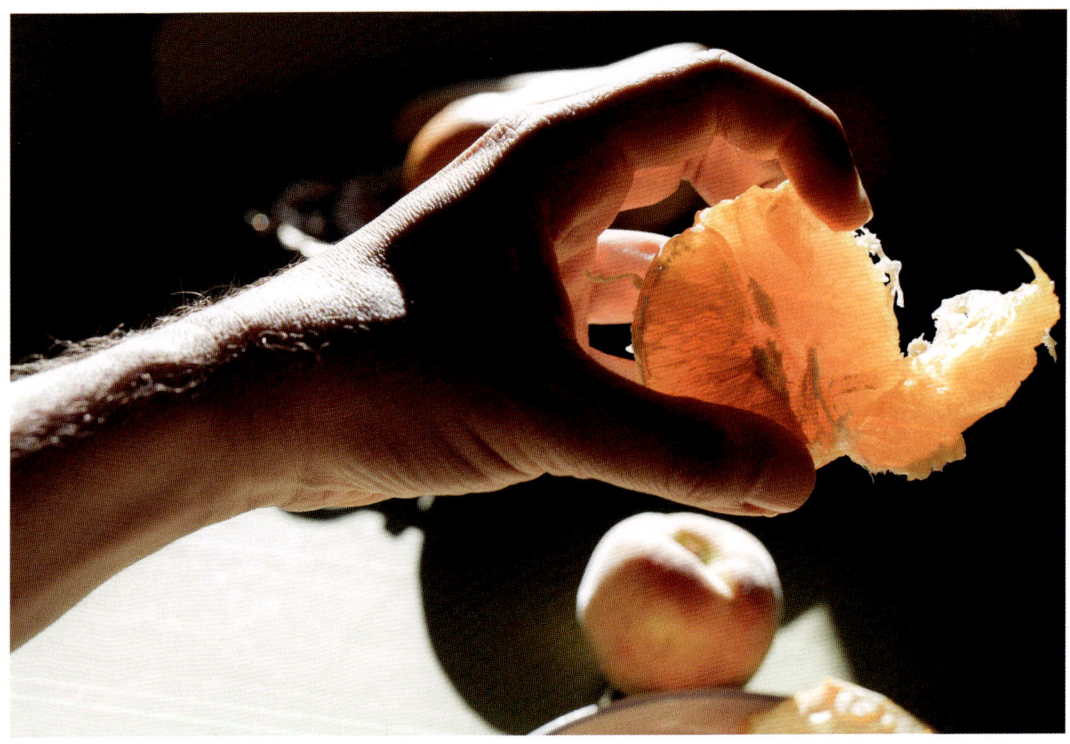

Prof Phyllida Barlow CBE RA
Untitled:Mantlestacked;2020
Mixed media
H 175 cm

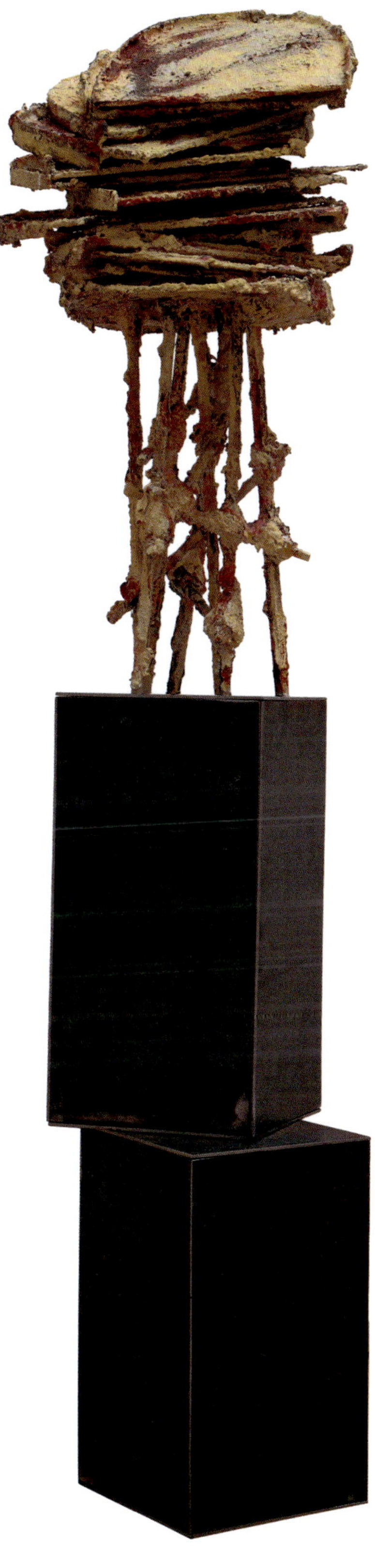

Anne Hardy
Threshold
Mixed media
300 × 348 cm

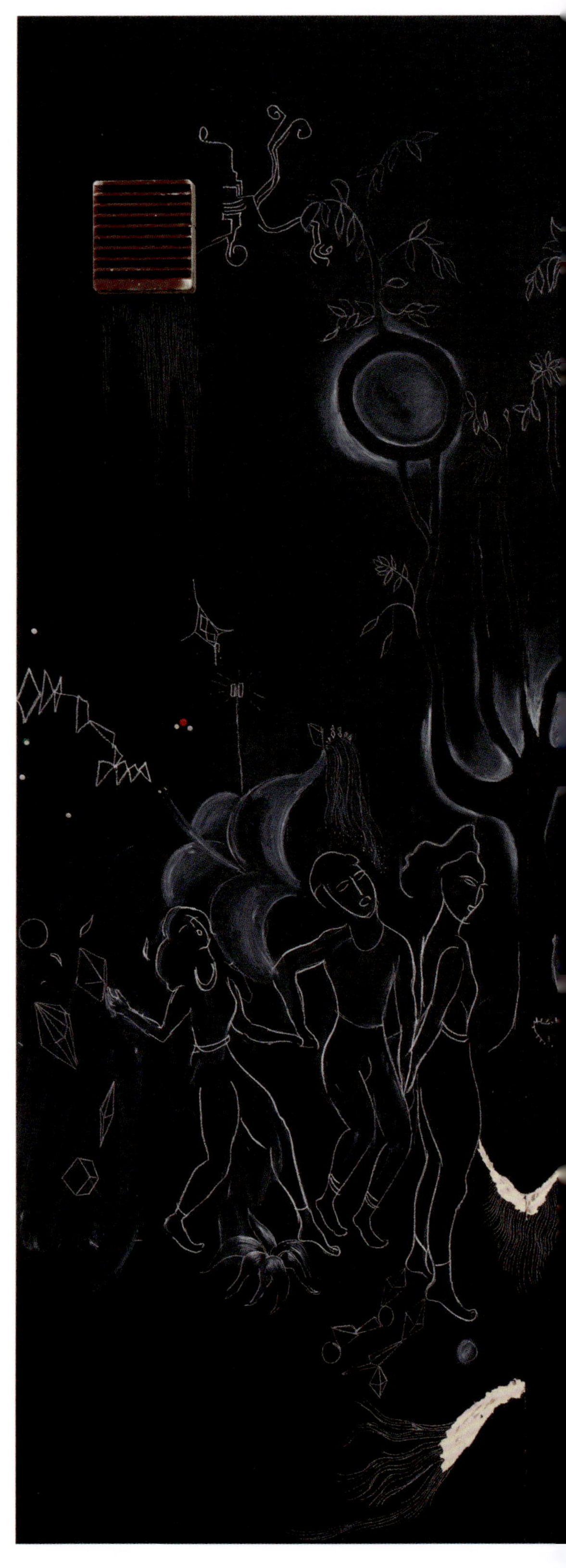

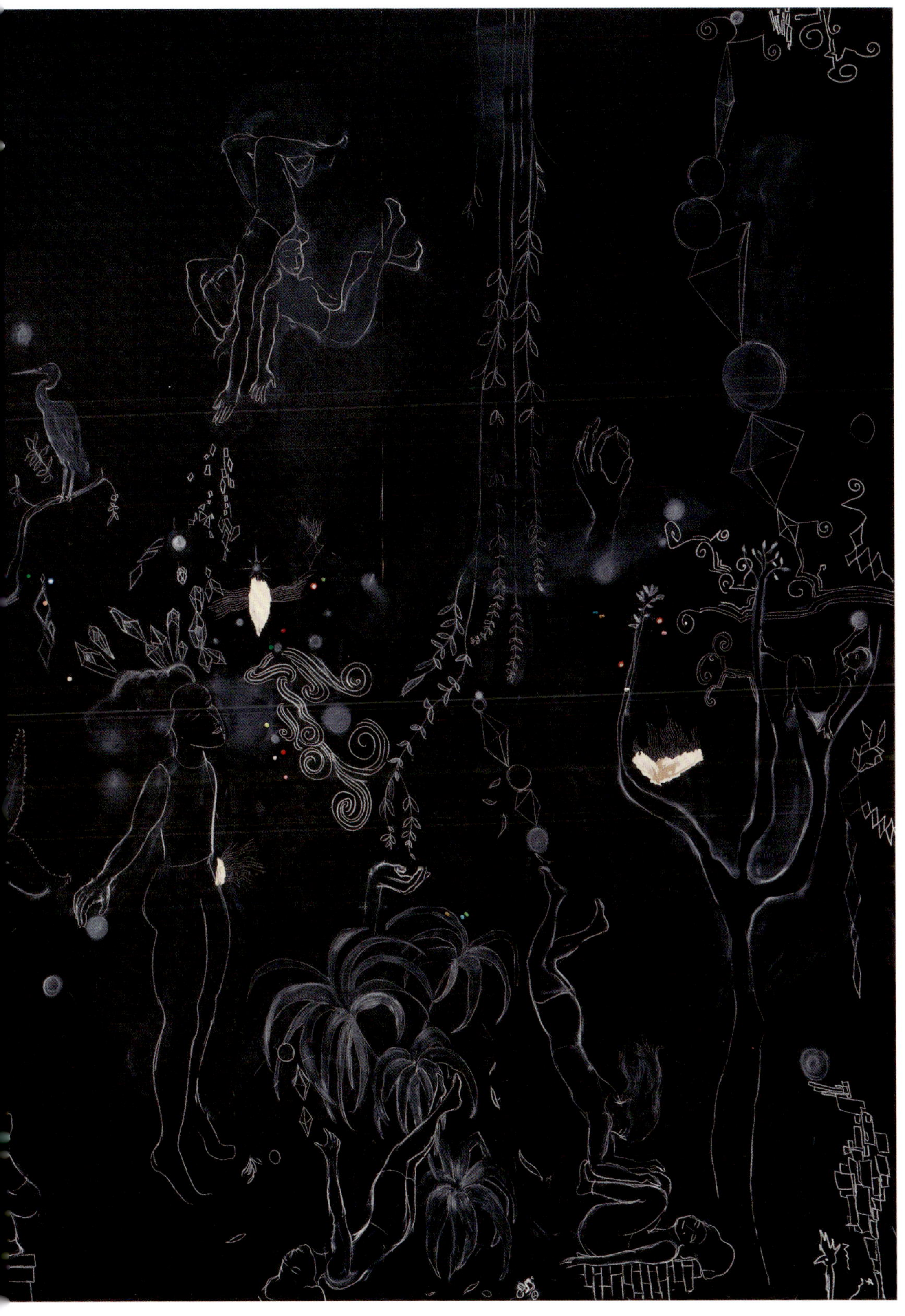

Jane and Louise Wilson RA
I'd Walk With You But Not With Her
LED net
800 × 540 cm

Marina Abramović Hon RA
Dozing Consciousness (Body) – Eyes Closed
Dye sublimation print
229 × 115 cm

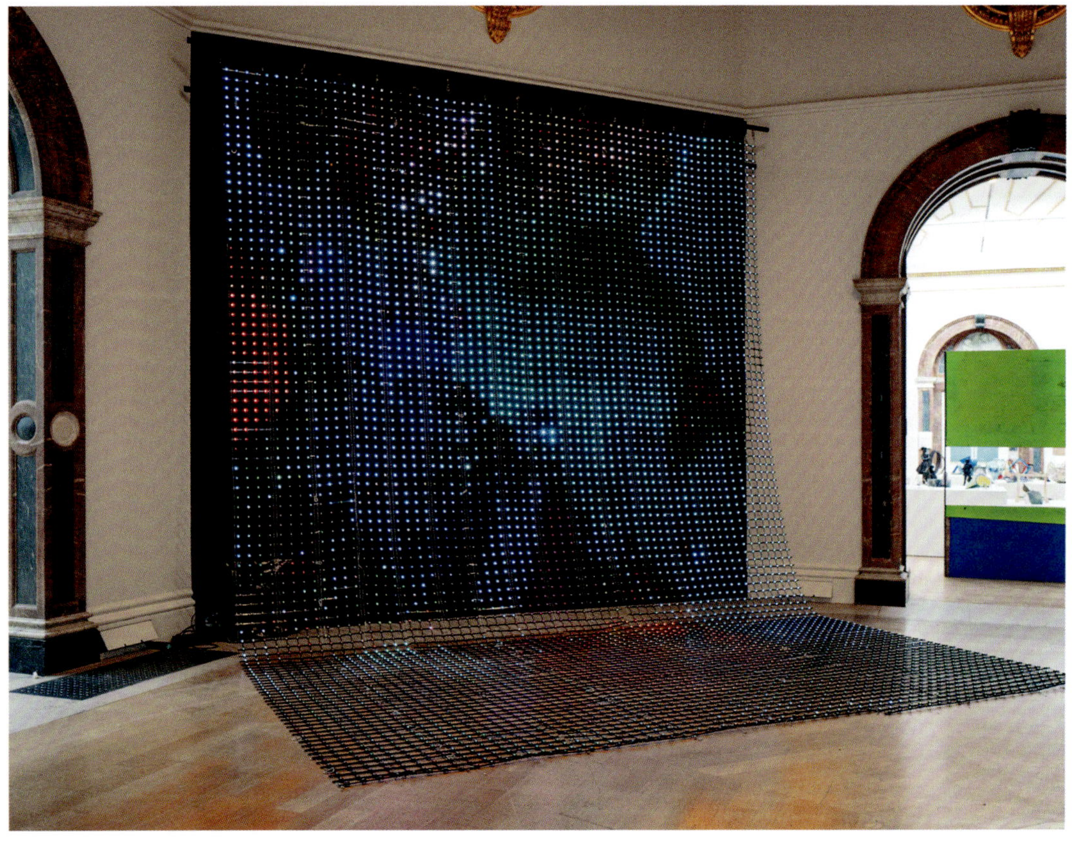

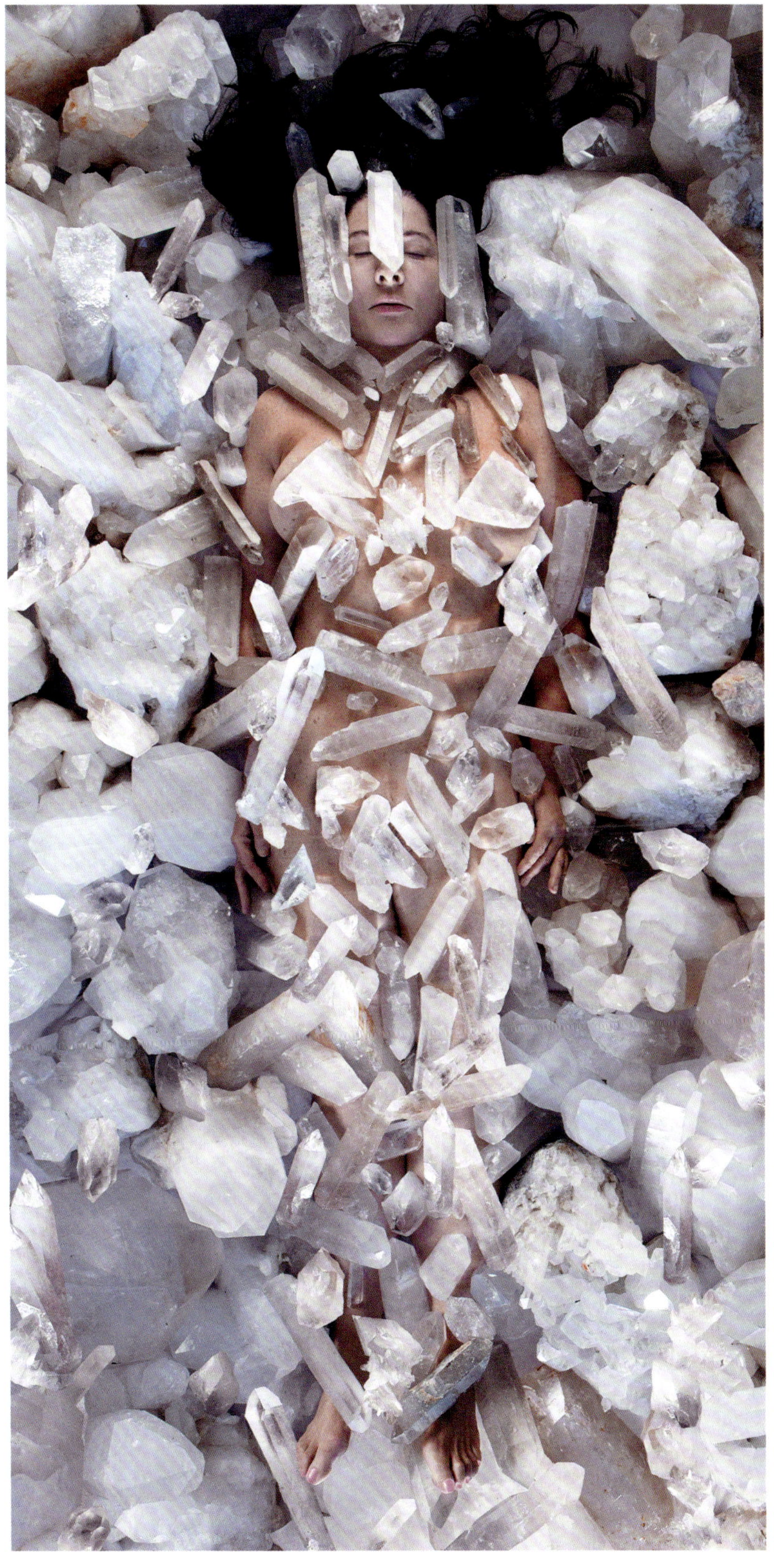

Ajamu
Self-portrait in Wedding Dress 1 and 2
Silver gelatin prints
8 × 5 cm (each)

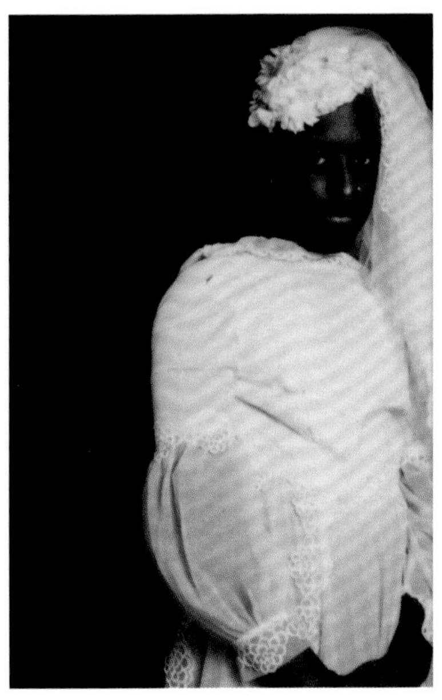

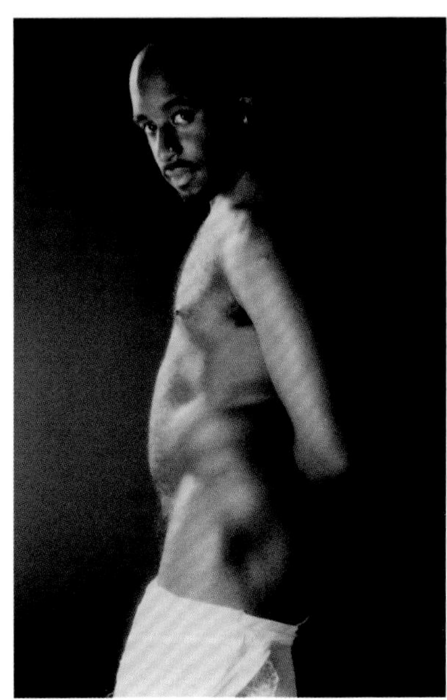

Michael Armitage
Untitled
Ink
23-31 × 23-31 cm (each)

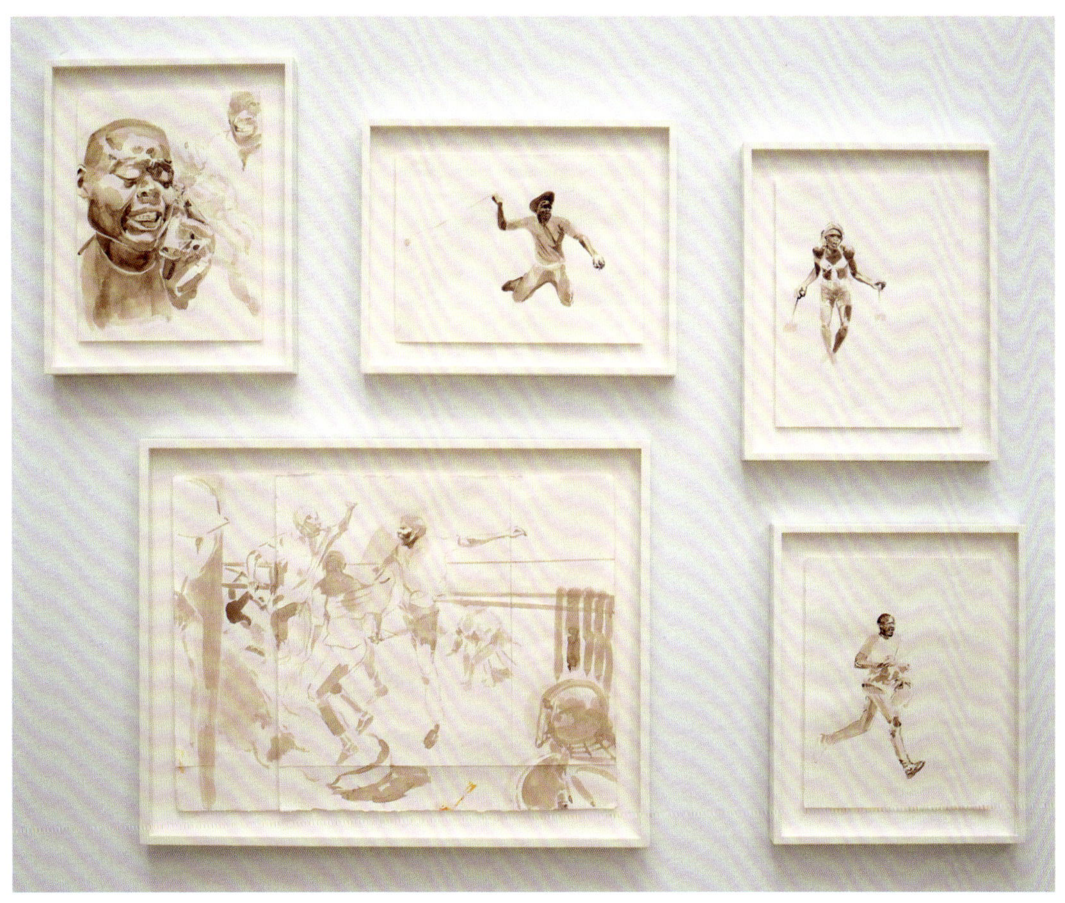

Korakrit Arunanondchai

History Painting (Frame)
Mixed media
218 × 163 cm

Painting with History (Bodypainting)
Mixed media
218 × 163 cm

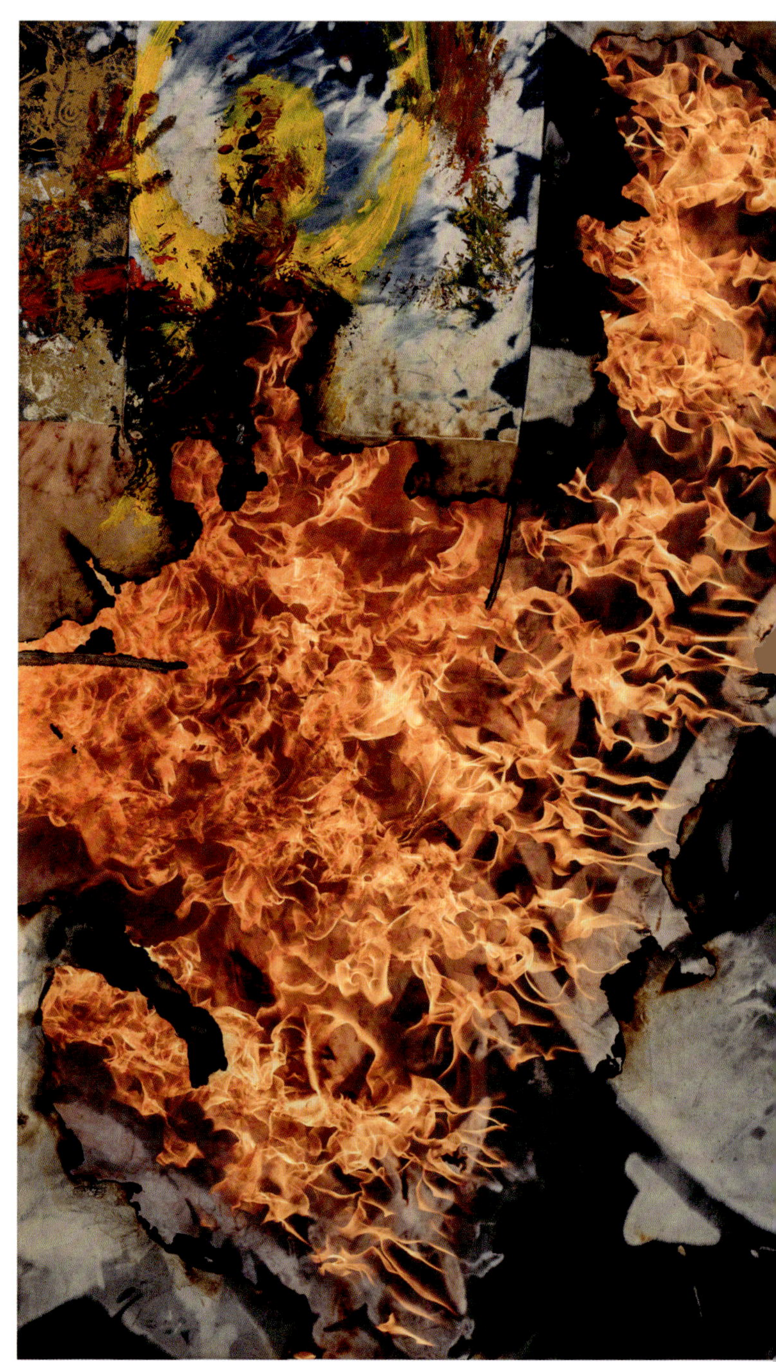

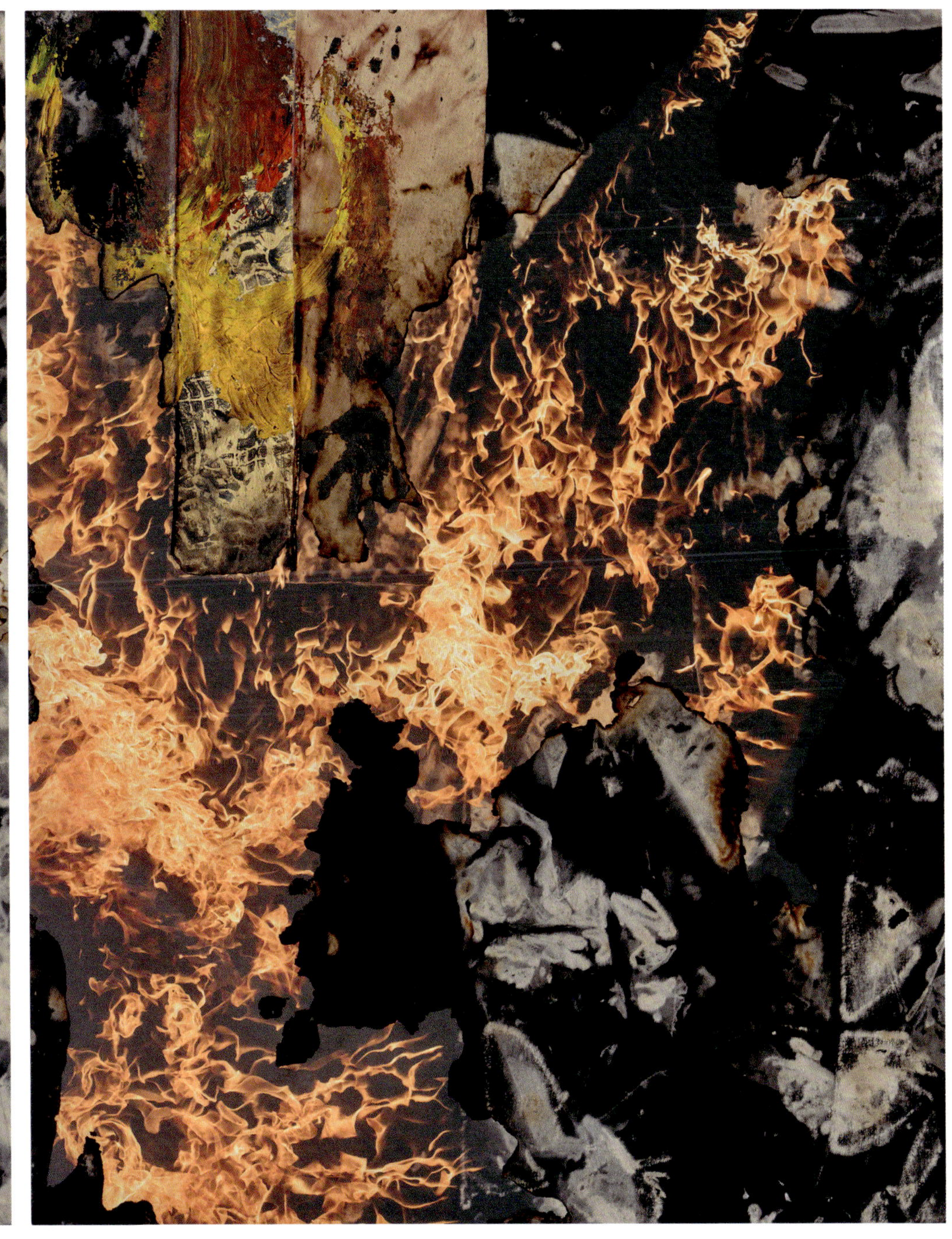

Index

Royal Academy of Arts in London, 2020

Registered charity number 1125383

Officers

President: Rebecca Salter PRA
Keeper: Cathie Pilkington RA
Treasurer: Chris Wilkinson OBE RA
Secretary and Chief Executive:
Axel Rüger

Senior Royal Academicians

Prof Norman Ackroyd CBE
Diana Armfield
Prof Phyllida Barlow CBE
Basil Beattie
Dame Elizabeth Blackadder DBE
Olwyn Bowey
Frank Bowling OBE
James Butler MBE
John Carter
Prof Sir Peter Cook
Sir Michael Craig-Martin CBE
Frederick Cuming HON D LITT
Gus Cummins
Prof Trevor Dannatt OBE
Dr Jennifer Dickson
Kenneth Draper
Jennifer Durrant
Anthony Eyton
Lord Foster of Thames Bank OM
Peter Freeth
Anthony Green
Sir Nicholas Grimshaw CBE PPRA
Nigel Hall
David Hockney OM CH
Sir Michael Hopkins CBE
Ken Howard OBE
Prof Paul Huxley
Bill Jacklin
Tess Jaray
* Eva Jiřičná CBE
Allen Jones
Prof Phillip King CBE PPRA
Prof Bryan Kneale MBE
Sonia Lawson
John Maine
Mick Moon
Prof Chris Orr MBE
Tom Phillips CBE
Dr Barbara Rae CBE
Dame Paula Rego DBE
* David Remfry MBE
Lord Rogers of Riverside CH
Michael Rooney
Prof Michael Sandle
Terry Setch
Philip Sutton
Joe Tilson
Dr David Tindle
William Tucker
Anthony Whishaw
Rose Wylie OBE

Royal Academicians

Sir David Adjaye OBE
John Akomfrah CBE
Ron Arad
Prof Fiona Banner
Rana Begum
Prof Gordon Benson OBE
Tony Bevan
* Prof Sonia Boyce OBE
Adam Caruso and Peter St John
Prof Brian Catling
Stephen Chambers
Sir David Chipperfield CBE
Ann Christopher
* Eileen Cooper OBE
Stephen Cox
Sir Tony Cragg CBE
* Richard Deacon CBE
Tacita Dean CBE
Anne Desmet
Tracey Emin CBE
* Prof Stephen Farthing
Sir Antony Gormley OBE
Piers Gough CBE
Spencer de Grey CBE
Thomas Heatherwick CBE
Prof Lubaina Himid CBE
Gary Hume
Louisa Hutton OBE
Timothy Hyman
Vanessa Jackson
Neil Jeffries
Chantal Joffe
* Isaac Julien CBE
Sir Anish Kapoor CBE
Michael Landy
Christopher Le Brun PPRA
Sir Richard Long CBE
Jock McFadyen
Prof David Mach
Prof Ian McKeever
Níall McLaughlin
Lisa Milroy
Prof Dhruva Mistry CBE
Mali Morris
Prof Farshid Moussavi OBE
David Nash OBE
Prof Mike Nelson
Humphrey Ocean
Hughie O'Donoghue
Cornelia Parker OBE
Eric Parry
Grayson Perry CBE
Cathie Pilkington
Fiona Rae
Peter Randall-Page
Prof Ian Ritchie CBE
Eva Rothschild
* Rebecca Salter PRA
Jenny Saville
Sean Scully
Tim Shaw
Conrad Shawcross
Yinka Shonibare CBE
Bob and Roberta Smith OBE
Alan Stanton OBE
Emma Stibbon
Wolfgang Tillmans
Rebecca Warren
Gillian Wearing CBE
Prof Alison Wilding OBE
Prof Chris Wilkinson OBE
* Jane and Louise Wilson
Richard Wilson
Bill Woodrow

* *Hanging Committee 2020*

Honorary Royal Academicians

Marina Abramović
Prof El Anatsui
Laurie Anderson
Prof Tadao Ando
Georg Baselitz
Jim Dine
Marlene Dumas
Olafur Eliasson
Frank O Gehry
Carmen Herrera
Jenny Holzer
Prof Rebecca Horn
Prof Arata Isozaki
Jasper Johns
William Kentridge
Anselm Kiefer
Jeff Koons
Daniel Libeskind
Bruce Nauman
Mimmo Paladino
Senator Renzo Piano
Ed Ruscha
Julian Schnabel
Richard Serra
Cindy Sherman
Kiki Smith
Frank Stella
Rosemarie Trockel
James Turrell
Bill Viola
Kara Walker
Ai Weiwei
Wim Wenders
Peter Zumthor

Supporting the Royal Academy of Arts

The Royal Academy of Arts has a unique position as an independent institution led by eminent artists and architects whose purpose is to promote the creation, enjoyment and appreciation of the visual arts through exhibitions, education and debate. The Royal Academy receives no annual funding via government, and is entirely reliant on self-generated income and charitable support.

You and/or your company can support the Royal Academy of Arts in a number of different ways:

- Donations from individuals, trusts, companies and foundations help support the Academy's internationally renowned exhibition programme, the conservation of the Collection and education projects for schools, families and people with special needs; as well as providing scholarships and bursaries for postgraduate art students in the Royal Academy Schools.
- As a company, you can invest in the Royal Academy through arts sponsorship, corporate membership and corporate entertaining, with specific opportunities that relate to your budgets and marketing or entertaining objectives. Upcoming sponsorship and entertaining opportunities for corporate partners include *Francis Bacon: Man and Beast* and *Marina Abramović: After Life*.
- By including a gift to the Royal Academy in your will, you could help to protect all that we stand for, and ensure we are there as a voice for art and for artists, whatever the future may hold. Your gift can be a sum of money, a specific item or a share of what is left after you have provided for your family and friends. Any gift, regardless of the size, can have an impact, and will allow art lovers to enjoy the Royal Academy in the years to come.

To find out ways in which individuals can support this work, or a specific aspect of it, please contact Isobel Morris on 0207 300 8055.

To explore ways in which companies, trusts and foundations can become involved in the work of the Academy, please contact the Sponsorship and Partnership Team on 020 7300 5706/5813.

For more information on remembering the Academy in your will, please contact Frances Griffiths on 020 7300 5677, or email legacies@royalacademy.org.uk.

Become a Friend of the RA

Redeem the cost of your exhibition tickets when you become a Friend today*

Enjoy free and prioritised entry to every exhibition and much more...

There's never been a better time to become a Friend of the RA. Join today for prioritised access to critically-acclaimed exhibitions including *Francis Bacon: Man and Beast*, *Tracey Emin / Edvard Munch: The Loneliness of the Soul*, *Marina Abramović: After Life* and many more.

- Free entry to exhibitions for you, a family member and up to four children
- RA Magazine and a weekly email newsletter
- 10% discount in RA shops*
- Relax in the Fine Rooms, a gilded eighteenth-century room available only to Friends, and much more

By joining as a Friend you help secure our future as a place where art is made, exhibited and debated for years to come.

Why not join today? | At the Friends Desk | Online at roy.ac/friends | By phone 020 7300 8090

* *Some exclusions apply, see terms and conditions.*

Head of Summer Exhibitions and Contemporary Curator
Edith Devaney

Summer Exhibition Organisers
Sinta Berry
Helena Cooper
Bronte Earl
Scott Lawrence
Alexandra Searle
Paul Sirr

Royal Academy Publications
Florence Dassonville, Production Co-ordinator
Rosie Hore, Project Editor
Carola Krueger, Production Manager
Peter Sawbridge, Editorial Director
Nick Tite, Publisher

Rights and Reproductions
Susana Vázquez Fernández

Editor's note:
All given dimensions are unframed, height before width (before depth).

Book design: Adam Brown_01.02
Colour reproduction: DawkinsColour
Printed in Wales by Gomer Press

British Library Cataloguing-in-publication Data
A catalogue record for this book is available in the British Library

ISBN 978-1-912520-52-7

Illustrations

Page 2: *Khnum* by Brian Eno in the Small Weston Room.
Page 4: detail of *Watermelon Bight* by Frank Bowling OBE RA.
Page 6: detail of *Cha Cha Cha (Triptych)* by Chris Ofili.
Page 9: detail of *I'd Walk With You But Not With Her* by Jane and Louise Wilson RA.
Page 10: *Transmission* by Jane and Louise Wilson RA in the Large Weston Room.
Page 11: the 2020 Summer Exhibition's co-ordinators Jane and Louise Wilson RA.
Pages 20–21: the Main Galleries during the 2020 Summer Exhibition selection and hang.
Pages 30–31: Gallery I, showing works by Prof Sonia Boyce OBE RA, El Anatsui HON RA, Frank Bowling OBE RA and Yinka Shonibare CBE RA.
Pages 38–39: Gallery II, showing works by Wangechi Mutu, Frida Orupabo and Njideka Akunyili Crosby.
Pages 48–49: the Large Weston Room.
Pages 80–81: Gallery IV.
Pages 82–83, 88–89: Gallery V.
Pages 104–05: Gallery VII.
Pages 116–17: Gallery VIII.
Pages 122–23: Gallery IX.
Page 133: the Lecture Room. *Tumultra* by Stephen Lewis is in the foreground.
Page 143: the Lecture Room. *SI02 Vessel – Twisted Pair* by Gareth Neal and *Stepman* by David Nash OBE RA are in the foreground.

Photographic Acknowledgements

Unless otherwise stated: John Bodkin, DawkinsColour
Page 2: courtesy Paul Stolper Gallery London, 2020
Pages 4, 24: courtesy the artist
Pages 6 (detail), 32–33: © Chris Ofili. Courtesy the artist, Victoria Miro and David Zwirner. Private collection
Pages 9, 150: with thanks to ArtAV and SFX George Dyson. Photo Matt Humphrey
Page 13: courtesy the artist
Pages 14, 43 (below): courtesy the artist and Tiwani Contemporary
Page 17: courtesy the artist, Victoria Miro, London/Venice, and Metro Pictures, New York
Page 18: courtesy the artist
Pages 20–21: with thanks to Sinta Berry, Adam Brown, Simon Streather and Nick Tite
Pages 22–23: courtesy the artist. Photo Jack Hems
Page 25: courtesy the artist
Pages 26, 38–39: © Njideka Akunyili Crosby. Courtesy the artist, Victoria Miro and David Zwirner
Page 27: courtesy the artist and Victoria Miro, London/Venice
Page 34: © Glenn Ligon. Courtesy the artist, Hauser & Wirth, New York, Regen Projects, Los Angeles, Thomas Dane Gallery, London, and Chantal Crousel, Paris. Photo Ben Westoby
Pages 35, 38–39: © Wangechi Mutu. Courtesy the artist and Victoria Miro
Pages 36–37: © Theaster Gates. Courtesy Gagosian. Photo Robert McKeever
Page 40: courtesy the artist (above); © Karen Kilimnik. Courtesy the artist, 303 Gallery, Sprüth Magers and Galerie Eva Presenhuber AG (below)
Page 41: courtesy the artist (below)
Page 44: courtesy the artist. Photo Lucy Dawkins
Page 47: courtesy the artist (above); © Simon Periton. Courtesy Sadie Coles HQ, London (below)
Page 50: courtesy the artist (above); © Eddie Peake. Courtesy CounterEditions.com and Team GB/ British Olympic Association (below)
Page 52: © Linder. Courtesy the artist and Modern Art, London (above); courtesy the artist (below)
Page 53: © Hans-Peter Feldmann. Courtesy 303 Gallery, New York (below)
Page 54: courtesy the artist
Page 55: courtesy the artist (below)
Page 56: © Michael Craig-Martin CBE RA. Courtesy the artist and Gagosian. Photo Lucy Dawkins
Page 57: courtesy the artist (above); © Paul Huxley RA. Photo Nelson Huxley (below)
Pages 58–59: courtesy the artist (left); © the artist. Courtesy the artist and Marlborough, London
Page 60: courtesy the artist (above); © Frederick Cuming HON DLITT RA. Photo Alex Brattell (below)
Pages 62–63: © the artist. Courtesy the artist and Marlborough, London
Page 64: courtesy the artist (above)
Page 65: courtesy Mimmo Paladino HON RA. Photo Peppe Avallone
Pages 66–67: © Anselm Kiefer HON RA. Photo © White Cube (Ollie Hammick)
Page 67: photo Simon Streather
Page 68: courtesy the artist (above); photo Colin Mills (below)
Page 70: courtesy the artist (above); courtesy the artist and Chris Beetles Gallery, St James's, London (below)
Page 71: courtesy the artist
Page 72: courtesy the artist (above); courtesy the artist and Chris Beetles Gallery, St James's, London (below)
Page 73: courtesy the artist
Page 74: © the artist. Courtesy the artist and Marlborough, London (above); courtesy Mick Moon RA and Cristea Roberts Gallery, London (below)
Page 76: courtesy the artist (above); courtesy the artist and Victoria Miro (below)
Page 77: © Eileen Cooper OBE RA. Photo Justin Piperger
Page 78: courtesy Cornelia Parker OBE RA and Cristea Roberts Gallery, London
Page 79: © Michael Landy RA. Courtesy the artist and Thomas Dane Gallery. Photo Ben Westoby (above); courtesy the artist (below)
Page 85: © Chris Orr MBE RA / www.chrisorr-ra (below)
Page 86: courtesy the artist and greengrassi, London. Photo Marcus J. Leith (below)
Page 87 (above): courtesy Jim Dine HON RA and Cristea Roberts Gallery, London
Page 90: courtesy the artist (below)
Page 92: © Hufton + Crow
Page 93: courtesy the architect (above)
Page 94: Sir David Chipperfield CBE RA for *Domus* 2020. Image: *Domus* April 2020 cover by Thomas Demand (above); © Sauerbruch Hutton (below)
Page 95: © Lifschutz Davidson Sandilands. Photo James Newton (above); courtesy the artist (below)
Page 96: Caruso St John Architects (above); © Grimshaw. Photo Robert Sims (below)
Page 97: © Norman Foster RA (above); © Cullinan Studio (below)
Page 98: courtesy the architect (above); courtesy the architect (below)
Page 99: © Rogers Stirk Harbour + Partners (above)
Page 100: courtesy the architect (above)
Page 101: © RPBW (above); © WilkinsonEyre. Photo Ben Bisek (below)
Page 102: © Rose Wylie OBE RA. Courtesy the artist and David Zwirner (below)
Pages 102–03: Grayson Perry CBE RA and Paragon | Contemporary Editions Ltd, London. Photo Stephen White & Co
Page 106: courtesy the artist (above); photo Fiona Robinson (below)
Page 107: © Georg Baselitz HON RA and Cristea Roberts Gallery, London
Page 108: courtesy the artist
Page 109: courtesy the artist
Page 110: © Dr David Tindle RA. Courtesy The Redfern Gallery
Page 112: courtesy the artist
Page 113: courtesy the artist
Page 115: courtesy the artist
Page 118: courtesy the artist (above)
Page 120: courtesy the artist and Ingleby, Edinburgh. Photo Andy Keate
Page 121: courtesy the artist (above); © Stephen Chambers RA. Photo FS@SCS (below)
Page 124: © Dr Jennifer Dickson RA
Page 125: courtesy the artist (above); courtesy the artist (below)
Page 126: © Ann Christopher RA. Photo Steve Russell Studios (left); courtesy the artist (right)
Page 127: courtesy Rana Begum RA and Cristea Roberts Gallery, London
Page 129: courtesy the artist
Page 130: courtesy the artist
Page 131: courtesy the artist
Page 132: courtesy the artist (above); © Sir Phillip King CBE PPRA. Courtesy the artist and Thomas Dane Gallery. Photo Ben Westoby (below)
Page 134: courtesy the artist
Page 135: © the artist. Photo Prudence Cuming Associates Ltd (above); courtesy the artist. Photo Richard Ivey (below)
Page 136: courtesy the artist
Page 137: courtesy the artist
Page 138: courtesy the artist
Page 139: courtesy the artist
Page 140: © Nigel Hall RA. Photo Colin Mills (above); © John Carter RA. Courtesy The Redfern Gallery (below)
Page 141: courtesy Sir Richard Long CBE RA and Cristea Roberts Gallery, London
Page 142: © Lisa Milroy RA 2020. Photo FXP
Page 144: © Ai Weiwei Studio. Courtesy Lisson Gallery
Page 145: courtesy the artist
Page 146: © Wolfgang Tillmans RA. Courtesy the artist and Maureen Paley, London
Pages 148–49: © Anne Hardy, courtesy Maureen Paley, London / Hove
Page 151: © Marina Abramović HON RA. Courtesy Lisson Gallery